Emerging Perspectives on Substance Misuse

Emerging Perspectives on Substance Misuse

Edited by

Willm Mistral

WILEY Blackwell

This edition first published 2013
© 2013 John Wiley & Sons, Ltd

Wiley-Blackwell is an imprint of John Wiley & Sons, formed by the merger of Wiley's global Scientific, Technical and Medical business with Blackwell Publishing.

Registered Office
John Wiley & Sons Ltd, The Atrium, Southern Gate, Chichester, West Sussex, PO19 8SQ, UK

Editorial Offices
350 Main Street, Malden, MA 02148-5020, USA
9600 Garsington Road, Oxford, OX4 2DQ, UK
The Atrium, Southern Gate, Chichester, West Sussex, PO19 8SQ, UK

For details of our global editorial offices, for customer services, and for information about how to apply for permission to reuse the copyright material in this book please see our website at www.wiley.com/wiley-blackwell.

The right of Willm Mistral to be identified as the author of the editorial material in this work has been asserted in accordance with the UK Copyright, Designs and Patents Act 1988.

Library of Congress Cataloging-in-Publication Data

Emerging perspectives on substance misuse / edited by Willm Mistral.
     pages cm
     Includes bibliographical references and index.
     ISBN 978-1-118-30664-2 (cloth) – ISBN 978-1-118-30212-5 (pbk.)
1. Substance abuse.   2. Substance abuse–Treatment. 3. Alcoholism.
4. Alcoholism–Treatment.   I. Mistral, Willm.
     HV4998.E44 2013
     616.86–dc23

                                                    2013013061

A catalogue record for this book is available from the British Library.

Cover image: © Paul Edmondson / Getty Images
Cover design by Simon Levy Associates

Set in 10/12.5pt Plantin by Aptara Inc., New Delhi, India
Printed in Malaysia by Ho Printing (M) Sdn Bhd

1   2013

Contents

Contents

Contributors

Professor Amanda Baker, Centre for Translational Neuroscience and Mental Health, University of Newcastle, Australia. Email: amanda.baker@newcastle.edu.au

Rebecca Brown, PhD candidate, Department of Gender and Cultural Studies SOPHI, University of Sydney, Australia. Email: rbro9702@uni.sydney.edu.au

Professor Robin Davidson, Consultant Clinical Psychologist, Northern Ireland. Email: robindavidson@hotmail.co.uk

Sarah Hiles, PhD Candidate, Centre for Translational Neuroscience and Mental Health, University of Newcastle, Australia. Email: Sarah.Hiles@newcastle.edu.au

Dr Louise Hill, Policy Implementation Officer, CELCIS, University of Strathclyde, Scotland. Email: louise.hill@strath.ac.uk

Dr Frances Kay-Lambkin, Senior Research Fellow, National Drug and Alcohol Research Centre, University of New South Wales, Australia. Email: f.kaylambkin@unsw.edu.au

Dr Peter Kelly, Senior Lecturer Clinical Psychology, School of Psychology, University of Wollongong, Australia. Email: pkelly@uow.edu.au

Tim Leighton, Director, Centre for Addiction Treatment Studies, Action on Addiction, England. Email: tim.leighton@actiononaddiction.org.uk

Professor Fiona Measham, School of Applied Social Sciences, Durham University, England. Email: f.measham@durham.ac.uk

Dr Willm Mistral, Honorary Senior Research Fellow University of Bath; for 18 years managed the Mental Health Research & Development Unit, Avon & Wiltshire Mental Health Trust and University of Bath, England. Email: w.mistral@bath.ac.uk

Dr Karenza Moore, Lecturer in Criminology, Department of Applied Social Science, Lancaster University, UK. Email: karenza.moore@lancaster.ac.uk

Professor David Nutt, Director Neuropsychopharmacology Unit, Division of Brain Sciences, Imperial College London, England. Email: d.nutt@imperial.ac.uk

Amanda Searl, Clinical Psychologist, Centre for Translational Neuroscience and Mental Health, University of Newcastle, Australia. Email: reception@greenhillspsychology.com.au

Dr Lesley Smith, Principal Lecturer Quantitative Research Methods, Department of Psychology, Social Work and Public Health, Oxford Brookes University, England. Email: p0073992@brookes.ac.uk

Lorna Templeton, Independent Research Consultant, Member of the Board of Trustees of Adfam, and Alcohol Research UK Grants Advisory Panel, England. Email: ltempleton72@googlemail.com

Dr Louise Thornton, Research Officer, Centre for Translational Neuroscience and Mental Health, University of Newcastle, Australia. Email: Louise.Thornton@newcastle.edu.au

Richard Velleman, Emeritus Professor of Mental Health Research, University of Bath, England. Email: r.d.b.velleman@bath.ac.uk

Stephen Wilkinson, Chartered Clinical Psychologist, Visiting Research Fellow, University of Bath, England. Email: steve.wilk@hotmail.co.uk

About the Editor

Dr Willm Mistral has a long research career related to alcohol, drug, and mental health problems. He is an Honorary Senior Research Fellow at the University of Bath. For over 18 years he managed a team of researchers in the Mental Health Research and Development Unit, a joint enterprise of the Avon and Wiltshire Mental Health Partnership Trust and the University of Bath. To date he has been involved in over 75 research projects, and has more than 50 publications in books and journals.

Preface

The Topic

Excessive consumption of drugs and alcohol is associated with widespread social problems, and policymakers as well as practitioners in the field are seeking effective means to reduce the impact on individuals, families, and wider society. A vast amount of research has been undertaken into the underlying and maintaining causes of substance misuse, and there is considerable evidence to support promising interventions for related social and psychological problems. However, much national policy and practice remains entrenched in the past, often for the want of a clear exposition, or application, of research findings.

Importantly, this book addresses theoretical, practice and policy issues with regard to problematic use of both alcohol and illicit drugs, and presents a wide range of emerging evidence-based perspectives. As well as professionals charged with devising and delivering policies and interventions to reduce alcohol- and drug-related harm, it will also interest an academic audience as problematic consumption and addictive behaviours are increasingly being studied within universities.

The Authors

The contributing authors represent expertise from a range of different specialisms and perspectives in the substance-misuse field. As such, different authors may use differing terminology, as does this preface, referring at times to substance use or misuse, problematic drug or alcohol use, excessive consumption, or addiction. No attempt has been made to homogenize these terms as the differences represent the way this complex, and sometimes divisive, subject is approached in the real world.

Acknowledgements

I am most grateful to all the contributors to this volume. They are busy people, and I feel both privileged and proud that they have made the time and effort to give of their particular knowledge, experience, and understanding of this important subject.

1

Changing Perspectives on Problematic Drug Use[1]

Richard Velleman

What is Drugs Policy?

Drugs policy can be said to comprise the various ways that governments and societies try to deal with substances that many people consume for pleasure or medicinal purposes but which can also have negative consequences for users, their families, or wider society. The difficulty with this view of drugs policy is that it includes so much – not only laws regulating the substances but also programmes for dealing with those who fall foul of the laws or who develop problems with substance use, and also programmes for prevention of use, or safer use. All these require efforts across a large number of sectors including policing and law enforcement, health, education, customs, 'homeland security', and community organizations. This is a very large canvas, and this chapter will look at only a part of it – primarily the overarching government policies that various countries have adopted, how these have changed over time, and challenges to these policy directions.

History

Societies have used, and attempted to control, intoxicating or psychoactive substances as far back as records go. In Western societies, alcohol was the substance mainly used, and correspondingly controlled, for most of recorded history. Although other substances were occasionally used

Emerging Perspectives on Substance Misuse, First Edition. Edited by Willm Mistral.
© 2013 John Wiley & Sons, Ltd. Published 2013 by John Wiley & Sons, Ltd.

(usually hallucinogens such as 'magic mushrooms'), this was relatively rare and it was not until a range of different intoxicants became more available that use increased, and society felt the need to control that use. Although policy responses have varied, there are some main ways that large-scale societies and governments have conceptualized the issues, and these have determined the policies applied.

Conceptualizations of Drug Use

Societies and governments have variously taken the view that issues surrounding drug use are:

- economic: some substances ought to be freely traded;
- moral: people are weak and so substance use needs to be prohibited, and users need to be reformed and/or punished;
- health: some substances cause addiction and dependency, so use needs to be prevented or users need to be treated;
- criminal justice: many behaviours, including drug use, need to be controlled, forbidden or punished.

Countries usually utilize different or overlapping responses, depending on factors such as the status of the majority of the users, and whether or not use is associated with social disruption.

The United Kingdom

The experience of the United Kingdom is an interesting example. Up until the middle to late 19th century, because drugs other than alcohol were not seen as a problem, there were no drug policies, no laws, and no regulations. Instead, the government's approach was centred on an economic concept: drugs were commodities that could be traded in and with other countries, with resulting economic benefits to the United Kingdom. As Babor et al. (2010) state:

> ... psychoactive substances were an obvious choice; once the demand for them has been created, it becomes self-sustaining. Thus psychoactive substances became a favourite commodity from which to extract revenues for the state... The most notorious of such cases were the Opium Wars that Britain fought with China in the 1840s and 1850s to force the opening of the Chinese market for Indian opium. (p. 203)

As a result of this aggressive marketing, smoking opium became very common in 19th-century China, and a great deal of money was made by the British. However, while this economic model was applied abroad, the position taken with regard to the 'home market' was somewhat different. Many sailors, traders, employees of the East India Company, and others associated with the opium trade, returned to the United Kingdom, and a market for opium started to develop across Europe. At first this was relatively unproblematic but, around the same time as the opium wars, the active ingredient within opium, morphine, began to be produced on a large scale within Europe and became the basis of many popular patent medicines, including laudanum. As very many people purchased these products without understanding the potential for overdose, calls arose for legislative control. This led in Britain to the Pharmacy Act of 1868, which is highly important for two reasons.

First, it established the policy of limiting availability of dangerous drugs, a policy then followed by other European nations. Second, it placed central responsibility on a health-related profession, the Pharmaceutical Society established in 1841, to oversee the Act's provisions. Thus as well as aiding public health by having dangerous drugs sold or dispensed by individuals knowledgeable about their qualities, the Act also provided a significant boost to the status (and profitability) of a health profession. This created the conditions for a very long-standing approach (which became known as the British System) of placing health professionals at the heart of the governmental and policy responses to the control of drugs.

The impact of the Pharmacy Act was that the vast majority of people who used opiates did not become dependent on them (as opposed to in China, where the British trade in opium meant that over a quarter of the male population were regular consumers by 1905). In fact, recreational or addictive use in nations where opium was not so aggressively marketed remained rare until the early 20th century, with very many recordings of high praise for the drug. Nevertheless, some people did become dependent, especially once the more potent form of morphine, heroin, was developed in 1874 (and marketed from 1897 as a nonaddictive morphine substitute and cough medicine for children). However, the large bulk of those dependent were either members of health-related professions (who had ready access to morphine and heroin), or people who had become dependent following initial use of a heroin- or morphine-based medicine.

When the problem of what to do about these people became sufficiently pressing, the government set up the Rolleston Committee, which reported in 1926. This laid down a policy framework, which remained largely unchanged for the next 40 years, the central position of which was maintenance-prescribing for dependent users of heroin (MacGregor & Ettorre, 1987; Velleman & Rigby, 1990). This Committee laid down guidelines for appropriate maintenance prescribing:

> Persons for whom, after every effort has been made for the cure of the addiction, the drug cannot be completely withdrawn, either because (i) complete withdrawal produces serious symptoms which cannot be satisfactorily treated under the ordinary conditions of private practice; or (ii) the patient, while capable of leading a useful and fairly normal life so long as he takes a certain non-progressive quantity, usually small, of the drug of addiction, ceases to be able to do so when the regular allowance is withdrawn. (Rolleston Committee, 1926)

These guidelines gave control over prescribing to general practitioners, who could use their discretion on the treatment/maintenance of dependent individuals. This centrality of prescribing, and the discretionary powers of doctors, confirmed the primary orientation for dealing with heroin use as within the health sphere. Prescribing was of course not the only plank of government policy, enforcement has always been included in the system of controlling drug use in the United Kingdom, but it was the primary focus. This system was the practice until the 1960s (Velleman & Rigby, 1990) and then followed by another health-oriented approach focused more on short-term prescribing of reducing amounts of opiates, leading to abstinence. It was not until the 1980s that the long-standing health orientation shifted towards a more confrontational, crime and enforcement approach, swayed by an increasingly USA-influenced United Nations and international 'war on drugs'.

The United States

While the main conceptual basis of British drugs policy was originally economic, followed by health, drug policy within the United States developed very differently. First, both medicine and pharmacy remained essentially unorganized in the United States until the First World War. Although the American Medical Association was founded in 1847, and the American Pharmaceutical Association in 1851, both remained small and nationally unrepresentative groups for the next 60–70 years; and crucially, both lacked the authority to license practitioners. As Musto (n.d.) states:

> Licensing of pharmacists and physicians, which was the central govern-ments' responsibility in European nations was, in the United States, a power reserved to each individual state .... any form of licensing that appeared to give a monopoly to the educated was attacked as a contradic-tion of American democratic ideals. (para. 5)

Thus within the United States, with respect to drugs policy, there was

* no practical control over the health professions;
* no control on the labelling, composition, or advertising of compounds that might contain opiates or cocaine;
* no representative national health organization to aid the government in drafting regulations, and
* no national system of developing laws or regulations relating to drugs (because the form of government adopted in the United States, a federation of partly independent states, was a conscious attempt to prevent the establishment of an all-powerful central government char-acteristic of Europe).

The result, unsurprisingly, was no drug policy at all with most states making little attempt to control addictive substances until quite late in the 19th century. Opiates were used in abundance for almost every ailment, with hypodermic syringes even advertised to consumers in the Sears Roebuck catalogue (Musto, 1973).

The second difference between the United Kingdom and the United States related to who became addicted. In the United States there was a large population of Chinese immigrants, especially on the West Coast, many of whom were already dependent on opium. United States' policy then, fragmented and with no lead from the health lobby, began with the stigmatization of Chinese immigrants and opium dens across California, leading rapidly from town ordinances in the 1870s to the formation of the (United States'-focused and led) International Opium Commission in 1909. During this period, the portrayal of opium in literature was squalid and violent, and purified morphine and heroin became widely available for injection (Brown, 2002).

The US approach towards illicit drugs was also greatly influenced by the temperance movement's approach to alcohol. This movement helped establish the attitude that there could be no compromise with the 'forces of evil' and that 'moderation' was a false concept when applied to alcohol: prohibition was the only logical or moral policy when dealing with this great national problem. As Musto (n.d.) argues, the significance for the control of 'narcotics' (in the United States this term covers most illicit drugs, including marijuana) is that 'The moral question of how to deal with a dangerous substance was being fought out over alcohol, but the case would be stronger even with narcotics when that issue was brought to national deliberation.'

As a result of these three factors – no strong health professional lobby, a stigmatized group being visibly addicted, and a strong Puritan prohibitory approach, the dominant conceptualization adopted was a moral and a criminal justice one: laws regulated use, and those breaching those laws were to be punished. Further, the strong moral approach, coupled with a belief that most of the drugs they were seeking to outlaw came from other countries, also meant that the United States felt a duty to ensure that other countries took a similar line. Accordingly, the United States pursued a twin approach from the start of the 20th century: strict controls at home, and an international approach to dealing with supply. The Harrison Narcotics Act of 1914 basically outlawed opiates. Providing maintenance prescriptions was unlawful, and the federal government could take action nationwide to arrest and convict health professionals who practiced this. In 1920 a prohibition policy was also adopted for alcohol. However, while alcohol prohibition laws were repealed in 1933, anti-drugs laws became increasingly draconian, and by the 1950s, punishment for violations included the death penalty (Musto, 1973; n.d.). Nevertheless, with regard to marijuana, there has been a recent shift in policy at state level in the United States, discussed below.

International Drug Policy

The United States' international approach to drug control started with an international meeting at Shanghai in 1909 to consider opium traffic among nations. The United States wished to join with China in its own efforts to eradicate the serious opium problem that British trade had left it with. This meeting resolved with almost unanimous agreement that opium for nonmedicinal uses should be prohibited or 'carefully regulated', and that all nations should 're-examine' their laws. Subsequently, the Hague Opium Conference, 1911, and Opium Convention of 1912, placed the burden on domestic legislation in each nation to control the preparation and distribution of medicinal opium, morphine, heroin, cocaine, and any new derivative with similar properties (Taylor, 1969). The Hague Convention was then incorporated into the Versailles treaty, which ended the First World War. Britain, therefore, passed the Dangerous Drugs Act of 1920, not because of any serious problems with addiction but because, by ratifying the Versailles treaty, it had committed to comprehensive domestic legislation (Berridge & Edwards, 1981).

Further international treaties followed, which continued the policy, started by the United States, of seeking to control and criminalize a wide range of drugs – mainly opiates and cocaine, but also marijuana. Although the United States' international influence on drug control waned during the 1920s due to an increasingly isolationist stance, by the outbreak of the Second World War it was again participating in international antidrug activities (Musto, 1973). The United States exercised drug control primarily via law enforcement and moral outrage both within its borders, by criminalizing possession and demonizing all drug use, and increasingly across the entire world by ensuring that the main organizations it underwrote financially and politically, such as the United Nations and the WHO, adopted similar terminologies and approaches.

In the 1970s the term 'war on drugs' was coined in the United States, and the power of this prohibitory, criminal justice approach, and the efforts put into ensuring international engagement, cannot be minimized. The 1988 United Nations Convention Against Illicit Traffic in Narcotic Drugs and Psychotropic Substances made it mandatory for the signatory countries to 'adopt such measures as may be necessary to establish as criminal offences under its domestic law' (UN, 1988, p. 3) all the activities related to the production, sale, transport, distribution, etc., of a range of restricted substances. Criminalization also applies to the 'cultivation of opium poppy, coca bush or cannabis plants for the purpose of the production of narcotic drugs', an element that the United States had tried unsuccessfully to introduce internationally in 1925.

Convergence of Policies

More recently there has been a move away from the 'war on drugs' ideology, and the US has started to accept the necessity of not only using a crime and punishment model, and begun to provide substitute medication (e.g. methadone) and sterile injecting equipment. The most recent US *National Drug Control Strategy* (2010) was presented as a new direction in drug policy, where drug use is seen mainly as a public health issue, and where the enormous demand is recognized as the prime cause of drug problems. The strategy emphasizes prevention, treatment and recovery from addiction, and calls for the integration of addiction treatment into mainstream medicine, as with other chronic disorders. Indeed, President Obama stated that while he was not in favour of legalization, he believed drugs ought to be treated as 'more of a public health problem . . . we've been so focused on arrests, incarceration, interdiction, that we don't spend as much time thinking about how do we shrink demand' (Reuters, 2011). A special situation has developed with regard to marijuana, and this is discussed below.

Although UK policy was influenced by the 'war on drugs', it still retained a primarily health and social care approach, with drug treatment being commissioned and performance managed via the National Treatment Agency for Substance Misuse (NTA), part of the National Health Service (NHS). This 'health' approach has been reinforced by the recent emphasis on 'recovery' (UKDPC, 2008). While earlier policies were primarily aimed at increasing the number of people accessing treatment, notably with provision of opioid substitute drugs, Britain has attempted to integrate all aspects of its drugs strategy, with successive policies focusing on treatment outcomes and social reintegration of users (Home Office, 2008) and on making recovery a key policy element (Home Office, 2010; Scottish Government, 2008), as well as on reducing the supply.

Other European countries also have made serious attempts to move away from a 'war on drugs' to rebalance drug policy objectives between reducing harms and promoting recovery. National drug strategies and action plans now exist in almost all of the 30 countries monitored by the European Monitoring Centre for Drugs and Drug Addiction (EMCDDA). Portugal's current drug policy is more than ten years old, but it has gained increased attention in recent years, first from drug-policy analysts and advocacy groups, but now also from governments in Europe and beyond. Central to the Portuguese policy is the decriminalization of drug use, discussed below.

Outside the European Union, a number of national or regional strategies have been published recently, notably by Australia, Russia, the United States and the Organization of American States (OAS). These documents reveal similar characteristics to the European approach. Hence the OAS's Hemispheric Drug Strategy describes drug addiction as a chronic relapsing disease that should be treated as such. The first Russian drug strategy (2010–2020) builds on a recognition of the scale of the drugs problem and its contribution to the spread of infectious diseases. The Australian drug strategy (2010–2015) has the broadest scope, with minimizing harm as the overarching approach to all psychoactive substances capable of causing addiction and health problems, including alcohol, tobacco, illicit and other drugs.

Decriminalization or Legalization

The picture presented above is of an increasing convergence in drug policies across the world, still with an emphasis on a 'war on drugs' and on prohibition and criminalization; but with a clear view that prevention, treatment, and harm reduction are important components as well.

A rather different approach is that of the drug liberalization movement, and its two component parts, legalization and decriminalization. There have always been strong voices arguing for a more libertarian view of drug policy, and since the early 2000s these voices have started to gain some political capital. Commentators have called attention to numerous factors that suggest that an antidrug policy may not be sensible, helpful or deliverable, including:

- most illicit drugs are less harmful than either alcohol or tobacco, which are legal in the vast majority of countries;
- the libertarian view, that as long as someone is doing no harm to others, they should be allowed to consume whatever they wish;
- the 'war on drugs' seems demonstrably not to be working, as very large amounts of drugs are still available, and (certainly until recently) the numbers of drug users worldwide has continued to increase;
- prohibition turns large numbers of citizens into criminals, and if significant numbers of people ignore a law, it suggests the law needs changing;
- prohibition increases price, which increases acquisitive crime and organized crime, with resulting rises in violence and corruption. Gamboa (2012) estimates that over 10,000 deaths a year in the United States are caused by the criminalization of drugs, and nearly 13,000 people died in drug-related violence in Mexico in the first 9 months of 2011 (BBC, 2012)
- prohibition also reduces quality, adulterated drugs are frequently sold, and negative health consequences, and deaths, rise.

Because of these factors, there have been increasing calls for either decriminalization, or legalization (or relegalization, reflecting the fact that drugs which are currently illicit used to be legal).

9

Decriminalization

Proponents of drug decriminalization call for reduced control and reduced penalties. Some support these ideas as a 'halfway house' towards legalization, and propose that illegal drug users be fined instead of imprisoned, or given other punishments that would not appear on their permanent criminal record. In many ways, decriminalization is a form of harm reduction. On the other hand, because decriminalization is in some ways an intermediate between prohibition and legalization, it has been criticized as being 'the worst of both worlds' in that drug *sales* would still be illegal, thus perpetuating the problems associated with organized crime while also failing to discourage illegal drug use by removing the criminal penalties that might otherwise cause some people to choose not to use drugs. Counter arguments include that decriminalization of possession of drugs would refocus law enforcement onto arresting dealers and big-time criminals, thus making it more effective.

Engaging with these arguments, in recent years 15 European countries have made changes to their penalties for possession of small amounts of drugs. Three broad types of penalty changes can be identified since the early 2000s: changing the legal status of the offence (criminal or non-criminal); changing categories of drugs, when the category determines the penalty; and changing the maximum penalty available. Most of the countries that have altered their penalties have used a combination of these types of change, complicating any concise analysis.

Changing the legal status of the offence is perhaps the most significant step. In 2001 Portugal became the first country to decriminalize personal possession of all drugs, reducing the *maximum* punishment from 3 months' imprisonment (already far smaller than in many other countries) to an administrative fine given by the new 'commissions for dissuasion of drug abuse', which prioritize health solutions over punitive sanctions. These changes have been extensively evaluated, and demonstrated positive results (Domoslawsk, 2011; Greenwald, 2009; Hughes & Stevens, 2010). In Luxembourg, since 2001, personal possession of cannabis incurs only a fine for the first offence, and maximum penalty for personal possession of all other drugs was reduced from 3 years in prison to 6 months. A similar change took place in 2003 in Belgium, and moves towards decriminalization were also made in Estonia and Slovenia.

Without changing the legal status, other countries (Romania, Bulgaria, Czech Republic, Italy, and the United Kingdom) changed the categorization of different drugs, with the category determining the penalty. The United Kingdom has been especially changeable, in 2004 reclassifying cannabis from Class B to Class C, lowering the maximum imprisonment for personal possession from 5 to 2 years; and national police guidelines were issued not to arrest, but to give an informal warning, if there were no aggravating circumstances. Then in January 2009, cannabis was reclassified to Class B, raising maximum penalties to 5 years' imprisonment again. Revised national police guidelines continued to advise an informal warning for a first offence, with a criminal fine for a second offence. A third group of countries, Finland, Greece, Denmark and France, reduced their penalties for personal possession, without addressing legal status or categories and, in 2005, Slovakia widened the definition of 'possession for personal use' from 1 to 3 doses of any illicit substance, while leaving the maximum punishment unchanged.

The situation in Holland has also given rise to a great deal of discussion. The possession of small quantities of drugs for personal use is accorded a much lower priority in Holland: anyone with less than 0.5 g of Schedule I drugs (e.g. heroin, cocaine) will generally not be prosecuted, and for cannabis a maximum of 5 g will not lead to investigation or prosecution. The Netherlands is the only country in Europe with a national system for the regulated supply of cannabis. When the principle of 'separating the markets' between dangerous drugs and cannabis was codified in 1976, *coffeeshops* emerged as a semi-legal sales channel for cannabis, albeit under strict conditions, including not serving alcohol. A *coffeeshop* is not to be confused with a *koffiehuis* (coffee house) or a *café* (the equivalent of a bar). *Coffeeshops* are tolerated as an attempt to keep young people away from other more dangerous drugs. Nevertheless, around three-quarters of Dutch municipalities do not allow *coffeeshops*; the total number has declined, and two new criteria were introduced in 2012 to tighten controls on these venues. The 'closed club criterion' limited *coffeeshop* access to registered members (maximum 2000), and the 'residence criterion' limited accessibility only to adults resident in the Netherlands. The rationale behind these developments was to reduce public nuisance and return *coffeeshops* to their original purpose: small-scale points of sale of cannabis for local users. However, the mayors of major Dutch cities have said that restricting access to *coffeeshops* will simply lead to an increase in street dealing and criminality. At the time of writing a new government has come into office, and there is ongoing debate as to whether these new laws will be enforced.

In the United States, in 2013, 19 states allow possession of small amounts of marijuana with a medical prescription. Two states, Colorado and Washington have just legalized possession of small amounts of marijuana for recreational use, bringing them into direct conflict with US federal laws and the 1988 UN Convention, which the US strongly supported. How this will play out is yet to be seen.

Thus, although laws vary across different countries, there are signs of a converging trend towards decriminalization or a reduction in penalties for personal possession of drugs, and no Western country has introduced new criminal penalties or increased prison sentences over the last ten years.

Relegalization

Drug relegalization calls for the end of government-enforced prohibition of the distribution or sale and personal use of specified (or all) currently banned drugs. Not all proponents of drug relegalization necessarily share a common ethical framework, and proposed ideas (e.g. Transform, 2009) range from full legalization, completely removing all government prohibition or control, to various forms of regulated legalization, which might mean:

- mandated labels with dosage and medical warnings;
- restrictions on advertising;
- age limitations;
- restrictions on amount purchased at one time;
- requirements on the form in which certain drugs would be supplied;
- ban on sale to intoxicated persons;
- special user licences to purchase particular drugs.

Any regulated legalization would probably have a range of restrictions for different drugs, depending on perceived risk, with some being sold over the counter in pharmacies or other licensed establishments, while those with greater risks of harm might only be available on licensed premises where use could be monitored and emergency medical care made available. Full legalization is often proposed by libertarians who object to drug laws on moral grounds, while regulated legalization is suggested by groups such as Transform (http://www.tdpf.org.uk/), and Law Enforcement Against Prohibition (LEAP, http://www.leap.cc/) who object to the drug laws on the grounds that they fail to achieve their stated aims and instead greatly worsen the problems associated with use of prohibited drugs. An important distinction that is often lost is that favouring drug relegalization does not imply approval of drug use.

New Drugs

The policy responses discussed so far in this chapter are all attempts to deal with a growing but relatively predictable set of substances: opiates (primarily heroin), stimulants (primarily amphetamine and cocaine), hallucinogens (primarily LSD), and marijuana. A major new phenomenon appeared in the 1980s: the rise of synthetic substances, designed to not fall within the remit of existing laws but to be very attractive to potential users. These new psychoactive substances have been referred to colloquially as 'designer drugs' or 'legal highs'. Drugs legislation generally covers specific substances, as opposed to whole classes of chemicals. Accordingly, each new drug synthesized is not covered by existing legislation, and needs to be added to the list of illegal substances, as evidence accrues of dangerousness (or as media-induced 'moral panics' create situations where politicians feel they need to declare a substance illegal, long before there is sufficient evidence as to whether or not the substance is dangerous, and if so, at what level). In the United Kingdom, the Chair of the Advisory Council on the Misuse of Drugs (ACMD, set up to advise the government), Professor David Nutt, suggested a more rational policy towards declaring drugs illegal, based on the level of harm the drug had the potential to cause (Nutt, King, Saulsbury, & Blakemore, 2007). Professor Nutt's championing of this idea was so politically unacceptable that senior politicians attempted to force him to resign; when he refused, he was sacked (Guardian, 2009).

Ecstasy (MDMA)

The first synthetic drug was Ecstasy (MDMA), which combined some of the properties of two classes of drug (stimulants and hallucinogens). Although first synthesized in 1912, it was largely forgotten over the next 65 years, until it began to be used recreationally in the late 1970s and rose to prominence via dances and 'raves' across the Western world. Ecstasy was made illegal in the United Kingdom in 1977 and in the United States in 1985. However, MDMA proved to be the proverbial 'tip of the iceberg'.

Other New Drugs

The new drugs market is distinguished by the rapidity by which suppliers respond to control measures by offering new alternatives to restricted products. This has led the European Monitoring Centre for Drugs and Drug Addiction to set up an 'early warning system' and a speedy risk assessment for any new drug that appears problematic, so that European governments can be ready to take action. A range of information sources and leading-edge indicators, including Internet monitoring and wastewater analysis (see below) are all used to help obtain a better picture of emerging drug trends in Europe. Between 1997 and 2010, more than 150 new psychoactive substances were formally notified through this early warning system, and all are now being monitored by the EMCDDA. The rate at which new substances appear on the market has increased, with 24 in 2009, 41 in 2010, and 49 in 2011. Many of these new substances have been detected through test-purchases of products sold on the Internet and in specialist shops (e.g. 'smart' shops, 'head' shops, 'legal high' shops). The number of online sources offering at least one psychoactive substance rose from 314 in 2011 to 690 in 2012 (European Monitoring Centre for Drugs and Drug Addiction, 2011a, 2012a).

Increasing Amphetamine Use

An emerging issue is the increased capacity and sophistication in the illicit amphetamine market (European Monitoring Centre for Drugs and Drug Addiction, 2011b) with changing patterns and trends in the production and trafficking of this widely used synthetic stimulant, as well as the chemicals for its manufacture. In many ways, amphetamine can be termed a 'European drug', with data suggesting Europe to be both the world's number one producer of the substance and a major consumer market. While, globally, methamphetamine is more widely used, amphetamine has stabilized as the second most widely consumed stimulant drug in Europe today (after cocaine). And in many countries, especially in the north and east of Europe, it is the second most widely used illicit drug after cannabis. This suggests that, although amphetamine attracts much less attention in media and policy circles than cannabis, cocaine or heroin, it should not be treated as a 'secondary issue'. Research published in 2011 showed that around 12.5 million Europeans had used amphetamines in their lifetime, some 2 million in the previous year. European amphetamine markets are therefore highly profitable 'business opportunities' for organized crime (European Monitoring Centre for Drugs and Drug Addiction, 2011b). There are distinct production and trafficking areas ('criminal hubs'), with large-scale production and organized crime involvement being found mainly in northern Europe, centred on the Netherlands and to a lesser extent Belgium. Significant production and trafficking of the drug also occurs in the north-east, notably in Poland, where production is reported to be on the rise.

Emerging Initiatives in Policy and Practice

The rapid spread of new substances is pushing governments around the world to rethink their standard responses to the drug problem, with policymakers demanding new, faster and effective ways of drug control to protect public health and deter suppliers from circumventing controls (European Monitoring Centre for Drugs and Drug Addiction, 2011a, 2012a). But there are both practical and legal obstacles facing countries when responding to such new substances. New drugs may pose health and other risks to individuals and the general public, yet hard data on these may initially be lacking. Testing products can be time consuming and expensive, which can hinder rapid, targeted responses by legislators. Legislative procedures to bring a substance under the control of the drug law can take over a year in some countries, and controlling a substance may have unintended consequences, such as the emergence of a more harmful, noncontrolled replacement. Faster processes have been introduced in some countries, including emergency systems that enable a substance to be placed under temporary controls, or fast-track systems placing substances under permanent control by shortening the consultation periods in the law-making process. But striking the right balance between swiftness of response to new substances on the one hand, and sufficient scientific evidence and legislative supervision on the other, is an important policy goal.

Wastewater Analysis

Wastewater analysis or sewage epidemiology is a rapidly developing scientific discipline with the potential for monitoring population-level trends in illicit drug consumption (European Monitoring Centre for Drugs and Drug Addiction, 2008). Advances in analytical chemistry have made it possible to identify urinary excretion of illicit drugs and their main metabolites at very low concentrations. This is comparable to taking a much-diluted urine sample from an entire community. With certain assumptions, it is possible to back-calculate from the amount of metabolite in the wastewater to an estimate of the amount of a drug consumed

15

in a community. While early research focused on identifying cocaine and its metabolites, recent studies have produced estimates on levels of cannabis, amphetamine, methamphetamine, heroin, and methadone. The identification of less commonly used drugs, such as ketamine and new psychoactive substances, looks promising. This area of work is developing in a multidisciplinary fashion, with important contributions from a number of disciplines including analytical chemistry, physiology, biochemistry, sewage engineering, and conventional drug epidemiology. At least 18 research groups in 13 European countries are working in this area (European Monitoring Centre for Drugs and Drug Addiction, 2011b). At the top of the current research agenda is development of consensus on sampling methods and tools, as well as the establishment of a code of good practice for the field.

In January 2012 the EMCDDA launched a multicity demonstration project, and by the end of that year the project had generated comparable data from 26 European cities, thanks to a specifically designed and agreed common sampling approach (European Monitoring Centre for Drugs and Drug Addiction, 2012b). This demonstration project will provide comparable information in real time on weekly patterns of use, trends and changing consumption habits in the participating cities. Wastewater analysis is an emerging science. While its methods do not provide the detailed consumption data currently yielded by drug surveys, its ability to provide timely estimates of illicit drug consumption in a given population make it a useful complement to existing methods for studying drug use trends in Europe.

Heroin Assisted Treatment

In the treatment of opiate addiction, both gradual reduction and methadone maintenance have long had their advocates. Indeed, the prescription of substitution drugs (e.g. methadone, buprenorphine) has become a mainstream, first-line treatment for opioid dependence, with around 700,000 of Europe's 1.3 million problem opioid users receiving substitution treatment today (Strang, Groshkova, and Metrebian, 2012). But there has always been a small minority of entrenched opioid users who have repeatedly failed to respond to interventions to either reduce use or substitute a different drug, and they used to be thought of as 'untreatable'.

Since the early 2000s there has been increasing interest in utilizing medicinal heroin as a substitute drug (Metrebian, Carnwath, Stimson &

Soltz, 2002; Strang et al., 2010; Uchtenhagen, 2010). Supervised injectable heroin (SIH) treatment was first introduced in Switzerland in the mid-1990s in the face of a growing national heroin problem. The new approach was a step on from prescribing heroin to addicts without supervision, practised in the United Kingdom throughout the 20th century – the British System referred to earlier in this chapter. By 2011, some 2,500 clients across the European Union and Switzerland were enrolled in SIH treatment, under direct medical supervision to ensure safety and to prevent diversion of diacetylmorphine (medicinal heroin) to the illicit market.

Strang et al. (2012) report that the research trials conducted since the mid-1990s provide strong evidence that, for this specific group of long-term heroin users, SIH treatment can be more effective than oral methadone maintenance treatment (MMT). Less positively, the risk of adverse events (e.g. fatal overdoses) was higher in SIH than MMT, underlining the need for clinical precautions. The cost of SIH treatment for this problematic target group was also considerably higher than that of MMT. But, according to the report, if analysis takes into account all relevant parameters, especially related to criminal behaviour, SIH treatment saves money. The very fact that SIH has been trialled in this way is a major policy and practice initiative; we will need to wait to see if it will be taken into the mainstream.

Opioid Maintenance in European Prisons

A recent systematic review and editorial published in *Addiction* (Hedrich et al., 2012; Hedrich & Farrell, 2012) describe opioid maintenance treatment (OMT) as an 'effective option for opioid-dependent prisoners', offering benefits similar to those reported in community settings. According to the findings of the systematic review, prison-based OMT offers important benefits, such as continued treatment for inmates in OMT before incarceration, and recruitment into treatment of problem opioid users previously untreated. For both groups, it reduces illicit opioid use, injecting and associated risks while in prison, and potentially minimises the likelihood of overdose on release. The papers also find prison-based OMT to be cost-effective, offering 'potential for important gains in public health and subsequent cost savings'. Of the 30 countries monitored by the EMCDDA, 24 now sanction prison OMT.

Although this implies that encouraging progress is being made in several European countries towards closing the treatment gap between community and prison, in most countries such equivalence of care is an aspiration rather than a reality. One major conclusion is that, in order to promote equivalence and continuity of treatment, it is important to challenge negative perceptions of prison-based opioid maintenance treatment among policymakers and prison administrators and to develop appropriate training programmes for prison staff and professionals.

Hepatitis C

Hepatitis C virus (HCV) infection is highly prevalent in injecting drug users (IDUs) across Europe, with national samples of IDUs showing between 22% and 83% infected. A large proportion of IDUs are now over 40, most of whom will have been living with HCV for 15–25 years. The natural history of chronic HCV (cirrhosis risk escalates after 15–20 years) and the ageing cohort effect in this population, mean that a large burden of advanced liver disease can be anticipated over the next decade. In spite of this burden and the recent improved treatment outcomes for HCV patients, available data show treatment uptake to be very low in this group (1–9%). Considerable improvements in HCV antiviral therapy have been reported in recent years and there is a growing recognition of the importance of providing HCV infection treatment to IDUs. Data show that this group can now be treated as successfully as non- or ex-injectors and that low rates of reinfection are recorded after successful treatment.

Conclusions

Babor et al. (2010) make a number of helpful points about where we are at present, and where we should we be going with international drugs policy. Several of these are especially relevant to this chapter:

1. *There is no single drug problem within or across societies; neither is there a magic bullet that will solve 'the' problem.* There are marked differences between and within societies in the types of drugs used at a particular time, how they are used, the problems caused by the drugs, and how a society responds.
2. *The drug policy debate is often dominated by false dichotomies that can mislead about legitimate options and expected impacts.* Law enforcement and health service approaches each contribute, as when, for example, police warn users of dangerously high-potency batches;

and health services treatment leads to fewer crimes. In addition, targeting drug use *per se* as well as targeting the drug-related harm is not inconsistent because harm-reduction approaches can lead to abstinence while abstinence can result in reduced harm.

3. *Perverse impacts of drug policy are prevalent.* Drug policies should be judged not only on intended effects but also on unintended consequences, using cost-benefit analysis.

4. *In terms of prevention, many policies that affect drug problems are not considered drug policy, and many specific drug policies have effects outside the drug domain.* Similar factors can predict problematic drug use and other problem behaviours, and policies in one domain can impact on others.

5. *Similarly, there is modest support for school, family and community prevention programmes,* especially those that focus upon improving overall behaviour and social skills, and not specifically on drug use.

6. *In terms of control, efforts by wealthy countries to curtail cultivation of drug-producing plants in poor countries have not reduced aggregate drug supply or drug use, and probably never will.* Significant expansion in cultivation curtailment, as in defoliation and alternative development programmes, has not produced desired results. One reason is that production can be simply moved to another area, or another country.

7. *Once drugs are made illegal, there is a point beyond which increased enforcement and incarceration yield little added benefit.* Increasing enforcement against drug dealers does not result in price increases beyond what would occur with routine enforcement.

8. *The legal pharmaceutical system can affect a country's prescription drug problem and drug policy options.* Because of increasing rates of misuse of psycho-pharmaceuticals, more efficient distribution and dispensing of medicinal products could be a first step towards an effective policy addressing misuse of prescription medications.

9. *There is virtually no scientific research to guide improvement of supply control and law enforcement efforts.* The lack of careful study of enforcement, interdiction, incarceration, and related measures poses a major barrier to effective application.

10. *Substantial investment in evidence-based services for opiate-dependent individuals usually reduces drug-related problems.* Injecting drug use poses a high risk of overdose and death, and has resulted in an epidemic of HIV/AIDS in many societies. Expansion of effective services for opiate dependent individuals will benefit not just drug users but society at large.

In conclusion, drugs policy has grown up piecemeal over many years, often strongly influenced, either overtly or covertly, by ideological positions. It is certainly rarely evidence based and, although available scientific evidence is neither perfect nor sufficient, it is equally certain that what is available is rarely used to best effect. It would be a move in the right direction if more leaders and policymakers were to apply the available evidence to create more effective drug policy.

Note

1. A longer and more detailed version of this chapter is available on the author's website: http://www.bath.ac.uk/psychology/staff/richard-velleman/ (accessed March 4, 2013).

References

Babor, T., Caulkins, J., Edwards, G., Fischer, B., Foxcroft, D., Humphreys, K., et al. (2010). *Drug policy and the public good.* New York: Oxford University Press.

BBC (2012). Retrieved March 4, 2013, from http://www.bbc.co.uk/news/world-latin-america-16518267.

Berridge, V. & Edwards, G. (1981). *Opium and the people: Opiate use in nineteenth-century England.* London: Allan Lane.

Brown, R. (2002). The opium trade and opium policies In India, China, Britain, and the United States: historical comparisons and theoretical interpretations. *Asian Journal of Social Science 30*(3), 623–656.

Domoslawsk, A. (2011). *Drug policy in Portugal: The benefits of decriminalizing drug use.* Warsaw: Open Society Foundations.

European Monitoring Centre for Drugs and Drug Addiction (2008). *Assessing illicit drugs in wastewater.* Lisbon: EMCDDA.

European Monitoring Centre for Drugs and Drug Addiction (2011a). *Responding to new psychoactive substances.* Lisbon: EMCDDA.

European Monitoring Centre for Drugs and Drug Addiction (2011b). *The state of the drugs problem in Europe: Annual report, 2011.* Lisbon: EMCDDA.

European Monitoring Centre for Drugs and Drug Addiction (2012a). *EMCDDA – Europol 2011 annual report on the implementation of Council Decision 2005/387/JHA.* Lisbon: EMCDDA.

European Monitoring Centre for Drugs and Drug Addiction (2012b). Drugs and Wastewater. Retrieved March 16, 2013 from http://www.emcdda.europa.eu/news/2012/wastewater.

Gamboa, F. (2012). The legalization of drugs: a form of euthanasia or a death cult? *The Americas Political Folio Strategic Analysis Bulletin, 1*(7), 1–8. Retrieved March 4, 2013 from http://praxispublica.org/en.

Greenwald, G. (2009). *Drug decriminalization in Portugal: Lessons for creating fair and successful drug policies*, Washington, DC: CATO Institute.

Guardian (2009). Retrieved March 4, 2013 from www.guardian.co.uk/politics/2009/nov/02/drug-policy-alan-johnson-nutt.

Hedrich, D., Alves, P., Farrell, M., Stöver, H., Møller, L. & Mayet, S. (2012). The effectiveness of opioid maintenance treatment in prison settings: a systematic review. *Addiction, 107*, 501–517.

Hedrich, D. & Farrell, M. (2012). Editorial: Opioid maintenance in European prisons: is the treatment gap closing? *Addiction, 107*, 461–463.

Home Office (2008). Drugs: Protecting Families and Communities. Retrieved March 16, 2013 from http://webarchive.nationalarchives.gov.uk/20100413151441/drugs.homeoffice.gov.uk/publication-search/drug-strategy/drug-strategy-2008.html.

Home Office (2010). Drug Strategy 2010. Reducing Demand Restricting Supply, Building Recovery: Supporting People to Live a Drug Free Life. Retrieved March 4, 2013 from http://www.homeoffice.gov.uk/publications/alcohol-drugs/drugs/drug-strategy/drug-strategy-2010?view=Binary.

Hughes, C. & Stevens, A. (2010). What can we learn from the Portuguese decriminalization of illicit drugs? *British Journal of Criminology, 50*, 999–1022.

MacGregor, S. & Ettorre, B. (1987). From treatment to rehabilitation – aspects of the evolution of British policy on the care of drug takers. In: Dorn, N. & South, N. (Eds.) *A land fit for heroin? Drug policies, prevention and practice.* London: Macmillan.

Metrebian, N., Carnwath, T., Stimson, G. V. & Soltz, T. (2002). Survey of doctors prescribing diamorphine (heroin) to opiate dependent drug users in the United Kingdom. *Addiction, 97*, 1155–1161.

Musto, D. (1973). *The American disease: Origins of narcotic control.* New Haven, CT: Yale University Press.

Musto, D. (n.d.). The History of Legislative Control over Opium, Cocaine, and their Derivatives. Retrieved March 4, 2013 from www.druglibrary.org/schaffer/history/ophs.htm.

National Drug Control Strategy (2010). Retrieved on March 16, 2012 from http://www.whitehouse.gov/sites/default/files/ondcp/policy-and-research/ndcs2010_0.pdf.

Nutt, D., King, L., Saulsbury, W. & Blakemore, C. (2007). Development of a rational scale to assess the harm of drugs of potential misuse. *Lancet, 369*(9566), 1047–1053.

Reuters (2011). Obama: drug abuse requires broader policy response. Retrieved March 5, 2013 from www.reuters.com/article/2011/01/27/us-obama-drugs-idUSTRE70Q8XR20110 127.

Rolleston Committee (1926). Departmental Committee on Morphine and Heroin Addiction (Rolleston) Recommendations 8b. Circumstances in which morphine or heroin may legitimately be administered to addicts. Retrieved March 5, 2013 from http://www.druglibrary.eu/library/reports/rolleston.html.

Scottish Government (2008). The Road to Recovery. A New Approach to Tackling Scotland's Drug Problem. Retrieved on March 16, 2013 from http://www.scotland.gov.uk/Publications/2008/05/22161610/0.

Strang, J., Metrebian, N., Lintzeris, N., Potts, L., Carnwath, T., Mayet, S. et al. (2010). Supervised injectable heroin or injectable methadone versus optimized oral methadone as treatment for chronic heroin addicts in England after persistent failure in orthodox treatment (RIOTT): A randomised trial. *Lancet, 375*, 1885–1895.

Strang, J., Groshkova, T. & Metrebian, N (2012). *New heroin-assisted treatment.* Lisbon: EMCDDA.

Taylor, A. (1969). *American diplomacy and the narcotics traffic, 1900–1939: A study in international humanitarian reform.* Durham, NC: Duke University Press.

Transform Drug Policy Foundation (2009). After the War on Drugs: Blueprint for Regulation. Retrieved 1 December 2012 from http://www.tdpf.org.uk/Transform_Drugs_Blueprint.pdf.

Uchtenhagen, A. (2010). Heroin-assisted treatment in Switzerland: a case study in policy change. *Addiction, 105*, 29–37.

UKDPC (2008). *A vision of recovery.* London: UK Drug Policy Commission Recovery Consensus Group.

UN (1988). *Convention against Illicit Traffic in Narcotic Drugs and Psychotropic Substances.* New York, United Nations.

Velleman, R. & Rigby, J. (1990). Harm-minimisation: old wine in new bottles? *International Journal on Drug Policy, 1*(6), 24–27.

2

Formulating Effective Alcohol Policy: Not as Simple as it Sounds

Robin Davidson

Introduction

This chapter summarizes some of the issues that determine the content and direction of national policies on alcohol. It is argued that evidence-based policy may still be talked about more in hope than expectation. Policy frameworks may be partly based on evidence but also on political ideology, media campaigns and ensuring preservation of an alcohol industry. The emphasis of this chapter is on the process of policy formulation rather than a detailed review of the evidence for and against popular policy initiatives.

It has often been said that alcohol is no ordinary commodity (Babor et al., 2010). It is a drug that is sold in supermarkets, there is no requirement for a prescription and it is legally used by most of us. The production, sale and consumption of alcohol impact on many aspects of our lives, providing jobs, tax revenues, an accompaniment to leisure activities, both positive and negative social and health effects, as well as contributing to public disorder and crime. Many of us enjoy alcohol and can be ambivalent about restricting its availability. On the other hand it can be harmful and addictive, and have a serious adverse influence on wellbeing and quality of life. Accordingly, clear policies for the manufacture, distribution and sale of alcohol are essential if we are not to re-experience the social and physical harm that dominated the United Kingdom, and many other countries, up to the mid-nineteenth century. Indeed, prior to this time alcohol use was largely unfettered and uncontrolled. In 1621

Emerging Perspectives on Substance Misuse, First Edition. Edited by Willm Mistral.
© 2013 John Wiley & Sons, Ltd. Published 2013 by John Wiley & Sons, Ltd.

Burton (1838, p. 148) commented that '. . . immoderate drinking is in every place, people flock to the tavern. There is no discouragement now to stagger in the streets, reel, rave, etc.' Public drunkenness seemed to be a normal feature of British life, punctuated at times by a belief in the spiritual advantages of temperance rather than influenced by any government policy initiatives.

Raistrick, Hodgson & Ritson (1999) suggest that one of first significant attempts to control the widespread misuse of alcohol in the United Kingdom through legislation and policy was the Duke of Wellington's Beerhouse Act of 1830. This abolished the tax on beer and allowed anyone, on payment of a small fee, to run premises from which the only alcohol sold was beer. This was aimed at reducing the consumption of spirits by altering the nature of retail outlets. Attempts by government to control alcohol use in this way have continued ever since with, however, various mediating influences. During the Industrial Revolution, policy (or its absence) had been underpinned by trading imperatives. In the mid-19th century it became primarily a moral issue, moving on to social reform in the late Victorian times. During the First World War, policy was driven by the need for national industrial efficiency. At that time no advertising of alcohol was permitted, the level of tax on spirits was increased fivefold and, in cities and industrial areas, public house opening hours, previously 5.30 a.m. to 12.30 at night, were limited at 12 noon to 2.30 p.m. and 6.30 to 9.30 p.m. In the 1960s alcohol policy became primarily a health issue, and latterly it has been influenced by leisure and tourism, as well as increasing concerns about public disorder. A news media emphasis on binge drinking, city centre disorder, night-time economies, A&E violence, safe levels of consumption, café culture and the like, reflects the tone of alcohol policy since the early 2000s in the United Kingdom.

Essentially, Babor (2009) defines alcohol policies as measures aimed at minimizing harm caused by alcohol abuse to both individuals and society. Possibly this is a little optimistic in view of the 'acceptable harm' test. As Vogel (2002, p. 5) argues

> . . . it is obviously not feasible to deny regulatory approval or restrict any or all commercial activities that might pose risks to consumers . . . a literal application of the precautionary principle would impose unacceptably high economic costs as well as unnecessarily restrict many potentially beneficial commercial activities . . . Accordingly, governments must make often difficult choices.

Kingdon (1995) reflects this in his work on the issues that shape the policy agenda. He describes what he calls 'three policy streams'. First, policy is driven by major events or high-profiled reports of commissions; second, policy can reflect the concerns and priorities of elite policymakers; and third is the arena of a public debate dominated by political interests. He goes on to say that successful policy initiatives generally require all three streams to flow together. Good alcohol policy must balance the positive and negative effects of this unusual commodity. On the one hand there is its capacity for contributing to public pleasure, and on the other the so-called 'acceptable level' of its harms.

There are numerous stakeholders in the policy debate, all of whom have a vested interest in how this balance is struck. These stakeholders include the elected government and opposition, the manufacturers, distributers and retailers of alcohol, the law and justice agencies, and the health and social care professionals. Indeed it could be argued that every one of us is a stakeholder in national alcohol policy. Generally there is strong public support for enforcing laws on underage drinking and drink driving, banning of alcohol at sporting events, and providing alcohol education in schools. There is moderate support for restrictions on advertising. There has however been relatively little support for restricting the hours of retail sales, the density of outlets, or fiscal control through what is now called minimum unit pricing (Pendleton et al., 1990). Nonetheless, recently, fiscal initiatives aimed at consumption control have possibly become more publicly acceptable. Following all party approval by the Scottish Assembly in 2008, a minimum unit price with 'protection of health' justification was to be established for the first time in Scotland on April 1, 2013 (Scottish Government, 2008). However, because of a legal challenge to the European Commission, sponsored by the alcohol industry, this start date has been indefinitely delayed. This is a demonstration of how, in recent years, alcohol policy has at times been predicated on the relationship of government with both the alcohol industry and the health lobbies, rather than necessarily on the contemporary evidence base.

Policy should reflect national changes in the pattern and nature of alcohol consumption. For example, since 2003, in the United Kingdom, there has been a gradual reduction in per capita consumption. This overview has however masked individual trends and a north-south gradient, with the rate of reduction being less in the northern areas of the United Kingdom. Consumption among older drinkers has also increased during this time, and there has been a marked increase in purchases from supermarkets (Anderson, 2007) and a marked decrease in purchases from public houses. Recent figures show that 18 pubs now close across the UK each week, with over 5,800 pubs having permanently closed since 2008 (Campaign for Real Ale, 2012). If closures continue at the present rate, the last pub in the United Kingdom will shut in the late 2020s. Although there has been this significant reduction in the number of traditional 'local' public houses, there has been an increase of bars and clubs in town centres focused on attracting a young clientele by offering music, 'happy hours' and 'two-for-one' offers. This changing environment means that policy needs to be flexible, fit for purpose and adaptable.

Policy and the Alcohol Industry

As would be expected, the alcohol industry is driven by the commercial imperative to make profits for shareholders. Each sector of the industry wants policies that are most commercially advantageous to them. It has been noted, for example, within the retail sector that the licensed traders (i.e. public houses, bars and clubs) support minimum unit pricing, whereas the off-licence traders (i.e. small retail shops and, particularly, large supermarkets) are opposed to it. This is simply because a minimum price per unit would not impact on pubs, but would impact on the cut-price, and sometimes less than cost-price, deals offered by stores. Thus, minimum unit pricing would increase the competitiveness of the licensed trade.

Adams, Buetow & Rossen (2010) comment that, until 2010, national UK alcohol policies were by and large closer to those advocated by the industry rather than the health-and-social-care lobby and the associated research evidence base. However, there is very little international evidence as to precisely how the alcohol industry influences governments in the formulation of policy. We have much more information on the processes of influence of the tobacco industry in this regard (Holden & Lee, 2009). We do know that tactics can include active lobbyists, campaign contributions, gifts, corporate hospitality, donations to charity, direct involvement in government networks, and executives who have alliances with special interests groups. There are also social aspect organizations (SAOs) like the Portman Group in the United Kingdom, established by the industry to promote, in a publically and politically acceptable way, alcohol policy initiatives that are acceptable to government but which do not impact too much on overall levels of consumption. Drinkwise in Australia and Drinkaware in the United Kingdom have occupied a central role in community education and public awareness campaigns about the dangers of acute intoxication. By and large the industry prefers policies that emphasize self-regulation, voluntary codes of practice and 'partnerships' with government, as illustrated by the so-called Responsibility Deal brokered between the UK government and the alcohol industry (Department of Health, 2011). Casswell (2009) notes that developing 'partnerships' with those government agencies charged with reducing alcohol-related harm has been a key strategy of the alcohol industry. However, Room (2004) argues that the primary role of an SAO is to 'claim a place at the table in any open discussion of alcohol policy, thus granting industry actors direct access to the policy process'.

Alcohol industry representatives argue that most alcohol-related harm is experienced by a small minority of disproportionately heavy drinkers for whom the primary intervention should be treatment. Other than that, they hold the view that the attitudes, cognitions and behaviour of the great mass of nonproblematic, average drinkers will be positively influenced by interventions based on education and health promotion. On the other hand, the health and academic lobby argues for statutory regulation of the number and location of retail outlets, availability control through properly enforced licensing restrictions, and measures to increase prices. These initiatives, they argue, will reduce consumption over the whole range of drinkers, heavy as well as social and light, and this reduction of per capita consumption will in turn reduce alcohol-related harms across the entire drinking spectrum.

Research and Policy

Because of the increasing influence of the industry on policy evolution, at least until 2010 in the United Kingdom, there has been considerable debate among academics and clinicians about the legitimacy of accepting industry funding for research. It is the view of some members of the research community that, provided firewalls and governance procedures are securely in place and complete autonomy is maintained by researchers in terms of topic choice and dissemination of findings, then industry money is acceptable. Other researchers and academics would argue that there are no circumstances under which industry can fund objective scientific research into alcohol harms and the most effective strategies to reduce these harms.

Robin Davidson

Politics and Policy

By and large the policy initiatives tend to reflect the overall ideological orientation of the political party in power. For example Hawkins et al. (2012) comment that policy in the United Kingdom, under the New Labour government 1997 to 2010, reflected that party's broader ideology on individual responsibility and a pro-business economic stance. The importance of alcohol in developing the leisure and tourism industry was taken into account and indeed for a time alcohol policy development was the prime responsibility of the Department of Culture, Media and Sport. New Labour's philosophy on alcohol policy tended to occupy a thin line between its traditional stance on state control and the free markets. It also began to suffer from what has been called *departmental pluralism*. This can come about because, although alcohol policy may apparently fall under the remit of one government department, in reality it is influenced by, and influences, many different departments with different priorities. For example some departments seek positive economic outcomes from the jobs and tax revenues provided by the alcohol industry, whereas others have to deal with the negative health and criminal justice consequences of excessive consumption. With many government departments involved there is a danger that alcohol policy becomes fragmented and aimless, and this often results in multiple and at times conflicting outcomes.

As well as political ideology and contemporary social issues the policy debate is shaped by the prevailing psychosocial models of lifestyle, choice and behaviour in the context of ever-changing cultural norms, the *weltanschauung* of the time. There is the issue of personal freedom versus social responsibility; there is the desire of governments to protect the economic sector, particularly in a recession; there are the financial benefits accruing from the alcohol industry pitched against the costs of policing and healthcare. With so many competing interests and multiple positive, as well as negative, outcomes it is hardly surprising that almost all new alcohol policy attracts more criticism than praise. As in so much of the work of government, it is impossible to please all of the people all of the time.

In the United Kingdom there have been a number of key policy initiatives since the early 2000s. In 2004 there was the Alcohol Harm Reduction Strategy, followed in 2007 by Safe Sensible and Sociable: The Next steps in National Alcohol Strategy. By and large, these policies promoted public information, media campaigns, health education, stepped-care treatment services, and measures to reduce crime and public disorder. As noted below, the strategies were largely based on the notion of promoting 'responsible drinking'. As Szmigin et al. (2008) point out, this idea underpins many government reports, research studies and marketing communications, implying that there is a normal or appropriate way to drink alcohol, and that not conforming to this leads to illness and crime. Problem drinking is seen as located with the individual, not the wider social context.

However, a report from the Academy of Medical Sciences just prior to publication of the 2004 Alcohol Harm Reduction Strategy was quite pivotal in changing, albeit gradually, the perceptions of key stakeholders to a more balanced interpretation of the already available evidence. 'It cannot be ignored that the *per capita* consumption of alcohol has risen by 50% in the UK since 1970 . . . Compelling recent evidence supports previous findings of a strong correlation between mean or median alcohol consumption and heavy or "problem" drinking' (Academy of Medical Sciences, 2004, p. 7).

This report concluded that the country had reached a point where it was 'necessary and urgent to call time on runaway alcohol consumption' and, as this position gradually gained credibility with the media and the public, the issues of pricing, availability and marketing became the subject of serious lobbying. It was also around 2004 that the UK media began to produce documentaries such as *Booze Britain* and *Binge Nation*, illustrating the culture of excessive consumption and 'determined drunkenness' seemingly prevalent in many towns and cities in the United Kingdom (Griffin, Bengry-Howell, Hackley, Mistral & Szmigin, 2009). Tabloid newspapers featured lurid headlines and articles detailing 'the scourge of binge drinking among young people'. And, in 2009 the Chief Medical Officer's report (Donaldson, 2009) detailed the impact of excessive consumption on individuals, families, and the wider community, and stated that adopting a minimum price of 50 pence per unit of alcohol would save an estimated £1billion every year, impact on heavy drinkers more than others, and eliminate cheap supermarket alcohol, which fuels binge drinking.

As the political pressure increased from media headlines, public pronouncements from senior figures in the medical establishment, and research evidence for greater controls to reduce the impact of excessive alcohol consumption, the new coalition government which came to power in the United Kingdom in 2010 began to place more emphasis on fiscal controls, including minimum unit pricing, as a policy imperative. However, as noted above, any move to introduce minimum unit pricing faces huge resistance from much of the alcohol industry, which is able to exert considerable influence via legal challenges and political lobbying.

Robin Davidson

New Approaches to Policy

It has been said that existing models of policymaking are inappropriate in the new world of decentralized services and complex multivariate outcomes (Hallsworth & Rutter, 2011). These authors argue that the fundamentals of good policy construction are clarity of goals, evidenced-based ideas, rigorous design, responsive external engagement, thorough appraisal, transparency, and effective mechanisms for feedback and evaluation. They go on to say there should be greater training for relevant government ministers on alcohol policy strategy and greater communication between civil servants and those ministers. A new Policy Skills Framework was launched by the Institute for Government (2011) in order that policy was able to 'make change happen in the real world'. The Framework recommends that a series of questions should be asked of any policy:

- Has proper account been taken of evaluations of previous policy?
- Has there been opportunity for innovative thinking?
- Have policy makers analysed ideas and experience from the front line, overseas and devolved administrations?
- Has policy been rigorously tested or assessed to ensure that it is realistic?
- Have those affected by the policy been engaged in the process?
- Are policies cost effective over the appropriate time horizon?
- Are they resilient to changes in the external environment?

Another observation in the Framework is that, broadly speaking, policy formulation and implementation should not be separate, as has been historically the case. A policy is not just made and then executed. It is a dynamic that is constantly evolving with the involvement of multiple players throughout layers of the system. It is said to be good practice to draw on multiple sources, for example local government, academics, research institutions or healthcare bodies. Furthermore, in this regard, it has been suggested that government departments should have standing contracts with Universities or Research Institutes/Commissioners to embed outsiders and project teams in the decision-making process. In other words, policymakers should have ready access to a network of high-quality current evidence and it should be routine to mobilize experts to challenge civil service advice. It has also been said that, as well as policymakers' political ideology, more benign influences such as cognitive bias can affect their decision-making process. For example it is well known that government ministers will often be more easily swayed by impressions gained at the beginning of their tenure. This is referred to as a 'primacy effect' by psychologists and as 'anchoring' in the policy development literature. Other potential biases can include over-optimism or problem minimization. Policymakers must also at times reflect the flexible, perhaps chaotic, nature of public decision making rather than clinging to some false idea of incremental rationality. While the whole process is intrinsically complex there is no reason not to strive for a resilient, robust, systematic approach to policy development.

Evidence-Based Policy

There is currently much debate on how we can develop a culture of evidence-based policy (Crawshaw, 2008). The idea of supposed evidence-based policy has been increasingly discussed in the United Kingdom since Prime Minister Blair's announcement in 1997 that the then New Labour government would replace what he called 'outdated ideology' with a concern for 'what works'. Despite this, there has been little clear guidance on how the robust evidence available at any particular time can be translated into effective policy. Indeed it has been noted by Monaghan (2010) that 'what counts as evidence' is in itself a political question. The subject of how policymakers address evidence has been recently the subject of qualitative research (Stevens, 2011) that suggested that there are a number of impediments at work in the policymaking behaviour of civil servants, in addition to the anchoring, minimization and overoptimism referred to above. These include selective interpretation of academic research, lack of awareness of the suitability of some types of research in answering policy questions, and career advancement. It concluded that at times the narrow and selective use of evidence can be ideological, promoting policies that are seen as 'tough' rather than necessarily addressing social issues and harm.

Furthermore, as the Policy Skills Framework above (Hallsworth & Rutter, 2011) recognizes, it is at times difficult to apply policy interventions in real-world settings. Humphries & Eisner (2010) suggest that without knowledge of real world application of interventions there is a risk of 'attributing cause and effects to prevention initiatives which might have been absent'. They cite the geographically variable effect of the UK Licensing Act 2003 on crime and disorder, public safety, public nuisance and protecting our children from alcohol-related harm. This Licensing

Act was perhaps one of the largest deregulation activities in the United Kingdom since the beginning of the 19th century. A primary component of this Act was removal of restrictions on trading times, allowing licensed premises to apply for extended hours of trade. The rationale underpinning this was that fixed closing times led to crowds of inebriated people emerging on to the streets at one time, in 'competition for scarce resources (food, more alcohol, transport, or sexual intercourse) within confined urban environments' (Humphries & Eisner, 2010, p. 45). It was presumed that venues would stagger their closing times, thus reducing the problematic situation on the streets. However, individual venues clustered in certain areas extended their hours in line with each other, thereby simply moving the closing-time crowd to later at night. It is argued by Humphries & Eisner (2010) that if greater attention had been paid to *implementation issues* this would have improved the Licensing Act effectiveness. As well as robust scientific methodology it is incumbent on evaluation researchers that their research designs take account of the variations in the local implementation of any particular policy before causal attributions can be implied.

Policy Parameters

It is helpful when trying to understand the breadth of potential policies to structure the nature of these policies into different categories. Holder (1998) argues that appreciating, understanding and intervening in the *community system* is the most effective way forward for prevention of alcohol-related problems. Holder has helpfully categorized a set of subsystems within the community, which he sees as natural groupings of factors that research has shown to be important in the understanding of alcohol use. These sub-systems comprise:

1. Consumption of alcohol as part of routine community life.
2. Social norms, community values and social influences that affect drinking.
3. Retail sales, alcohol availability and promotion.
4. Formal regulation, rules, administration, and enforcement.
5. Legal sanctions or prohibition of alcohol.
6. Social, economic, and health: community identification of, and organized responses to, alcohol problems.

Policies in the consumption category could include initiatives like price controls and outlet density regulation. The social norms category could include product placement restrictions, media advocacy, didactic programmes in the schools and workplaces, public health, safe limits and unit labelling. The retail category could include things like management of the night time economy, server training, contextual manipulation, changes in pub architecture and initiatives aimed at altering the balance of commercial activity in drinking environments. The controls category could include advertising regulation, the sponsorship of alcohol at sporting events, local council initiatives in town centres and the like. The legal category clearly includes issues around drink driving, retailers' liability, licensing and age limits. Finally in the social, economic and health category, it is important to have policies that define the minimum competencies of individuals who provide specialist health and social care for the casualties of alcohol misuse, the definition of interventions which are both efficient and effective and the optimum conditions under which these should be delivered. It is important to have an appropriately balanced mix of all of these categories. Holder (1998) concludes that alcohol problem-prevention policies should abandon approaches that target particular groups seen as problematic, as we will never prevent nor substantially reduce alcohol-related problems by simply treating dependent drinkers, or by targeting other groups, typically young people, within the community.

Policy and Stigma

By and large the alcohol policy initiatives in the UK since *Sensible Drinking* (Department of Health and Social Security, 1995) have been primarily aimed at changes in attitudes, and to what is generally described as 'responsible drinking'. The Safe Sensible and Social strategy (Department of Health, 2007) referred on numerous occasions to responsible and irresponsible consumption. Information on 'sensible drinking' has dominated subsequent strategies. Education and persuasion measures and media campaigns are encouraged to enhance responsible drinking as are new kinds of 'information and advice'. An emphasis on public information campaigns has persisted despite the fact that education and persuasion strategies focused on changing knowledge and attitudes have had a chequered history of ineffectiveness in altering drinking behaviour. The 'responsible drinking' and 'self-discipline' style of national alcohol policy tends to minimize the extreme difficulty that many individuals have in controlling alcohol use, and the compulsive nature of dependence is understated. This is somewhat at odds with the UK coalition government's Drug Strategy published in 2010 where the ambition is to reduce dependence among the heaviest users.

The idea of a sensible drinking message has been identified as a feature of alcohol control policies in numerous countries, for example New Zealand's Alcohol Reform Bill and Canada's National Alcohol Strategy (National Alcohol Strategy Working Group, 2007), the latter stating that there was a need to cultivate 'a culture of moderation'. Williamson (2011) argues that this policy emphasis constitutes implicit stigmatization. There is an implication that dependent drinkers are simply 'irresponsible'. She also notes the sanctions on benefit claimants whose alcohol dependence does not improve (Department for Work and Pensions, 2011) and draws a distinction between this rather uncomfortable policy position and the National Institute for Health and Clinical Excellence guidance in England, which emphasizes the importance of a nonjudgemental approach to treatment (National Institute for Health and Clinical Excellence, 2011). The implication that dependent drinkers should not be left on benefits is, at best, unintentionally stigmatizing alcohol dependence in UK policy. There should perhaps be more joined-up work between published NICE clinical guidance and evidence-based policy initiatives. It is important that there is a policy framework which unites prevention and public health with an integrated treatment system and which is sensitive to the cultural and social environment.

Some Central Policy Initiatives

It is not the purpose of this chapter to provide a comprehensive review of the literature about the main influences on drinking and related problems, which should inform policy initiatives. However there is a broad consensus on a number of general conclusions that can inform decisions in the main policy arenas. Control of consumption by increasing the price of alcohol has arguably been scrutinized more than any other policy initiative. There is clear and unambiguous evidence that the price of alcohol impacts on all levels of consumption. Numerous studies have modelled national consumption against price increases and the UK government is currently working with the University of Sheffield in this regard. Some time ago Godfrey and Maynard (1992) suggested that a 5% annual increase in price will reduce national consumption by about a third over a 10-year period. Of course all kinds of caveats are built into this calculation; not least that price elasticity for alcohol not only varies across countries but also varies across beverages. In other words a price increase does not lead to uniform reduction in consumption. The essential rule of thumb here is that consumption of the most popular drink in the country is usually the least responsive to price manipulation. For example price responsiveness for wine would be less in continental Europe, and for beer would be less in the United Kingdom. However it is clear that attention must be given to the affordability of alcohol.

The influence of media campaigns and national education programmes continues to be less effective than it is often portrayed. At the moment there is no strong evidence to suggest that the ever-popular school-based didactic approaches impact on adult health decision making in general and alcohol consumption in particular.

There is probably a link between the availability of alcohol at any one time and the impact of advertising restrictions. In other words, during times of high availability and high affordability, alcohol advertising seems to have a greater impact on beverage switching than general consumption. There have been several international reviews on alcohol advertising regulation that addressed the question of marketing communication and its impact on the volume and pattern of consumption across various demographic groups (e.g. Anderson, Foxcroft, Kaner, Moskalewicz & Nociara, 2009). The alcohol industry would generally say that advertising does not increase consumption but simply promotes product switching or enhances brand loyalty. The available evidence would suggest that this is not the case although there are there are differential effects across the various demographic groups. In the United States, youth exposure to alcohol advertising has increased by almost 50% in the first decade of the 21st century and it has been said that each additional advertisement seen increases the number of drinks consumption in this group by about 1%. In terms of legislative regulation it is clear that UK legislation has been and continues to be enacted in a somewhat geographically inconsistent way. By and large, research studies would suggest that an effective way to reduce consumption, especially among young people, is something akin to France's Loi Evin, which prohibits alcohol advertisements on television or in cinemas, imposes strict control over messages and images, and the inclusion in all advertisements of a message to the effect that alcohol abuse is dangerous to health.

Outlet density and opening times not only impact on national consumption, but also on public order. Current evidence clearly shows that increased access to alcohol through more outlets and longer trading hours is linked to a range of alcohol-related harms and, in certain circumstances, higher national consumption. However, the relationship between availability and alcohol-related harm is complex. The best evidence comes from ecologically valid, opportunistic studies that measure consumption before and after policy changes that impact on availability. A large Canadian study found a clear increase in overall consumption when the number of off-licence outlets increased by a third (Stockwell et al., 2011). In the United Kingdom it was found that the consumption of beer was correlated with increases in the number of outlets but this did not apply to wine or spirits. Such mixed results have been seen in similar opportunistic trials in other countries although the link between higher outlet density and alcohol-related harms is reasonably well established (Livingstone, 2011). These harms include not only alcohol-related health problems but also local levels of public disturbance, related road-traffic accidents, self-reported injuries, child neglect, and domestic violence. On the relationship between opening hours and alcohol-related problems the evidence is mixed. A review of the literature looking at the impact of the England and Wales 2003 Licensing Act found no increase in alcohol-related violence but noted changes in consumption.

The strongest evidence is that the increased affordability of alcohol in the UK from the 1970s to the turn of the century has arguably been the major cause of the rising rates of alcohol consumption and harm. There would appear to be complex interaction between affordability and availability (Popova, Giesbrecht, Bekmuradov & Patra, 2009). When affordability goes up the density outlet has a disproportionately greater effect on the extent of harmful alcohol use. In other words, easier access to alcohol, either through more retail outlets or relaxed licensing hours, can compound the harm associated with rising affordability. On the other hand, regulation of availability can modulate the effect of price change. What this evidence demonstrates is that while there is a clear relationship between availability, affordability, consumption and harm, the relationship is dynamic and is not simple cause and effect.

It is evident that the multivariate influences on national alcohol consumption are complex and interactive. There is a variety of stakeholders with competing and often vested interests. There are many outcomes and a range of research methodologies to investigate these outcomes. Policy preference is a product of one's political ideology, academic background, personality, career choice and material aspirations. Regulating consumption of this far from ordinary commodity is not a simple task.

References

Academy of Medical Sciences (2004). *Calling time: The nation's drinking as a major health issue.* London: Academy of Medical Sciences.

Adams, P., Buetow, S. & Rossen, F. (2010). Vested interests in addiction research and policy: poisonous partnerships. *Addiction, 105,* 585–590.

Anderson, P. (2007). Safe sensible and social. New Labour and alcohol policy. *Addiction, 102,* 1515–1521.

Anderson, P., Foxcroft, D., Kaner, E., Moskalewicz, J. & Nociara, R. (2009). *Does marketing communication impact on the volume and patterns of consumption of alcoholic beverages, especially by young people? A review of longitudinal studies.* Brussels: European Alcohol and Health Forum.

Babor, T. (2009). Alcohol research in the alcohol beverage industry: Issues concerns and conflicts of interests. *Addiction, 104,* 34–47.

Babor, T., Caetano, R., Casswell, S., Edwards, G., Giesbrecht, N., Graham, K., et al. (2010). *Alcohol: No ordinary commodity: Research and public policy* (2nd ed.). Oxford: Oxford University Press.

Burton, R. (1838). *The anatomy of melancholy by Democritus Junior.* London: Blake.

Campaign for Real Ale (2012). Urgent Action on Beer Tax Needed as Britain's Pub Closure Rate Soars by 50%. Retrieved March 5, 2013 from http://www.camra.org.uk/article.php?group_id=7834.

Casswell, S. (2009). Alcohol industry and alcohol policy: The challenge ahead. *Addiction, 104* (Suppl. 2), 3–5.

Crawshaw, P. (2008). Implementing the new scientific spirit: Response to de Leuuw et al. *Critical Public Health, 18,* 5–20.

Department for Work and Pensions (2011). *Analysis of incapacity benefits: Detailed medical condition and duration.* London: Department for Work and Pensions.

Department of Health (2007). *Safe sensible social. The next steps in the National Alcohol Policy.* London: Department of Health.

Department of Health (2011). Public Health Responsibility Deal. Alcohol Network. Retrieved March 5, 2013 from http://responsibilitydeal.dh.gov.uk/category/alcohol-network/.

Department of Health and Social Security (1995). *Sensible drinking: The report of an inter-departmental working group.* London: Department of Health and Social Security.

Donaldson, L. (2009). 150 years of the Annual Report of the Chief Medical Officer: On the State of Public Health 2008. Passive Drinking: The Collateral Damage from Alcohol. Retrieved March 5, 2013 from http://webarchive.nationalarchives.gov.uk/+/www.dh.gov.uk/en/Media Centre/Media/DH_096274.

Godfrey, C. & Maynard, A. (1992). *A health strategy for alcohol: Setting targets and choosing policies.* YARTIC Occasional paper 1. Leeds Addiction Unit, University of York.

Griffin, C., Bengry-Howell, A., Hackley, C., Mistral, W. & Szmigin, I. (2009). The allure of belonging: young people's drinking practices and collective identification. In M. Wetherell (Ed.) *Identity in the 21st century: New trends in changing times* (pp. 213–230). London: Palgrave.

Hallsworth, M. & Rutter, J. (2011). *Making Policy Better: improving Whitehall's core business.* London, Institute for Government.

Hawkins, B., Holden, C. & McCambridge, J. (2012). Alcohol industry influence on UK Alcohol Policy. *Critical Public Health, 22*, 297–305.

Holden, C. & Lee, K. (2009). Corporate power and social policy: the political economy of the transnational tobacco companies. *Global Social Policy, 9*, 328–354.

Holder, T. (1998). *Alcohol and the community. A systems approach to prevention. International research monograms in addictions.* Cambridge: Cambridge University Press.

Humphries, D. & Eisner. M. (2010). Evaluating a natural experiment in alcohol policy: The Licensing Act 2003, and the requirement for attention to implementation. *Criminology and Public Policy, 9*(1), 41–67.

Institute for Government (2011). *Policy making in the real world: evidence and analysis.* London: Institute for Government. Retrieved March 5, 2013 from http://www.instituteforgovernment.org.uk/sites/default/files/publications/Policy%20making%20in%20the%20real%20world.pdf.

Kingdon, J. (1995). *Agendas, alternatives and public policies.* New York: Longman.

Livingstone, M. (2011). A longitudinal analysis of alcohol outlet density and domestic violence. *Addiction, 106*, 919–925.

Monaghan, M. (2010). The complexity of evidence: Reflections on research utilization in a heavily politicised policy area. *Social Policy and Society, 9*, 1–12.

National Alcohol Strategy Working Group (2007). Reducing Alcohol Related Harm in Canada: Toward a Culture of Moderation. Retrieved March 5, 2013 from http://www.ccsa.ca/2007%20CCSA%20Documents/ccsa-023876-2007.pdf.

National Institute for Health and Clinical Excellence (2011). *Alcohol use disorders: Diagnosis, assessment and management of harmful drinking and alcohol dependence.* London: National Institute for Health and Clinical Excellence.

Pendleton, L., Smith, C. & Roberts, J. (1990). Public opinion on alcohol policies. *British Journal of Addiction, 85*, 125–130.

Popova, S., Giesbrecht, N., Bekmuradov, D. & Patra, J. (2009). Hours and days of sale and density of alcohol outlets. Impacts on alcohol consumption and damage: A systematic review. *Alcohol and Alcoholism, 44*(5), 500–516.

Raistrick, D., Hodgson, R. & Ritson, B. (eds.) (1999). *Tackling alcohol together. The evidence base for a UK alcohol policy.* London: Free Association Books.

Room, R. (2004). Disabling the public interest: Alcohol strategies and policies for England. *Addiction, 99*, 1083–1089.

Scottish Government (2008). *Changing Scotland's relationship with Alcohol. A discussion paper on our strategic approach.* Edinburgh: The Scottish Government. Retrieved March 5, 2013 from http://www.scotland.gov.uk/Publications/2008/06/16084348/0.

Stevens, A. (2011). Telling policy stories. Ethnographic study of the use of evidence in policy-making in the UK. *Journal of Social Policy. 40*(2), 237–255.

Stockwell, T., Zhao, J., Macdonald, S., Vallance, K., Gruenewald, P., Ponicki, W. et al. (2011). Impact on alcohol-related mortality of a rapid rise in the density of private liquor outlets in British Columbia: A local area multi-level analysis. *Addiction, 106*, 768–776.

Szmigin, I., Griffin, C., Mistral, W., Hackley, C., Bengry-Howell, A., Weale, L. et al. (2008). Re-framing binge drinking as calculated hedonism. *International Journal of Drug Policy, 19*(5), 359–366.

Vogel, D. (2002). The Politics of Risk Regulation in Europe and the United States. Retrieved March 5, 2013 from http://faculty.haas.berkeley.edu/vogel/uk%20oct.pdf.

Williamson, L. (2011). Editorial. Nice but needy. *Alcohol and Alcoholism, 46*(6), 647–650.

3

Binge Drinking: Consumption, Consequences, Causes and Control

Willm Mistral

This chapter considers binge drinking, its consequences, its causes, and efforts to control it, in the context of the general drinking culture of wider society; the huge amount of money spent on advertising by the alcohol industry; the economic importance of the alcohol industry as a generator of employment, and the contribution that sale of alcohol makes to government taxation revenues.

In recent years there have been numerous, and often sensational, news media reports about 'binge drinking' by young people. The term 'binge drinking' is, however, both nebulous and contested. In the United States, SAMHSA (2011) defines it as having five or more drinks within a couple of hours of each other on at least 1 day a month. In the United Kingdom, one government department has defined it as 'too much alcohol over a short period of time, e.g. over the course of an evening, and it is typically drinking that leads to drunkenness' (Department of Health, Home Office, Department for Education and Skills, and Department for Culture, Media and Sport, 2007, p. 3) while another has opted for consumption of twice the government's guidelines of a maximum daily intake of 3–4 units for men or 2–3 units for women (POST, 2005). The situation is complicated further by the fact that what constitutes a 'drink' varies from nation to nation. For example, Herring, Berridge, and Thom (2008) tell us that five standard US drinks contain 70 g of alcohol while five standard UK drinks contain 40 g of alcohol. The variety of 'cutoffs' employed leads to a perplexing array of statistics and a lack of clarity about the measurement and prevalence of binge drinking. However as

Emerging Perspectives on Substance Misuse, First Edition. Edited by Willm Mistral.
© 2013 John Wiley & Sons, Ltd. Published 2013 by John Wiley & Sons, Ltd.

Bartlett and Grist (2011) point out, in the view of the general public, government, and mass media, 'binge drinking' is not simply a matter of the number of drinks consumed. It conjures up an image of young adults recklessly and very publicly drinking to excess, putting themselves and others at risk of harm.

Consumption Levels

Before focusing on young people and the amount they drink, however defined, it is interesting to consider the general level of alcohol consumed across the world. The World Health Organisation (WHO) publishes estimates of alcohol consumption by adults, classified as those aged 15 years and older. The World Health Organisation (2012) report shows that, over the years 2003–2005, average consumption of pure alcohol per capita in the United States was 9.4 litres; in New Zealand 9.6 litres; in Australia 10; the UK 13.4; and France 13.7; whereas across north and sub-Saharan Africa, the middle east and southern Asia, per capita consumption was less than 2.5 litres per annum. These latter regions contain large populations of the Islamic faith, with very high rates of abstention. The European region has the highest level of alcohol use, with the average adult (aged 15+ years) consuming more than double the world average (Anderson, Møller & Galea, 2012).

The European School Survey Project on Alcohol and Other Drugs (ESPAD) monitors trends within and between European countries on substance use among 15–16 year-old students. The first study in 1995 covered 26 countries, whereas in 2011 reports came from 36 countries and included over 100,000 students. The 2011 data revealed that, on average, 87% of students had had alcohol at least once in their life; nearly 60% by the age of 13 years, and 12% had been drunk at that age. Of course, these averages were derived from some highly divergent figures from individual countries. Consumption of larger quantities appeared mainly among students in the Nordic countries and British Isles, whereas lower levels were more often found in south-eastern Europe. On their most recent drinking day, Danish students on average drank more than three times as much as students in Albania and Romania (European School Survey Project on Alcohol and Other Drugs, 2012).

In the United States the Substance Abuse and Mental Health Administration (SAMHSA) undertakes annual national surveys of substance use. In 2010, it found rates of binge alcohol use (five or more drinks within a couple of hours of each other on at least 1 day a month) among young people in the US were approximately 1% of 12–13 year olds, 15% of 16–17 year olds, 33% of persons aged 18–20, and peaked among those aged 21–25 at 46%. Being a full-time US college student appears to increase consumption, as 63% were current drinkers, 42% were binge drinkers, and 16% heavy drinkers. Young people not enrolled full time in college had substantially lower rates of 52%, 36% and 12%, respectively (Substance Abuse and Mental Health Administration, 2011).

Heavy episodic, or binge, drinking (five drinks or more on the same occasion during the past 30 days) among teenage girls has undergone one of the most striking changes across the European surveys. In 1995, 29% of girls consumed at this level, but by 2007 this had increased to 41%, dropping slightly to 38% in 2011. Among boys, the figure increased from 41% in 1995 to 45% in 2007, but fell back to 43% in 2011 (European School Survey Project on Alcohol and Other Drugs, 2012). In line with the reductions above, a survey in the United States (Johnston, O'Malley, Bachman & Schulenberg, 2012) of 46,700 students aged 13 to 18 years, in 400 secondary schools nationwide, found that all measures of alcohol use (lifetime, annual, 30-day, and binge drinking in the past 2 weeks) had reached historic lows, following a peak in the 1990s. The percentage binge drinking reduced by 52% for those aged 13–14 years, 39% for 15–16 year olds, and 31% for those aged 17–18 years.

Despite the finding (European School Survey Project on Alcohol and Other Drugs, 2012) that students in the United Kingdom are more likely to drink alcohol than their peers in many other European countries, the latest in a series of surveys in England (Fuller, 2011) of 7,296 school pupils aged 11 to 15 shows that, similarly to the US, there has been a decline in the proportion of pupils drinking alcohol. In 2010, 45% of pupils had drunk alcohol at least once in their lifetimes, compared with 61% in 2003. The proportion of pupils who had drunk alcohol in the week prior to the survey was 26% in 2001 but halved to 13% in 2010. Similar proportions of boys and girls had been drinking in the last week, the mean amount consumed being 12.9 units. Although Asian pupils were less likely to have been drinking than their White counterparts, no other ethnic differences were significant (Sutton & Bridges, 2011). It would also appear that pupils are becoming less tolerant of drinking and drunkenness among their peers. In 2003, 46% agreed that it was okay for someone of their age to drink alcohol once a week, while in 2010 this dropped to 32%. At the same time the proportion who thought it okay for someone of their age to get drunk once a week also fell, from 20% to 11% (Sutton & Bridges, 2011). However this perceived shift in alcohol-related attitudes and behaviours does not yet appear to have undermined a pervasive culture of 'determined drunkenness' in which excessive drinking is a normal part of many young adult's social lives (Griffin, Bengry-Howell, Hackley, Mistral & Szmigin, 2009).

Consequences of Excessive Consumption

The World Health Organisation (2012) reports that alcohol is a causal factor in 60 types of diseases and injuries, and a component cause in 200 others. It accounts for 4% of all fatalities worldwide, more than are caused by HIV/AIDS or tuberculosis, and is the leading risk factor for death among males aged 15–59 years. Excessive alcohol consumption is also associated with many serious social issues, including road traffic accidents, violence, child neglect and abuse, and workplace absenteeism. There is a strong association between adolescent alcohol use and an array of negative behaviours or conditions such as smoking, illegal drug use, risky sexual behaviour, disruptive behaviour, depression, anxiety, eating disorders and obesity, as well as suicidal and homicidal behaviour (Newbury-Birch et al., 2009). The most recent ESPAD survey (2012) showed teenage boys across Europe exhibiting more problematic behaviours than girls. Engaging in a physical fight was reported, on average, by 17% of boys but 6% of girls. Other behaviours more common among boys include trouble with the police (8% versus 4%), unprotected sex (11% versus 7%), regretted sex (8% versus 5%) and accident or injury (12% versus 9%).

Nevertheless, many young women in the United Kingdom and in Holland are reported to be engaging in heavy drinking at the weekends, and this is associated with accidents, assaults, and the risk of sexual assault or rape (Mohler-Kuo, Dowdall, Koss & Wechsler, 2004) especially with underage drinking in unsupervised places such as parks. Furthermore, any unplanned or risky sexual activity while under the influence of alcohol may lead to regrets, pregnancy and/or sexually transmitted infections (STI). In New Zealand a 30-year prospective longitudinal study of the health, development and adjustment of a birth cohort of 1,265 individuals found clear and consistent trends linking increasing involvement with alcohol with increased risk of STI diagnoses (Boden, Fergusson & Horwood, 2011). In London, alcohol-related hospital admissions for young people aged 11–21 years increased by 91% between 2002 and 2006 and, despite the ESPAD findings above, admissions rates for girls aged 11–15 years were twice as high as for boys of the same age (Institute of Alcohol Studies, 2009). In Holland, Bouthoorn, van Hoof & van der Lely (2011) found that girls aged 13 and 14 years had significantly higher hospitalization prevalence due to alcohol intoxication than boys of the same age, despite the girls having lower blood alcohol levels. Although rates of hospitalization were similar among boys and girls of other ages, girls generally had lower blood alcohol levels, an indication of lower tolerance.

Alcohol use is one of the most important risk factors in both causation and severity of road traffic accidents. Across the whole European region, road traffic injuries are the leading cause of death in children and young adults aged 5–29 years (Mitis & Sethi, 2012). Drivers younger than 21 are more vulnerable than older drivers to the impairing effects of alcohol. Male drivers aged 21–24 years with a blood alcohol concentration of 0.04–0.05 g/dl are nearly twice as likely to be in a road accident as men aged 35–49 years with the same blood alcohol concentration (Sethi, Racioppi & Bertollini, 2007). Injuries, many of which are alcohol related, are the main cause of death among young people. In England, for example, alcohol is a factor in 26.6% of deaths in males aged 16–24 years (Jones, Bellis, Dedman, Sumnall & Tocque, 2008). Despite the fact that young people's binge drinking and its consequences attracts the attention of many headline writers, politicians, and researchers, it is older men and women who are more likely to need alcohol-related hospital admissions than younger people, and middle-aged men who are the most likely to die from the long-term effects of alcohol misuse (British Liver Trust, 2012). This toll of death, disease and injuries has substantial economic and social impacts, including medical and policing costs incurred by governments, and a financial and psychological burden on individual families.

Causes of Excessive Drinking

Following a major review of the research literature Velleman (2009) tells us that, by the time children start to drink, they have well developed knowledge, attitudes, and expectations about alcohol. These have been acquired through a process of socialization involving significant influence from parents, close relatives, peers, advertising and other media representations of alcohol use, as well as school, community, religious, and cultural social environments.

In a national survey in England, Fuller (2011) found that pupils aged 11 to 15 were most likely to believe that their peer group drinks to look cool in front of their friends (76%), to be more sociable (65%), because of peer pressure (62%), or because it gives them a rush or buzz (60%).

However, pupils' drinking behaviour is also very strongly influenced by the attitudes and behaviour of their families. Of pupils who said that their parents would not like them to drink, 85% had never had alcohol, compared with only 27% of those whose parents did not mind. Of students who drank alcohol in the past week, 26% were living with three or more people who drank alcohol, compared with only 4% of those living in nondrinking households. These factors are supported by the findings of Bremner, Burnett, Nunney, Ravat, and Mistral (2011) in their survey of 5,700 school pupils aged 13–16, in England. This study concluded that young teenagers are more likely to drink, to drink frequently, and to drink to excess if:

- they receive less supervision from a parent or other close adult;
- they are exposed to a close family member, especially a parent, drinking or getting drunk;
- they have friends who drink, or they spend multiple evenings a week with friends;
- they have positive attitudes towards and expectations of alcohol;
- they have easy access to alcohol.

On the other hand, those who had an adult present when they first tried alcohol were less likely to report being drunk more than once, and this may again suggest the positive impact of adult supervision on young people's behaviour.

The influence of close social networks on alcohol consumption was explored in the United States by Rosenquist, Murabito, Fowler & Christakis (2010). Data collected over 32 years on 12,067 friends, co-workers, siblings, spouses, and neighbours, were analysed to see whether alcohol consumption behaviour spreads from person to person. Being closely surrounded by heavy drinkers increased reported alcohol consumption by about 70% compared with those who were not connected to any heavy drinkers. Conversely, being surrounded by abstainers decreased consumption by half. The analyses ruled out, as far as possible, the confounding effects of shared environment and the tendency of people to seek out others with shared interests.

The above studies show the impact that attitudes and behaviours of families and friends have on levels of alcohol consumption. However, other powerful factors also contribute to excessive drinking by young adults. Following a systematic review of relevant research studies, Smith & Foxcroft (2009) indicate a clear association between young people's exposure to advertising and increased consumption of alcohol. And young people are a heavily targeted group in advertising on television, radio, newspapers, billboards, posters, the Internet, as well as experiencing depiction of alcohol use in movies, prime-time TV programmes, music videos, song lyrics, and promotional activities such as give-away t-shirts and other items bearing alcohol brand logos.

Measham & Brain (2005) develop a cogent argument that, from about 1990, alcohol consumption by young people became increasingly central to the development of night-time economies in British towns and cities. By catering for a new generation of young, culturally diverse consumers, licensed premises have brought large crowds into town centres, particularly at weekends. These drinkers often move from one establishment to another, attracted by 'happy hours' and other special price offers in large numbers of specially designed venues such as café bars, dance clubs, themed pubs, and 'high volume vertical drinking establishments', large-capacity sites with loud music and no seating, which have been seen to encourage rapid consumption of alcohol (Home Office, 2012b). This congregation of large numbers of young people in public drinking venues and surrounding streets is associated with high levels of public disorder, violence, road traffic accidents, and unintentional injury (Hughes & Bellis, 2012).

At the same time, the alcohol industry has created a wide range of new products aimed at the youth market, including alcopops, ready-to-drink spirit mixers, flavoured alcoholic beverages, 'buzz' drinks containing stimulants such as caffeine, and spirit 'shots', which are often sold in city centre bars by staff mingling among the crowd and marketing them directly, as opposed to customers making a decision to go to the bar. This encourages mixing of different shots, rapid consumption of spirits as shots are usually taken in one swallow, and a general increase in the amount consumed as they are an addition to customers' usual bottled beers or ready-to-drink spirit mixers. Also in recent years the strength of traditional alcohol products such as wines and beers has increased by up to 50%, in a direct attempt to appeal to a new generation of psychoactive consumers (Measham & Brain, 2005).

Fry (2011), reporting research in Australia, tells us that the contemporary market economy packages alcohol consumption as cool, fashionable, desirable, and exciting. Excessive consumption of alcohol is an integral component of young adults' pursuit of pleasure, and also acts as a signifier of identity. It confirms identity as an adult, indicates a lifestyle of fun and socializing, and confers status as part of a group. All these factors can be seen as contributory to the findings by Measham & Brain (2005) from over 350 young adult weekend drinkers in a major UK city, that the pursuit of 'determined drunkenness' was a specific aim of week-end drinking, and central to socializing with friends. The importance of drinking within young friendship groups has also been highlighted by Griffin et al. (2009), who used a series of focus groups to explore young adults' alcohol-related behaviours. Their participants recounted stories of drinking to the point of vomiting, loss of memory, unconsciousness and waking up in hospital. However, these events always took place in the context of group outings and were seen as a source of entertaining stories, to be told and retold within friendship groups. There appeared to be an integral relationship between excessive drinking, its sometimes undesirable, unpleasant or 'weird' consequences, and 'fun' as a key element of the young people's social lives (Griffin et al., 2009; Szmigin, Griffin., Mistral, Bengry-Howell, Weale & Hackley, 2008). This social dimension is played upon by the alcohol industry, with sophisticated marketing and advertising campaigns showing young people in strange, exciting adventures with their mates and, of course, in association with alcohol (Griffin et al., 2009).

Another important factor leading to excess consumption of alcohol, in the UK and Australia at least, is that many supermarkets have been using alcohol as a loss-leader, selling at extremely low prices, with some own-brand products on sale for less than the duty (tax) the supermarket paid. While drinkers still go out to pubs, bars and clubs to enjoy the social aspects of drinking, it has become a more affordable option, especially for young people with limited finances, to 'preload' by drinking at home before going out.

Although these developments within the alcohol industry have been primarily focused on people of legal drinking age, the behaviours of young adults often serve as drinking role models for younger people, as has been noted above. In this way excessive consumption and 'determined drunkenness' becomes normalized.

Effective Alcohol Control Policies

Governments appear to have difficulties in both devising and applying effective policies to control alcohol-related harm. In the first quarter of the 20th-century major controls, including total prohibition of the manufacture and sale of alcohol, were tried in many countries including the United States, Canada, Iceland, Finland, Norway, as well as both czarist Russia and the Soviet Union. Many of these laws were repealed after a few years as they were difficult or impossible to police, they encouraged organized criminal activity, and had massive unintended negative economic affects.

The importance of the alcohol industry to many national economies cannot be overstated. Wine was the European Union's highest value export in 2008–10, at 4.6 billion euros, and whisky exports accounted for 2.7 billion euros (Monitoring Agri-trade Policy, 2011). The financial revenues going to European governments from the production and sale of beer, that is taxes paid by breweries, beer consumers and employees together, total around 38 billion euros a year (Ernst & Young, 2005). United Kingdom households spend around £15 billion a year on the consumption of alcoholic drinks, 18% of their total expenditure on food and drink, and in 2009–2010 this generated £9 billion in alcohol duties for the UK Government (Collis et al., 2010). The US alcohol beverage industry contributes nearly $388 billion to the economy, being responsible for over 3.9 million jobs, and paying over $21 billion in direct taxes annually, in addition to corporate and payroll taxes (Distilled Spirits Council of the United States, 2003).

The economic power of the alcohol industry means that it wields considerable political influence, and many governments are loath to confront the risk to jobs and tax revenues inherent in curtailing alcohol sales. Also, the neoliberal free market ideology underpinning most governments in the developed world has militated against state alcohol monopolies, increases in taxation, or other restrictions on the availability of alcoholic beverages. So, despite all the well documented problems and socio-economic costs arising from excessive alcohol consumption, it generally remains low on the public policy agenda, while many lesser health risks are given a higher priority.

Many governments have relied upon education and public information campaigns to reduce alcohol-related problems. This approach includes setting guidelines for maximum daily intake, mass media campaigns showing young people getting into dangerous situations after drinking, and working with the industry to encourage 'responsible drinking'. Numerous research studies have shown, however, that these have very little effect on behaviour (Anderson. Foxcroft, Kaner, Moskalewicz & Nociara, 2012). Young people especially do not see government warnings or drinking guidelines as realistic, especially as advertising by the alcohol industry bombards them with images associating alcohol with mates, music, flirting, and fun. Also, alcohol is potentially very addictive and the industry appears very willing to target the young, impressionable, and vulnerable, with spending on advertising in the United Kingdom

45 times higher than the government budget for alcohol education (Gilmore & Atkinson, 2010).

Public policy documents often imply or explicitly state that individual choice to consume excessively, in spite of attempts to inform and educate, is the root of problem drinking. A clear example can be seen in the 2004 alcohol strategy for England, which introduced legislation allowing licensed premises to open 24 hours, 7 days a week, with the aim of reducing public disorder associated with crowds of intoxicated people coming onto the streets after fixed closing times. The introduction to this strategy stated

> . . . alcohol misuse by a small minority is causing two major, and largely distinct, problems: on the one hand crime and anti-social behaviour in town and city centres, and on the other harm to health, as a result of binge and chronic drinking. (Prime Minister's Strategy Unit, 2004: 5)

Many researchers saw the strategy's focus on 'misuse by a small minority' as a simplistic and naïve (if not disingenuous) view of the extent of overconsumption and resultant problems in the wider population. In part this was because, although the strategy explicitly recognized a clear association between alcohol price, availability, and consumption levels, it argued that using price as a key lever to moderate consumption risked major unintended side effects. These possible side effects were not spelled out, but the document stated that policies need to be publicly acceptable in order to succeed. Some argued that the 'public' referred to was the alcohol industry, which would not have been pleased with increased taxes or other measures to reduce alcohol availability, which would in turn lead to a reduction in per capita consumption (e.g. Room, 2004).

The discourse in the 2004 strategy document, as well as in a later version (Department of Health, 2007) also implicitly positions 'binge' drinking by young people, aged under 25 years, in opposition to 'normal' drinking by the general population, with the former seen as the cause of inappropriate and criminal behaviour. This dichotomy of problematic versus nonproblematic drinking may be seen as part of tendency to portray young people as lacking in self-control in relation to alcohol, while the effects of marketing practices of the alcohol industry, government legislation liberalizing alcohol licensing, and the negative effects of excessive consumption across the wider population, are played down (Hackley, Bengry-Howell, Griffin, Mistral & Szmigin, 2011). United Kingdom government policy (Department of Health, 2011) has relied on a voluntary 'partnership' with alcohol producers and retailers, in a 'responsibility deal', with industry commitments to act to reduce consumption and harm. However as Sheron, Gilmore, Parsons, Hawkey & Rhodes (2012) point out, the primary aim of the alcohol industry is to deliver profit, which in a competitive marketplace is by maximizing consumption, and so there is a fundamental, although never mentioned, conflict of interest at the very heart of this initiative. More recently, in what many saw as a welcome, albeit belated, response to the failure of the alcohol industry to act 'responsibly', the UK government proposed setting a minimum retail price per unit of alcohol, in order to substantially increase the price of the cheapest high alcohol content drinks (Home Office, 2012a). However, this proposal was later dropped.

Despite the evident difficulties or reluctance exhibited by governments in challenging the industry, the World Health Organisation (2012) argues that the health, safety and socio-economic problems attributable to alcohol can be effectively reduced by the application of a range of evidence-based alcohol policies. According to the Alcohol and Public Policy Group (2010), among the best practices in alcohol harm-prevention policies are interventions to increase the price and reduce the availability of alcohol, such as by increased alcohol taxes and increased minimum purchase age; government alcohol retail monopolies; and restrictions on the times of sale and the density of outlets selling alcoholic beverages. These should be coupled with drink-driving countermeasures, brief interventions for at-risk drinkers, and treatment for those with alcohol dependence.

Price

One of the most effective ways of reducing alcohol consumption is to increase its cost by increasing taxes or by setting a minimum price per unit of alcohol. Concern is sometimes expressed that price increases do not make any impact on heavy drinkers while unfairly penalizing light drinkers. However, using the most recently available UK data, alcohol in 2011 was 45% more affordable than it was in 1980 (National Statistics, 2012); and, with some variation between countries, there has been an overall trend of increasing affordability across the European Union (Osterberg, 2012), Australia (Carragher & Chalmers, 2011), and the United States (Kerr, Greenfield & Patterson, 2012). So, concern for the extra expense to light drinkers could be said to be misplaced. A recent analysis of 112 studies confirmed that when the price goes up, drinking goes down, including among problem drinkers and young people (World Health Organisation, 2012). The Alcohol and Public Policy Group (2010) tells us that dozens of studies have shown this leads to a reduction in related problems, including mortality rates, crime and traffic accidents.

Minimum Legal Age

A review of 132 studies published between 1960 and 2000 found strong evidence that increasing the minimum legal drinking age can have substantial impact on reducing alcohol-related harm, often lasting well after young people reach the legal age (Wagenaar & Toomey, 2002). In the United States, since 1988, all states require people to be at least 21 years old to purchase alcohol. In contrast, most European countries have minimum legal drinking ages between 16–18 years, while in Canada, Australia and New Zealand it is 18 years. Research in the United States has found that a higher drinking age results in lower alcohol consumption among young people aged 16–20, is an effective deterrent to underage drinking and driving, and substantially reduces alcohol-related car accidents among young drivers. Road deaths have been shown to go up when the drinking age is lowered, and go down when it is raised (McCartt, Hellinga & Kirley, 2010).

Lower BACs for Drivers

For drivers, any blood alcohol concentration (BAC) greater than zero increases the risk of being involved in a road accident. For the general driving population this risk rises significantly at levels higher than 0.4 g/l (Peden et al., 2004). Setting low maximum BACs, of at least 0.5 g/l for experienced drivers and 0.2 g/l for novices, and enforcing these with random breath testing, reduces road traffic accidents. Such interventions have been shown as both effective and cost effective, yet despite the susceptibility of young drivers under the influence of alcohol to being in car accidents, only 43% of 49 European countries have set the blood alcohol concentration limit for young and novice drivers at 0.02 g/dl, and 66% of these countries reported that enforcement was suboptimal (World Health Organisation, 2009).

A study by Paschall, Grube & Kypri (2009) examined the relationship between alcohol control policies and adolescents aged 15–17 years who participated in the 2003 ESPAD survey and other national secondary school surveys in Spain, Canada, Australia, New Zealand and the United States. This study found that more comprehensive and stringent alcohol control policies, particularly policies affecting alcohol availability and marketing, are associated with higher age of first use, and lower prevalence and frequency of adolescent alcohol consumption. However, these analyses also suggested that the level of alcohol use in the general population may impact on the relationships between control policies and youth consumption. Thus, if the culture among the adult population is to drink excessively then policies to control drinking by young people will be less effective.

Measham (2006) argues that a primary focus on harm reduction and demand reduction is constrained by a contemporary emphasis on economic deregulation and a culture of excessive consumption. Nevertheless, with political will, change may be possible, as has happened with tobacco use in many countries. In Britain in 1948, 82% of men smoked, but by 2010 the rate had fallen to 21% (Office for National Statistics, 2012). Dramatic falls in tobacco use have also been seen in the United States, Australia, and across many northern countries of the European Union, among others. A combination of government interventions including education, health warnings, tax increases, bans on advertising, and smoke-free legislation has contributed to this fall. All these measures have been implemented despite highly organized and well-funded opposition from the tobacco industry. This suggests that a similar combination of interventions could be applied to reduce alcohol consumption across the wider population. Also, as Rosenquist et al. (2010) point out, excessive alcohol consumption is both a public health and clinical problem that involves interconnecting groups who share behaviours, both positive and negative, and therefore targeting perceived negative behaviours should involve addressing populations and not just individuals or specific groups.

As noted above, there is much evidence demonstrating that parents play a major role in influencing their children's alcohol use, and there are a number of key parental behaviours, which either increase or reduce related problems. Basic attitudes and intentions are initially most influenced by parents, and it is crucially important that parents' own behaviour models appropriate alcohol use, or non-use. In situations where parents' own drinking behaviour conveys a 'norm' of excessive use, or they fail to supervise drinking behaviour, or condone excessive use, young people are at greater risk of excessive consumption and of developing alcohol-related problems (Bremner et al., 2011; Galvani, 2012). Parents' child-management practices need to balance care and control by clear communication of expectations about alcohol use and poten-tial disapproval if expectations are not met; by clear and consistent rules that are enforced; by high levels of supervision or monitoring in terms of knowing where children are and what they are doing; and by high levels of family bonding, including eating an evening meal together five or more times a week. These all serve as protective factors against young people's misuse of alcohol (Fuller, 2011).

However, in opposition to the research evidence indicated above are aligned the forces of unfettered neoliberal capitalism, the pursuit of profit, and governments' reliance on the alcohol industry to create jobs, produce tax revenues, and keep the great mass of the population happy by provid-ing distraction and immediate satisfaction – in other words the modern equivalent of 'bread and circuses' as described by Juvenal in the 2nd century (Rudd, 1992). Hayward & Hobbs (2007) argue that within the economic and the cultural context of neoliberalism, young people's dis-plays of 'extreme drinking' and 'determined drunkenness' are not simply allowed, but commanded by the motive of corporate profits. The force of this argument is seen in the restructuring of the night-time economy to attract young drinkers, the ubiquitous marketing of cheap deals, and the increase in the strength and volume of alcohol consumed by drinkers of every age, all of which play an important role in shaping a culture of intoxication (Griffin et al., 2009).

Despite complaints and flurries of 'moral panic' about the public behaviours of groups of young people (Cohen, 1972), excessive con-sumption by the general adult population, as long as they do it quietly, has become normalized in the minds of many people, including those who devise and implement alcohol policies. The term 'binge drinking' is seldom used to describe the alcohol consumption behaviours of any group other than young people appearing drunk and disorderly in public places. Private 'bingeing' is rarely referred to, and is seldom linked with alcohol-associated diseases, with accidents in the home, with domestic violence, or child abuse (Hayward & Hobbs, 2007). In fact, as Griffin et al. (2009, p. 471) conclude, 'young people's public displays of "extreme drinking" help to constitute the equally excessive (but altogether more private) alcohol consumption of the middle-aged middle classes as civi-lized and moderate.'

As argued by Hackley et al. (2011), to place the blame for exces-sive drinking on young people, and define alcohol problems in terms of a deficit of individual self-control and personal responsibility, is to ignore the role of overwhelming social, cultural, political and economic forces that promote drinking in this way. Young people drink alcohol, and drink alcohol in excessive quantities because older people drink alcohol and drink alcohol in excessive quantities. And a great number of people drink to excess because alcohol is readily available, relatively cheap, and extensively marketed as a requisite component of an enjoyable life.

Demonizing young people, moralizing about their binge drinking, problematizing it, and attempting to do something about it, without taking into consideration the liberalization of alcohol policies, the constant promotion of alcohol as a necessary accompaniment to 'fun', the reliance on alcohol production and sales for large sectors of the economy and for substantial tax revenues, and the alcohol-consuming example set by a substantial proportion of the adult population, is delusional, hypocritical and deliberately deceitful. Meanwhile, many people of all ages and the wider society of which they form a part are bearing the personal and economic cost of alcohol-induced illness, accidents, public disorder, private suffering and, ultimately, untimely death.

References

Alcohol and Public Policy Group (2010). Alcohol: No ordinary commodity. A summary of the second edition. *Addiction, 105,* 769–779.

Anderson, P., Møller, L. & Galea, G. (Eds.) (2012). *Alcohol in the European Union: Consumption, harm and policy approaches.* Copenhagen: World Health Organisation.

Bartlett, J. & Grist, M. (2011). *Under the influence: Interim report.* London, Demos.

Boden, J. M., Fergusson, D. M. & Horwood, L. J. (2011). Alcohol and STI risk: Evidence from a New Zealand longitudinal birth cohort. *Drug and Alcohol Dependence, 113*(2–3), 200–206.

Bouthoorn, S. H, van Hoof, J. J, van der Lely, N. (2011). Adolescent alcohol intoxication in Dutch hospital centers of pediatrics: characteristics and gender differences. *European Journal of Pediatrics, 170,* 1023–1030.

Bremner, P., Burnett, J., Nunney, F., Ravat, M. & Mistral, W. (2011). *Young people, alcohol and influences.* York: Joseph Rowntree Foundation.

British Liver Trust (2012). *Reducing alcohol harm: Recovery and informed choice for those with alcohol related health problems.* London: British Liver Trust.

Carragher, N. & Chalmers, J. (2011). *What are the options? Pricing and taxation policy reforms to redress excessive alcohol consumption and related harms in Australia.* Sydney: NSW Bureau of Crime Statistics and Research.

Cohen, S. (1972). *Folk devils and moral panics.* London: MacGibbon & Kee.

Collis, J., Grayson, A. & Johal, S. (2010). *Econometric analysis of alcohol consumption in the UK. HMRC Working Paper 10.* London: HM Revenue & Customs.

Österberg, E. (2012). Availability of alcohol. In P. Anderson, L. Møller, & G. Galea (Eds.) *Alcohol in the European Union: Consumption, harm and policy approaches.* Copenhagen: World Health Organisation.

Paschall, M. J., Grube, J. W. & Kypri, K. (2009). Alcohol control policies and alcohol consumption by youth: a multi-national study. *Addiction, 104,* 1849–1855.

Parliamentary Office of Science and Technology (2005). *Binge drinking and public health.* Retrieved March 6, 2013 from http://www.parliament.uk/ documents/post/postpn244.pdf.

Peden, M., Scurfield, R., Sleet, D., Mohan, D., Hyder, A. A., Jarawan, E. et al. (Eds.) (2004). *World report on road traffic injury prevention.* Geneva: World Health Organisation.

Prime Minister's Strategy Unit (2004). *Alcohol harm reduction strategy for England.* London: Cabinet Office.

Room, R. (2004). Disabling the public interest: alcohol strategies and policies for England. *Addiction, 99*(9), 1083–1089.

Rosenquist, J. N., Murabito, J., Fowler, J. H. & Christakis, N. A. (2010). The spread of alcohol consumption behavior in a large social network. *Annals of Internal Medicine, 152,* 426-433.

Rudd, N. (transl.) (1992). *Juvenal: The satires.* Oxford: Oxford University Press.

SAMHSA (2011). *Results from the 2010 national survey on drug use and health: Summary of national findings.* Rockville, MD: Substance Abuse and Mental Health Services Administration. Retrieved March 6, 2013 from http://www.samhsa.gov/data/NSDUH/2k10NSDUH/2k10Results.htm#2.9.

Sethi, D., Racioppi, F. & Bertollini, R. (2007). Preventing the leading cause of death in young people in Europe. *Journal of Epidemiology and Community Health, 61,* 842–843.

Sheron, N., Gilmore, I., Parsons, C., Hawkey, C. & Rhodes, J. (2012). Projections of alcohol-related deaths in England and Wales – tragic toll or potential prize? *The Lancet, 379*(9817), 687–688.

Smith, L. & Foxcroft, D. (2009). The effect of alcohol advertising, marketing and portrayal on drinking behaviour in young people: systematic review of prospective cohort studies. *BMC Public Health, 9*(51), 1–11.

Sutton, R. & Bridges, S. (2011). Drinking alcohol. In Fuller, E. (Ed.) *Smoking, drinking and drug use among young people in England in 2010.* London: National Centre for Social Research.

Szmigin, I., Griffin, I., Mistral, W., Bengry-Howell, A., Weale, L. & Hackley, C. (2008). Re-framing 'binge drinking' as calculated hedonism: Empirical evidence from the UK. *International Journal of Drug Policy, 19,* 359–366.

Velleman, R. (2009). *Children, young people and alcohol: How they learn and how to prevent excessive use.* York, Joseph Rowntree Foundation.

Wagenaar, A. C. & Toomey, T. L. (2002). Effects of minimum drinking age laws: Review and analyses of the literature from 1960 to 2000. *Journal of Studies on Alcohol and Drugs,* (Suppl. 14), 206–225.

World Health Organisation (2009). European Status Report on Road Safety. Towards Safer Roads and Healthier Transport Choices. WHO Regional Office for Europe, Copenhagen. Retrieved March 16, 2013 from http://www.euro.who.int/__data/assets/pdf_file/0015/43314/E92789.pdf.

World Health Organisation (2012). *Global Status Report on Alcohol and Health 2011*. Retrieved March 6, 2013 from http://www.who.int/ substance_abuse/publications/global_alcohol_report/en/index.html.

4

A Picture Tells a Thousand Stories: Young Women, Mobile Technology, and Drinking Narratives

Rebecca Brown

Over recent years young women's public alcohol consumption has been the focus of intense media and political attention. Images of intoxicated 'ladettes' lacking in self-control and composure are commonplace in newspapers, voyeuristic documentaries, and reality TV (Jackson & Tinkler, 2007; Redden & Brown, 2010). Fiona Measham and Jeanette Østergaard (2009) therefore argue that young women are the 'public face' of anxieties over 'binge drinking', particularly within the United Kingdom. Alcohol policy in both Australia and Britain blames young people in particular for the problem of excessive alcohol consumption (Hackley, Bengry-Howell, Griffin, Mistral & Szmigin, 2008; Keane, 2009). The official response to this issue typically involves public health campaigns that attempt to teach young people the value of moderate drinking by highlighting the unpleasant outcomes of intoxication. Interestingly, the representations of these scenarios are often divided according to gender and are either male- or female-focused.

Official rhetoric on young women's alcohol use employs a 'pedagogy of regret' in attempts to reduce consumption levels (Brown & Gregg, 2012). Alcohol education campaigns in both the United Kingdom and Australia target young women by reminding them that remorse and shame inevitably follow drinking. These campaigns typically use interrogative devices to encourage women to reflect on their feelings regarding intoxication. For example, Australian government campaigns asked women 'How will you feel tomorrow?' (Commonwealth Department of Health and Family Services, 1996), 'What are you doing to yourself?'

Emerging Perspectives on Substance Misuse, First Edition. Edited by Willm Mistral.
© 2013 John Wiley & Sons, Ltd. Published 2013 by John Wiley & Sons, Ltd.

(New South Wales Health Department, 2009); and a British health authority campaign concludes with 'Too much alcohol ever ruined your night?' (Derbyshire Primary Care Trust, 2009). The 'pedagogy of regret' functions through notions of responsible and 'respectable' femininity (Skeggs, 1997) by suggesting that intoxication leads to a variety of regrettable outcomes such as unwanted casual sex, sexual assault, masculinity, and ugliness. For example, the British 'Know Your Limits' campaign (Home Office, 2008) targeted women by appealing to notions of beauty and desirability. A TV advertisement presents a conventionally pretty, young white woman getting ready for a night out. Rather than accentuate her femininity however, she subverts the typical grooming routine by ripping her clothes to reveal her bra, smearing make-up across her face and combing vomit through her hair. The advertisement concludes with the tagline 'You wouldn't start a night like this, so why end it that way?'. A recent Australian campaign more explicitly employs a rhetoric of regret by linking alcohol consumption to sexual reputation (Department of Health and Aging, 2008). This advertisement begins with the protagonist (again pretty, young, and white) having fun drinking with her female friends. The night starts to unravel when the woman leaves the party to be alone in the garden with a young man. After removing her knickers, sexual activity is implied until a sudden flash indicates the couple have been caught on camera. As a group of teenagers huddle round a device, a stark message informs viewers: 'One in two Australians aged 15–17 who get drunk will do something they regret.' Both ads assume that women's sober selves would find deviating from appropriate femininity undesirable and regrettable, and as such, be persuaded to drink less alcohol.

The 'pedagogy of regret' overlaps with concerns about youthful online practices. Both public and academic discourse on young people's engagement with social media is couched in anxieties about risk, reputation, privacy and propriety (Christofides, Muise & Desmarais, 2012; Livingstone, 2008; Privacy Victoria, 2012; Sydney Morning Herald, 2009). The Australian campaign described above responds to this by highlighting the risk that recently emerged technology brings to bear on alcohol consumption. The damaging photo is likely to be shared virally and, as such, the advertisement links the young woman's alcohol consumption to her professional, as well as sexual, reputation. Such anxieties emerge from the apparent increase in employers vetting potential candidates by accessing their online profiles to seek evidence of hedonism (Brown & Vaughn, 2011; Rosen, 2010). Users of social media are therefore advised to avoid posting material that could jeopardize future employment opportunities and are encouraged to recognize the risks of disclosure (Ridout, Campbell & Ellis, 2012). As such, a large proportion of the literature on young people's social networking use revolves around exploring issues of risk, self-presentation and privacy (there is an overwhelming amount of literature in this area but a few examples are Debatin, Lovejoy, Horn & Hughes, 2009; Livingstone 2008; Taraszow, Aristodemou, Shitta, Laouris & Arsoy, 2010; and for a recent review of Facebook literature see Wilson, Gosling & Graham, 2012). This discourse suggests that, while celebrated in the present, alcohol consumption will be regretted at some point in the future.

However, recent literature on young people's drinking narratives disturbs these notions of inevitable regret. Telling stories and discussing nights out are one of the most pleasurable and significant dimensions of young people's drinking practices. These narratives provide entertainment and engender intimacy among friends. Interestingly, tales of drunkenness, danger and drama are the most memorable and enjoyable of drinking stories (Cullen 2010, 2011; Griffin, Bengry-Howell, Hackley, Mistral & Szmigin, 2009; Waitt, Jessop & Gorman-Murray, 2011). Sheehan & Ridge (2001) argue that young women refract behaviour defined as 'harmful' and 'risky' through the trope of the 'good story'. Actions that a public health perspective interprets as harmful, such as vomiting, lead to entertaining anecdotes to share among friends and, paradoxically, through these narratives, circumstances deemed as unpleasant and regrettable are interpreted as enjoyable. This provides a counterpoint to discourse that positions women's drunkenness as inevitably regrettable. Sheehan & Ridge (2001, p. 355) therefore ironically suggest that campaigns asking women to reflect on how they will feel the next day are likely to get the response: 'Looking forward to next time!' Fjær (2012) describes how young people spend the day after partying hanging out together, laughing and reminiscing about the night before. While they suffer from hangovers, this time becomes enjoyable via drinking stories and, as such, helps to minimize any suffering. Fjær argues that this period of time is an integral part of the overall drinking experience. As he suggests, the pleasures of drinking go beyond the 'liminal period' of intoxication. The significance of drinking stories therefore blurs the temporal boundaries of a night out.

The research on young women's drinking practices suggests that technology is becoming an intrinsic part of their night out. For example, nights out involve 'intricate planning' via online message boards (Cullen, 2011) and texting (Szmigin, Griffin, Mistral, Bengry-Howell, Weale & Hackley, 2008). At the time Griffin et al. (2009) collected their data mobile, phones with video capability had recently emerged and young people were beginning to use them to document narratives. In Cullen's research, which she conducted in 2003–5, photography was inseparable from young women's alcohol consumption and drinking stories. Her participants used phone cameras and still photography throughout their drinking sessions, later uploading the images to photosharing websites. Nights out can thereby be revisited through stories and photos, allowing young women to discuss, dissect and celebrate the aftermath. The *process* of constructing and creating narratives is an enjoyable and meaningful activity in itself. Cullen argues that young women's drinking stories are part of friendship work. Thus, the sessions of talking and telling are equally as significant as the content of the narratives. Given the speed of technological change, however, none of these studies considers how newer technology such as smart phones and social media impact on these practices.

Recent research on social networking points to a nexus between hedonism, online cultures and friendship. Van Doorn (2009) demonstrates that drugs, alcohol, and sex are the main topics of conversation on social media and argues that these discussions are used to strengthen friendship bonds. In a similar vein, Amy Dobson (2010) shows that the most popular photos on young Australian women's MySpace profiles are those displaying intoxication and a 'party lifestyle'. Dobson argues that such images are primarily displays of intimacy between groups of female friends. This work suggests that young people find posting alcohol-related material online to be meaningful and valuable rather than risky. Elsewhere, with Melissa Gregg (Brown & Gregg, 2012), I argue that social media provide a lens to explore the relationship between young women's drinking practices, social media, pleasure, and regret. Drawing on our own experiences of Facebook, we suggested that young women's use of this platform to broadcast hedonism disturbs notions of inevitable remorse. Drawing on empirical data from my doctoral research, here I build on these arguments by exploring the ways that social media and technology are embedded in young women's alcohol use and drinking narratives.

Background

My doctoral research explores young women's drinking practices in two post-industrial night-time economies. A total of 20 women were interviewed; 12 from Sunderland, a coastal city in the north-east of England, and eight from Newcastle, a regional coastal city in New South Wales, Australia. Interviews were complemented with both participant and nonparticipant observations. The interviews and fieldwork were conducted between December 2010 and July 2012. The women were recruited via a Facebook group, email circulars and snowball sampling. A Facebook group advertised the research and asked those who 'joined' the group to contact the author directly for further information. In this way, participants' identities remained confidential. Participants were aged between 19–29, came from a variety of backgrounds and occupations, were predominately white, although two of the Australian women were of South Asian descent, and heterosexual. The study also includes an online ethnography that draws on my own experiences of Facebook. Although I became Facebook friends with a number of the women over the course of the research and bore witness to their weekend antics, the study does not specifically analyse the content of their Facebook profiles. Rather, the use of technology and social media emerged as key themes within the interviews. I base my arguments on these narratives while also drawing from the ethnographic data.

The women's use of photos, and technology more broadly, changed throughout the course of the research. Since beginning my project in 2009, Facebook has grown exponentially and the ever improving interface capabilities encourage photo uploading and viewing. The emergence of smart phones and social media apps allow photos be uploaded in real time rather than the following day. The women considered digital cameras to be obsolete or likely to get lost or broken in the midst of intoxication. Some of the older women had used disposable cameras before the advent of camera phones, but this option was now deemed unnecessary. Only few of the women spoke of using videos despite this technology being widely available. A significant development during the research was the take-up of Facebook as a marketing tool by licensed premises and, by the second half of the fieldwork period, various drinking venues in both research locations had Facebook pages. During the evening, employees cruise the venues taking shots of groups of friends with their consent. Over the following days, the photos are uploaded to the venue's profile and the albums appear on the newsfeed of their 'friends'. Individuals can then browse the photos in order to tag themselves. This means that on any given weekend there are hundreds of photos to look at from across various venues. For the majority of the women, being in and looking at these albums is now part of the ritual of the night out.

Safety and Surveillance

The recent literature on young women's alcohol consumption demonstrates that safety and care are paramount during a night out (Griffin et al., 2009; Leyshon, 2008; Lindsay, 2009; Moore, 2010; Rudolfstoddir & Morgan, 2009; Sheehan & Ridge, 2001; Szmigin et al., 2008; Waitt et al., 2011). The desire to stay safe typically revolves around feelings of vulnerability, the perceived risk of sexual assault by predatory men, and the need to negotiate the hetero-normativity of bars and clubs. Interestingly, this research shows that safety practices are mediated through friendship. On a night out there is a strong emphasis on being responsible for each other, staying together and never leaving anyone alone. As they traverse night-time spaces, women avoid 'sleazy' or violent venues, and any unwanted male attention is managed as a group. One of the main ways the women in the present study ensure group safety on a night out is by employing strategies of surveillance. The participants spoke of the importance of being able to see each of their friends at all times and know when part of the group was visiting the toilet. The women position themselves strategically so that eye contact can be made with every member of the group, even if some individuals are at the bar, dancing, or being chatted up. One Australian participant described this as having the 'magic eye'. This term also encompasses having a sense of whether one's friends are happy or if they need rescuing from an awkward situation. There are times, however, when one's friends fall out of view and the group becomes separated. Here mobile technology adds a level of surveillance and safety during the night out.

Rebecca (interviewer): How do you take care on a night out?
Sam, 26, Sunderland: Basically we just all stick together when we're out, y'know, we never lose each other, if one of us is not in sight we either ring or send a text saying 'where are you?' straight away. So y'know we are on the ball and keep an eye on each other that way. And if they're taking their time in the toilets we'll either go to the toilets and shout for them or send a text saying 'where are you? we're at the bar'. So we're always on the ball that way.

In Sam's comments, sight emerges as a key motif in her friendship group's safety practices, and mobile phones enable surveillance when direct sight is not possible. While calling or sending texts are the main ways in which technology is harnessed to safety, Facebook's 'checking in' capability also gives women a way to know each other's location should a group be separated. Some women commented however, that such safety tactics can be undermined by intoxication, loud music, and also the loss of connectivity in underground venues.

Louise, 24, Sunderland: Like, going for nights out somewhere else, I don't know my way round as much, so if I got separated from my friends, like you have your phone, but people don't pick up their phone on a night out, people don't see that they've got text messages for ages. So, if you get separated from people... I don't like the thought of not knowing where I am.

Both Sam's and Louise's comments demonstrate that young women embrace technology to enhance already existing practices of safety and care. Szmigin et al. (2008) argue that women need a combination of planning, safety practices and trustworthy friends to be able to 'let go' and enjoy intoxication, and I would add mobile technology to these criteria. Louise avoids heavy intoxication in unfamiliar locations because the thought of losing mobile contact with her friends is unsettling. Here technology and connectivity act as a 'security blanket' for mobile (and roaming) youth (Gregg, 2011). This turns concern about online privacy, risk and exposure on its head. The point of mobile technology on a night out is to *allow* for surveillance and ensure that one is 'seen' by known others. Rather than being concerned about privacy and maintaining anonymity, for young women the risk is inherent in being undetectable.

Discuss and Dissect

While some of the drinking-story literature briefly points to the use of technology to document nights out, it generally depicts conversations as face-to-face or over the telephone. Here I demonstrate that social media enhances, or is used instead of, face-to-face discussions about the night out. Some of the women in the study occasionally see their friends the day after drinking, but for many this is impossible or undesirable due to distance, employment, childcare demands, or in some cases, feeling too sick. Some women phone their friends or send texts on awakening. This is primarily to establish wellbeing and the severity of each other's hangover, before moving on to talk about the previous evening. For the majority of the women however, these discussions take place on Facebook. Even among those who speak by phone, their evaluation of the night continues online, and the primary way the women use Facebook to document and discuss nights out is through photographs. This involves uploading images, tagging oneself and one's friends in photos, looking at others' or the pubs' photos and also commenting on images. For example, Michelle does not speak to her friends the next day; she informed me that any contact 'normally comes with pictures'. Looking at and commenting on photos on Facebook takes precedence over other forms of conversation and analysis. The way in which Facebook is a space for discussion is clear in Sam's interview:

Rebecca: Do you take photos on a night out?
Sam, 26, Sunderland: Aww the camera's *always* out. I love the camera. And I always upload them on Facebook as well so everybody can see.
Rebecca: So you put the photos on Facebook? And do you look at other people's photos?
Sam: I do yes. Talk about the night out on Facebook.

A few of the women prefer to leave the night behind rather than recall their drunken antics, but the prevalence of Facebook as the primary site for constructing drinking narratives makes this hard to avoid. Amira doesn't particularly enjoy talking to her friends the next day. While she enjoys her nights out, Amira appears to want to distance herself from the previous evening. I asked her if she spoke to her friends the next day:

Amira, 22, Newcastle: I usually don't. I don't know, I just don't wanna rehash things all over again. So unless someone calls me, I don't call them.
Rebecca: No?
Amira: No, I won't start discussions, but now it just happens on Facebook. When you log on it's there, so it's like aww god.

Cullen (2011) argues that young women use drinking stories and photos to 'archive' their friendship. Facebook enhances this process and also provides a shared space for the archive to be located. For most of the women in the study, photographs are one of the most pleasurable and memorable dimensions of going out. Some of the women spoke indifferently about intoxication but in contrast, however, when discussing taking, and in particular *looking at*, photographs the women became highly animated. Photo taking was ubiquitous among young women during my observations and, for the majority of the participants, a night out involves taking or being included in photos. Group photos are taken, followed by an obligatory huddling round the device to decide if the image needs to be reshot. One or two individuals in each friendship group are the key instigators of taking and uploading images. Some women find being responsible for taking photos disruptive to their night out, or feel the novelty of uploading images to Facebook is waning, but they nonetheless enjoy being in and looking at others' photos. As well as using Facebook to talk about and document recent nights out, older photos are also highly pleasurable and engender a sense of nostalgia. This meant that some women had spent time taking digitals shots of print photos in order to upload them. A night out from years previously can be recalled, discussed and laughed at through these images.

Given that their drinking stories are constructed through social media, the women take photos *for* Facebook. Some of the women said that while they intend to take photos, they often 'forget' to do so as the evening progresses. This implies that they feel they *should* be taking photos. There was a sense that that the women felt compelled to capture images and upload them to Facebook. The default assumption among friends is that photos will be shared online.

Rebecca: Do you and your friends take photos on the night out?

Steph, 27, Sunderland: Yeah it's obviously mainly on everyone's phone. We take quite a few pictures, you start taking them but then as the night gets on and you're more drunk you forget, you kind of forget that you've got a phone to take pictures, and them are the best times to actually take a picture! When you're absolutely mortal! But then in a way it's good cos they're not on Facebook for the whole world to see.

Rebecca: So is that what normally happens the next day, you put them on Facebook?

Steph: Aye they would go on Facebook. They would go straight on just so everybody can see how drunk (you are).

Here there is an expectation that all photos will appear on Facebook. Steph presents photos as being automatically uploaded, bypassing the need for a human to decide on and upload particular images. In this dialogue Steph attributes agency to the photos rather than the individual responsible for uploading the night's album. The prevalence of taking photos with Facebook in mind demonstrates that social media and intoxication are entwined practices.

Appropriate Impropriety

Recent research on young women's drinking practices demonstrates that acting 'inappropriately' is one of the most pleasurable aspects of consuming alcohol (Cullen 2010, 2011; Montemurro & McClure 2005; Sheehan & Ridge, 2001; Skeggs, 1997; Waitt et al., 2001). For example, the highlights of alcohol consumption involve discussing sex, swearing, being aggressive to unwanted predatory men, being sexually assertive, fighting, being rude, singing, vomiting, stealing, engaging in minor vandalism and urinating in public. This research also shows, however, that in order to be pleasurable and acceptable, transgression on a night out must be grounded in the safe space of friendship. So while being 'inappropriate' is enjoyable, it must be validated through being part of a group. This was reflected in the women's narratives about photos. In terms of content, the most enjoyable photos to take, appear in, upload and comment on, are those capturing instances of a lack of composure, inappropriateness, and intoxication. The women described images that depict them as extremely intoxicated or engaging in 'wild' behaviour, such as dancing on tables and chairs.

Steph, 27, Sunderland: There was a time when we went out and we went into the [pub name] and there was a band on, so we were in there and there was this guy singing away and I was *mortal* and I just walked over and took the microphone off him and started singing! [bursts into laughter]. There's a picture of us on Facebook singing down the microphone.

Michelle, 24, Sunderland: And we're standing outside the [pub name] and flashing our knickers and stuff like that. That's like a really good night to me. That's like when I'm drunk. I think a picture tells a thousand stories.

Michelle and Steph clearly find the photos and the accompanying memories pleasurable. Michelle uses the photo to construct her memory of how pleasurable the night was and also her level of intoxication. Despite images of her underwear being in the public domain, Michelle feels positively about what could be deemed unfeminine and inappropriate behaviour. In the quotes both women place emphasis on their intoxication and the group context. Any potential feelings of shame and the risk of stigma are mediated through the context of friendship, fun, intoxication, and the value of photos. As such, sharing the images online and constructing a drinking narrative renders such behaviour meaningful, valuable, and appropriate. There are, however, limits to the content that can be posted online, especially if it goes beyond the boundaries of 'respectable' femininity (Skeggs, 1997). Cullen (2010, 2011) argues that young women's drinking practices and stories are grounded in broader discourses of femininity. While drunken excess was celebrated among Cullen's teenage participants, stories were nevertheless entwined with notions of respectability and responsibility. They therefore had to avoid portraying themselves as being out of control, disrespectable, or a 'slag'. Michelle gives an example of a photo considered inappropriate for Facebook. She uploaded it as a joke, but took it down soon after at her friend's request:

Michelle, 24, Sunderland: There's a picture of me friend, and she's pushing her boobs up, and you can see the top of her nipple, and she's just... like... I removed *that*. Like I put it on, and fair enough I removed it.

While there is no issue with taking such a photo, Michelle's comments suggest the solitary, sexualized and decontextualized nature of the image means it is unacceptable for social media. By contrast, concerns about professionalism, privacy and risk were not apparent in the women's conversations about photos and their content. Only one Australian participant commented that some of her friends in the medical profession had to filter online material to make sure it was 'okay' for Facebook. What was highly important to the women however, was looking 'nice' and attractive. Acting inappropriately does not necessarily preclude being attractive but the women avoid posting unflattering or 'ugly' photos of themselves, and untag themselves from friends' photos they don't like. I asked Sam if there were some she didn't tag herself in:

Sam, 26, Sunderland: It happens all the time to be honest even pictures that I've took meself, or even the professional [licensed premises] pictures, if me hair's not in the right way, I just look ridiculous, I think I'm not tagging meself in there, or if me face looks bigger than the previous photograph I won't, it just depends, but no, if they're not very nice I won't tag meself in them, only nice.

Nevertheless, putting 'bad' photos on is a form of teasing between friends and often part of the ritual of the night out. The majority of the women felt in control by having the choice to untag themselves, but some felt the ubiquity of posting photos online meant maintaining an attractive appearance was difficult. Any concerns about photo content, however, were connected to being seen by a known audience in the present, rather than an unknown audience in the future.

Alleviating Anxiety

While acting inappropriately is fun, women are nevertheless more likely than men to feel ambivalent towards their intoxication (Griffin et al., 2009; Leyshon, 2008; Measham, 2002). As such, drinking narratives go beyond providing entertainment and engendering intimacy, as they enable young women to take a positive view of their alcohol consumption and subsequent behaviour (Cullen, 2010, 2011). For example, Sheehan and Ridge (2001) argue that these narratives allow young women to make sense of partaking in a stigmatized activity that is subject to contestation. This process ensures that excessive drinking is interpreted as fun, pleasurable, and meaningful rather than inappropriate, confusing, and shameful. Young women therefore use drinking stories to reconcile any ambivalent feelings they have towards their alcohol consumption and of the night out. Fjær (2012) argues that the process of talking about the night out allows young people to deal with feelings of worry over how one's drunken behaviour has been perceived. Telling stories and piecing together a shared memory enabled his participants to minimize anxiety and feel more positively towards their intoxication and consequent behaviour. Similarly, the women in the present study used Facebook to make sense of their intoxication and also to construct a memory of the night out. Carly often feels anxious the day after drinking as she worries about how her friends have perceived her, generally in case she's been 'talking rubbish'. Apart from a few texts, she rarely has contact with her friends the next day.

Rebecca: Do you ever upload photos onto Facebook after a night out?
Carly, 28, Sunderland: No, I know it's a big thing for some people, but I do like, like when I went out the other night, the comments you would get on Facebook and stuff like that, the next day, it just sort of helps you to think that you've had a good night with people. And knowing that they've had a good night as well and stuff.

Here Carly uses Facebook to evaluate the previous evening, to construct a positive memory, and also to work out her friends' feelings about the night. Discussions on Facebook alleviate her feelings of anxiety. In the following conversation Jo uses Facebook to reconsider an incident involving the risk of sexual assault. Jo described a night out where she woke up at a young man's house to find he was 'forcing himself' on her. She has only partial memories in regard to meeting him and leaving the pub. When she realized what was happening, Jo grabbed her belongings and quickly left. The young attempted to follow her saying he was sorry, but she ran away, telling him to leave her alone. Interestingly, the next day, Jo used Facebook to try and make sense of the situation and justify his behaviour.

Rebecca: Did you know him beforehand?

Jo, 19, Newcastle: No, definitely didn't. I could remember his name though and I looked him up the next day on Facebook, and he had posted all these statuses about how he had being crying and sent home from work and, like, he clearly didn't know what he was doing . . . I was okay about it cos . . . I don't know, I was very drunk and he was clearly very drunk and wasn't . . . but I wouldn't want to put myself in that kind of situation again, in a circumstance where it *was* somebody different. He was definitely emotionally unwell, from what I could tell from his Facebook.

Rebecca: Did you ever see him again when you were out?

Jo: No. But I did add him on Facebook. But to tell him mainly that he shouldn't do that . . . and he shouldn't . . . but at the same time I apologized for acting the way I did as well.

The comments from Carly and Jo suggest that feelings of shame, anxiety and confusion can emerge following intoxication. Although in differing ways, both women use Facebook to make sense of their own and others' feelings and behaviour following a night out. Social media emerges as a route to alleviate negative emotions and has the potential to prevent them from developing any further.

Pleasures of the Unexpected

In a study of young English people's experiences of alcohol consumption, Christine Griffin et al. (2009) found that narratives of a loss of consciousness were central to their participants' drinking practices. Narratives of memory loss allowed middle-class women in particular to abdicate responsibility for any drunken behaviour and therefore retain a hold on their respectable femininity. Beyond this, though, memory loss was experienced as enjoyable in that pleasure resided in recalling memories the following day. Fjær (2012) argues that memory loss leads to feelings of anxiety over what shameful behaviour one *might have* engaged in. He suggests that constructing shared drinking stories and recalling the night out allows anxiety to dissipate, resulting in more positive feelings towards one's memory loss. The notion that memory loss is enjoyable resonates in the present study, and again technology enhances and enables practices and pleasures already in place. Among the young women the most enjoyable photos to look at are those that they cannot remember being taken and also those that prompt 'flashbacks' of the night.

Sia, 22, Newcastle: (Laughing) Yeah it's pretty funny to look back at them the next day and sometimes you don't really remember stuff that happened or you might have forgotten something and that kind of reminds you of it.

Rebecca: Why is that enjoyable?

Sia: Um, I dunno, I guess just because... you don't remember that moment, and... then it's kind of like proof that you actually... that that happened. Rather than somebody just telling you, 'oh you did that'. Cos sometimes you're like, 'no, you were drunk too so you're probably just making that up'.

Here Sia uses photos not only to prompt memory recall about the evening's antics, but also as a reliable and impartial source of information to piece together the night and construct drinking narratives. The pleasure of memory loss disturbs the idea of a moderate, rational and controlled neoliberal self that is central to harm-minimization campaigns. This ideal form of selfhood emerged in tandem with the social, economic and cultural developments associated with neoliberalism, which is a dominant Western political rationality that promotes profitability, entrepreneurialism and a free market. Under this social order individuals are expected to be responsible, controlled, disciplined, self-aware, reflective, ethical subjects who are continuously in a process of self-transformation and self-improvement (Griffin et al., 2009; Skeggs, 2005). Intoxication enables a temporary suspension of this form of selfhood, leading Griffin et al. to argue that young people enjoy taking 'time out' from neoliberal subjectivity. While self-suspension and memory loss may be enjoyable for their own sake however, here I argue that pleasure particularly resides in the *unexpectedness* of what is recalled or witnessed in the photos.

Michelle, 24, Sunderland: Yeah I love looking at photos.
Rebecca: So that's (Facebook) the main place you see them?
Michelle: Yeah, it's been about a year since I had a photo developed! But normally I'll look at a picture and if I comment it'll be like 'can't remember this'! or 'what you doing!' Sort of like shocked. Rather than like 'oh my god can you remember this and this'.
Rebecca: So is looking at photos one of your favourite parts of the night?
Michelle: Yeah, and I would say one of the good parts is like *remembering* the night out, yeah, unexpected. Then it comes back to you!

This pleasure of the forgotten and unexpected is also clear in the following quote from Abigail, who is a moderate drinker compared to many of the other participants. She avoids extreme intoxication as it makes her feel vulnerable. Nonetheless, she finds delight in unexpected photo content that make one's memory loss apparent.

Abigail, 28, Sunderland: Love looking at them [photos] the next day and you think eeee I can't remember that and eeee I can't remember this, and I can't remember getting that taken. So love the photographs, and I think when you get them unexpected, or you get other people to take them, they're always the best ones, cos you're like eeee I can't remember that, or I can't remember this being took.

The pleasure of the unexpected explains why photos of venues are popular. They are accompanied by an element of anticipation and surprise, replacing that of print photography and disposable cameras. Unless one experiences memory loss, the immediacy of digital photography means that it is unable to provide a sense of the unknown and unexpected. The sense of anticipation technology provides can been seen in the following quote from Amy. She laughs as she describes her morning-after ritual and its relationship to technology:

Amy, 20, Sunderland: You wake up in the morning and check if you've got your phone, purse, keys passport and everything. So I'm running round the house looking for all this stuff, and you just *dread* looking at your photos on your phone. You're like 'Who are these people? Why've I took this photo?' Like, I'll have pictures of someone's sick!

Like why have I took it! Or like with my friends, if you leave your phone about they're gonna go on your phone right, so you always look at your texts to see if you've text someone anything embarrassing or if they've text someone off your phone and you've got to apologize. When you read them everything's misspelt and you've got like six 'where are yous' all the way down [referring to vertical SMS conversation on phone screen].

Amy's quote highlights how technology is bound to the night out in numerous ways. As well as using her phone to take photos during the night and to attempt to locate her friends when they become separated, Amy's phone's content provides a humorous evidence trail that she uses to piece together the night and recall it. Significantly, though, Amy demonstrates that pleasure, anxiety and anticipation are simultaneously located in memory loss and the unexpected. These emotions are at once enhanced, mediated and relieved through photos and smart phone technology. Here pleasure is not so much in self-suspension or memory loss, but in looking at photos the following day and being informed of and reminded of this loss. Technology, and the forums it provides for documenting and capturing the night out, allow for memory loss to be pleasurable. Any potential anxiety over the unknown is minimized because photos and phones allow the unknown to be knowable and retrievable.

Sunday Suffering

While extreme intoxication and hangovers are considered unpleasant and undesirable for young women, such instances are translated into 'funny' stories and therefore become pleasurable in the recounting and sharing (Griffin et al., 2009; Cullen, 2010, 2011). This is reflected in the way the women use Facebook to reference the night out by broadcasting the extent of their hangovers. A steady flow of self-mocking status updates and empathizing comments detail the extent of the suffering, typically involving the obligatory promise 'never again'. Visceral tales of severe hangovers were common in the interviews. Broadcasting one's pain on Facebook, however, helps make the suffering more bearable. Steph purposefully drinks to intoxication on nights out and occasionally uses cocaine. She eats little before going out, partly because of excitement and also because working in a retail environment means she does not have time to eat on Saturdays. She suffers from intense hangovers, spending Sundays vomiting and crying. Nevertheless, Steph continues to go out and repeat the process regularly. I asked if she talked about her hangovers on Facebook and she burst into laughter.

Steph, 27, Sunderland: Aww all the time! You can guarantee on Sunday morning if I've been out the Saturday night it's like 'Why on earth did I do this?' 'I'm hanging out me arse!' 'I can't cope with this anymore!' 'I'm not doing it again!' Yeah, until next weekend!

Despite her suffering, Steph's hangovers translate into a good story accompanied by much laughter. There was no sense of remorse, shame or regret surrounding Steph's intoxication or hangovers and there is little impact on her future consumption levels. Through contact with her friends the next day and minimizing the effects of the hangover to some extent via social media, the self-inflicted torment is enjoyable. Her hangover becomes a form of entertainment for herself and her friends, and Facebook is a space to find empathy and support. Steph doesn't interpret her hangover or heavy drinking as harmful. Rather, reliving the night out through photos and comments remind her that her pain was worth it.

Conclusion

This chapter has brought to light the symbiotic relationship between contemporary young women's drinking cultures and mobile technology. Adding to work that extends the temporal boundaries of a night out, my arguments here also blur the *spatial* boundaries. Facebook is a key space during nights out no less than bedroom getting-ready sessions, bars, and clubs. Rather than being a site of risk, here technology adds to existing forms of harm minimization, offering a layer of security to groups of friends, assisting to make a hangover (somewhat) more tolerable, and minimizing any negative feelings or ambivalence towards intoxication. It also enhances the pleasures of drinking and the subsequent memorable stories. Technology, therefore, has an *enabling* function in regard to young women's alcohol use. It facilitates friendship and transgression and also allows memory loss to be both pleasurable and recoverable. The result is that intoxication is safer and less anxiety provoking. Drunken antics become all the more meaningful and worthwhile if the moment can be captured in order to linger in the online archive. This work further strengthens claims that women's drinking is grounded in friendship. Social media allows women to capture and relive moments of shared fun, often in the face of demanding schedules that leave little room for time out.

Throughout the chapter I have drawn on women's use of social media to disturb notions of inevitable regret. The pleasures of unexpected 'forgotten' photos, constructing memories of being 'wild', and mocking one's hangover, highlight that the relationship between intoxication, pleasure and regret is by no means straightforward. It also shows that young women dispense with middle-class concerns that interpret posting alcohol-related material on Facebook as risky and damaging to one's potentially successful future. Of course, it can be argued that Facebook gives no indication of an individual's 'real-life' emotions and that women do experience regret following excessive alcohol consumption. As we have seen, intoxication does lead to feelings of ambivalence and anxiety. The point is, however, that Facebook provides a space for such emotions to be relieved. Further to this, technology and social media play an instrumental role in documenting and celebrating precisely what official representations deem as regrettable. When shame and suffering do occur, young women do not necessarily change their future behaviour in the way harmminimization campaigns presuppose. As such, this renders the 'pedagogy of regret' a futile strategy. I therefore implore public-health officials to move beyond a tactic that seeks to make young women feel ashamed about their alcohol consumption. Campaigns would do well to harness technology in the same manner as licensed premises, and draw on the strategies of care and surveillance that many young women already utilize.

References

Brown, R. & Gregg, M. (2012). The pedagogy of regret: Facebook, binge drinking and young women. *Continuum: Journal of Media and Cultural Studies*, 26(3), 357–369.

Brown, V. R. & Vaughn, E. D. (2011). The writing on the (Facebook) wall: The use of social networking sites in hiring decisions. *Journal of Business and Psychology*, 26(2), 219–225.

Christofides, E., Muise, A., Desmarais, S. (2012). Hey mom, what's on your Facebook: Comparing Facebook disclosure and privacy in adolescents and adults. *Social, psychological and personality science*, 3(1), 48–54.

Commonwealth Department of Health and Family Services (1996). *How will you feel tomorrow*. Canberra: Australian Government Publishing Service.

Cullen, F. (2010). 'I was kinda paralytic': Pleasure, peril and teenage girls' drinking stories. In C. Jackson, C. Paechter, & E. Renold (Eds.) *Girls and education*

3–16: Continuing concerns, new agendas (pp. 183–196). Maidenhead: Open University Press.

Cullen, F. (2011). 'The only time I feel girly is when I go out': Drinking stories, teenage girls and respectable femininities. *International Journal of Adolescence and Youth, 16*(2), 119–138.

Debatin, B., Lovejoy, J. P., Horn, A. & Hughes, B. N. (2009). Facebook and online privacy: Attitudes, behaviors, and unintended consequences. *Journal of Computer-Mediated Communication, 15*(1), 83–108.

Department of Health and Aging (2008). Don't turn a Night Out into a Nightmare. Commonwealth of Australia, Canberra. Retrieved 7 March 2013 from http://www.drinkingnightmare.gov.au.

Derbyshire Primary Care Trust (2009). *Bloody Mary*. Chesterfield: Derbyshire County Primary Care Trust.

Dobson, A. S. (2010). The representation of female friendships on young women's MySpace profiles: the all-female world and the feminine other. In E. Dunkels, G. Franburg & C. Hallagren (Eds.) *Youth Culture and Net Culture: Online Social Practices* (pp. 126–152). Hershey: IGI Global.

Fjær, E. G. (2012). The day after drinking: interaction during hangovers with young Norwegian adults. *Journal of Youth Studies, 15*(8), 995–1010.

Gregg, M. (2011). *Work's intimacy*. Cambridge: Polity Press.

Griffin, C., Bengry-Howell, A., Hackley, C., Mistral, W. & Szmigin, I. (2009). 'Everytime I do it I absolutely annihilate myself': Loss of (self-) consciousness and loss of memory in young people's drinking narratives. *Sociology, 43*(3), 457–467.

Hackley, C., Bengry-Howell, A., Griffin, C., Mistral, W. & Szmigin, I. (2008). The discursive constitution of the UK alcohol problem in Safe, Sensible, Social: A discussion of policy implications. *Drugs: Education, Prevention and Policy, 15*(suppl. 1), 61–74.

Home Office (2008). *Know your limits*. London, Home Office. Retrieved March 16, 2013 from http://webarchive.nationalarchives.gov.uk/200808210 82130/units.nhs.uk/.

Jackson, C. & Tinkler P. (2007). 'Ladettes' and 'modern girls': 'Troublesome' young femininities. *The Sociological Review, 55*(2), 251–272.

Keane, H. (2009). Intoxication, harm and pleasure: An analysis of the Australian National Alcohol Strategy. *Critical Public Health, 19*(2), 135–142.

Leyshon, M. (2008). 'We're stuck in the corner': Young women, embodiment and drinking in the countryside. *Drugs: Education, Prevention and Policy, 15*(3), 267–289.

Lindsay, J. (2009). Young Australians and the staging of intoxication and self-control. *Journal of Youth Studies, 12*(4), 371–384.

Livingstone, S. (2008). Taking risky opportunities in youthful content creation: teenagers' use of social networking sites for intimacy, privacy and self-expression. *New Media and Society, 10*(3), 393–411.

Measham, F. (2002). Doing gender – doing drugs: Conceptualizing the gendering of drug cultures. *Contemporary Drug Problems, 29*(2), 335–373.

Measham, F. & Østergaard. J. (2009). The public face of binge drinking: British and Danish young women, recent trends in alcohol consumption and the European binge drinking debate. *Probation Journal, 56*(4), 415–434.

Montemurro, B. & McClure, B. (2005). Changing gender norms for alcohol consumption: Social drinking and lowered inhibitions at bachelorette parties. *Sex Roles, 52*(5–6), 297–288.

Moore, D. (2010). Beyond disorder, danger, incompetence and ignorance: Rethinking the youthful subject of alcohol and other drug policy. *Contemporary Drug Problems, 37*(3), 475–498.

New South Wales Health Department (2009). *Binge Drinking: What are you doing to yourself?* Retrieved March 7, 2013 from http://www.whatareyoudoingtoyourself.com/.

Privacy Victoria (2012). Information for young people. Office of Victorian Privacy Commissioner. Retrieved March 16, 2012 from http://www.privacy.vic.gov.au/domino/privacyvic/web2.nsf/pages/information-for-young-people #think.

Redden, G. & Brown, R. (2010). From bingeing booze bird to gilded cage: teaching girls class and gender on Ladette to Lady. *Critical Studies in Education, 51*(3), 237–249.

Ridout, B., Campbell, A. & Ellis, L. (2012). Off your Face(book): Alcohol in online social identity construction and its relation to problem drinking in university students. *Drug and Alcohol Review, 31*(1), 20–26.

Rosen, J. (2010). The end of forgetting. *The New York Times Magazine,* July 25.

Rudolfsdottir, A. G. & Morgan, P. (2009). 'Alcohol is my friend': Young middle class women discuss their relationship with alcohol. *Journal of Community and Applied Social Psychology, 19*(6), 492–505.

Sheehan, M. & Ridge, D. (2001). 'You become really close . . . you talk about the silly things you did, and we laugh': The role of binge drinking in female secondary students' lives. *Substance Use and Misuse, 36*(3), 347–372.

Skeggs, B. (1997). *Formations of class and gender: Becoming respectable.* London: Sage.

Skeggs, B. (2005). The making of class and gender through vizualizing moral subject formation. *Sociology, 39*(5), 965–982.

Sydney Morning Herald (2009). Obama's Facebook warning: watch out for 'stupid' posts. *Sydney Morning Herald,* September 9. Retrieved March 7, 2013 from http://www.smh.com.au/technology/technology-news/obamas-facebook-warning-watch-out-for-stupid-posts-20090909-fgfn.html.

Szmigin, I., Griffin, C., Mistral, W., Bengry-Howell, A., Weale, L. & Hackley. C. (2008). Re-framing 'binge drinking' as calculated hedonism: Empirical evidence from the UK. *International Journal of Drug Policy, 19*(5), 359–366.

Taraszow, T., Aristodemou, E., Shitta, G., Laouris, Y. & Arsoy, A. (2010). Disclosure of personal and contact information by young people in social networking sites: An analysis of Facebook as an example. *International Journal of Media and Cultural Politics*, 6(1), 81–101.

Van Doorn, N. (2009). The ties that bind: the networked performance of gender, sexuality and friendship on My Space. *New Media and Society*, 11 (8), 1–22.

Waitt, G., Jessop, L. & Gorman-Murray, A. (2011). 'The guys in there just expect to be laid': Embodied and gendered socio-spatial practices of a 'night out' in Wollongong, Australia. *Gender, Place and Culture*, 18(2), 255–275.

Wilson, R. E., Gosling, S. D. & Graham, L. T. (2012). A review of Facebook research in the social science. *Perspectives on Psychological Science*, 7(3), 203–220.

5

Exploring Emerging Perspectives on Gender and Drug Use

Karenza Moore and Fiona Measham

Summary

In this chapter we consider developments in the field of gender and drugs research. Reviewing feminists' pioneering work on gender and drug use from the 1980s onwards, we draw attention to Ettorre's more recent call to 're-vision' our understandings of female drug use. In the context of over two decades of rave, dance and club drug research, which has paid attention to gendered drug use in innovative ways, we explore gendered patterns of drug use across diverse leisure spaces. We highlight how post-rave club drug-using cultures both challenge and reinforce gender and sexuality norms, drawing on our own and others' work on drug-using experiences in these socio-cultural contexts. Finally we discuss the emergence of new directions in research on gender and drug use, notably those developed through critiques of postfeminism, and highlight three key strands for future research.

Introduction

The emergence of challenges to medical, psychiatric and criminological models of offending from within the social sciences in the second half of the 20th century opened up the possibility of understanding criminals, including drug users, in ways that questioned prevailing stereotypes. Labelling and new deviancy theories presented a critical challenge to the

Emerging Perspectives on Substance Misuse, First Edition. Edited by Willm Mistral.
© 2013 John Wiley & Sons, Ltd. Published 2013 by John Wiley & Sons, Ltd.

then entrenched understanding of drug use as a pathology, a moral failing and/or a disease ('addiction') involving loss of autonomy and rationality. Yet subsequent feminist historical critiques have highlighted that research on women's experiences of deviancy, drugs, and the social control exercised upon female drug users was largely absent during this otherwise exciting intellectual period (Millman,1982). Early radical scholarly works in the sociology of crime and deviance in the 1960s and 1970s focused predominantly on male drug users (Young, 1971), male drinkers (Parker, 1974) and male-dominated music cultures (Hebdidge, 1979) and did little to address the experiences of female drug users. Consequently, in 1980, Kalant argued that research on women and drug use was effectively a 'non-field' (Ettorre, 2002; Kalant, 1980). Where the female drug user did appear, she was sicker, more deviant and more psychologically disturbed than her male counterpart (see Ettorre, 2007, for a critique). Following the emergence of 'second-wave' feminism (for a critique of 'era-thinking' and 'waves' within the history of feminist theorizing see McRobbie, 2009), a keener focus on women's experiences opened up a space for more nuanced understandings of female drug users.

It took the grassroots women's movement combined with feminist scholarly activity in the early 1980s, with its focus on experience and the privileging of previously subjugated knowledges, to prompt a seismic shift in the trajectory of gender and drugs research. With classical assumptions about female drug users' naturalized embodied deviance directly challenged (Ettorre, 2007), the social, cultural and economic aspects of female drug use emerged through the efforts of feminists (including feminist criminologists) at the time. Careful attention was paid to women's own accounts of their drug use, using methods such as the qualitative interview to theorise how female drug use was shaped by oppressive gendered social relations. Ettorre's (1992) ground-breaking work on women's use of tranquilizers, for example, understood (male) doctors prescribing tranquillizers to women confined to the domestic sphere through the lens of patriarchal dominance. Curran and Golombok (1985) argued that tranquilizing women should be viewed as a feminist issue because historically the medical, and particularly the psychiatric profession, has reproduced a belief that women are 'naturally inferior' to men, are 'neurotic', and that they should be 'passive' and dependent on the men in their lives (their doctors, psychiatrists, fathers, and husbands).

Medicalizing and psychologizing tendencies produce drug use as an individualized problem to be solved by expert intervention: some abhorrent (capital punishment), some brutal (imprisonment and forced detoxification), others perhaps less so (methadone maintenance treatment, MMT). The lived experiences of users and of interventions within the 'war on drugs' are profoundly gendered, racialized and classed. Fraser and valentine (2008), for example, highlight that, in a bid to give structure – itself a paternalistic undertaking – to those assumed to have chaotic lives, MMT builds a gendered notion of passivity which produced variable expectations with regards male and female clients. When (verbally) challenged by female clients, this produced them as transgressive of 'traditional ideals of femininity . . . quiet, retiring and subject to, rather than sovereign of, expert discourse' (Fraser & Valentine, 2008, p. 153). Mulia's (2002) qualitative study of American female drug users also noted the informal as well as formal institutional practises, which restrict and control women's access to drug services, leading to strategies of resistance and defiance such as non-disclosure of medical information. Such resistance, often interpreted as manipulative and self-destructive by the authorities, could lead to a negative impact on the quality and quantity of drug services for female users.

Given that drug interventions are often undertaken within criminal justice settings, feminist criminologists have also been critical of the ways and means by which prisons and other 'correctional' institutions actively gender penal subjects. Feminist criminological theorizing on gender and penal policy has explored how maternal relations are used by prison and probation services in order to govern 'risk' (Hannah-Moffat, 2007). Parenting programmes in Canadian prisons for example are gendered through the deployment of discourse around female drug users' 'inability' to keep their families together (with no mention of imprisoned male drug users' failure to do so), attesting to the use of normative understandings of white middle-class femininity and a woman's idealized role within the traditional family (Hannah-Moffat, 2007, p. 230; see also Fraser & Valentine, 2008). Pregnant drug-using bodies represent an anathema to this feminine and familial ideal. Feminist writers have highlighted the disciplinary practices directed towards these 'disordered, polluted bodies or vessels' in a society preoccupied with regulating reproductive bodies and 'protecting the foetus' (Ettorre, 2007), as salient to women's use of legal and illegal drugs. In the mid-1980s, for example, low-income minority ethnic women giving birth to 'crack babies' were the target of repressive drug-war policies following a drug scare produced by the media and the medical profession (Reeves & Campbell, 1994; Reinarman & Levine, 2004). Project Prevention has been working to sterilize female drug users, often from low-income and minority ethnic groups, in the United States and more recently in the United Kingdom in return for a one-off payment (Gregory, 2010).

82

'Woman as victim' remains the dominant model through which women's relationships with substances and with other people are understood; a model often internalized by women themselves. There has been growing concern for example, in the media, amongst policy makers and enforcement agencies, about 'drug-facilitated sexual assault' (DFSA) in which a substance is administered to the victim without their knowledge with the premeditated purpose of assisting an assault. If the drug is surreptitiously added to a drink that the victim willingly consumes then it is commonly known as 'drink spiking'. When surveyed, young British women were found to perceive 'spiking' with an illicit drug as a plausible threat to their safety in the night-time economy (NTE) (Burgess, Donovan, and Moore, 2009). Moore (2009) demonstrates that women are being simultaneously portrayed as victims of drink spiking with illicit drugs but also potentially blamed for their own victimization, as they are in relation to sexual assault more generally, both in the media and in the British criminal justice system. However, there is less concern amongst women regarding men 'spiking' their drinks with (additional) alcohol; men buying women double/triple measures of spirits or shots of unknown alcoholic strength; or of women's voluntary consumption of (sometimes large quantities of) alcohol and the often misogynist attitudes towards women at leisure in the night-time economy (Winlow & Hall, 2006).

'Woman as victim' is also reinforced through media coverage of drug-related deaths. Drug-related deaths selected by the media tend to be framed in terms of the innocent victim, typically a young woman, usually white and often from a 'respectable' family background, with similarities, for example, between the media coverage of the death of Leah Betts in 1995 after taking ecstasy, the death of Hester Stewart in 2009 after taking GBL and ecstasy, and the death of Gabrielle Price in 2009 after taking mephedrone, ketamine and other drugs. By contrast, the deaths of female injecting drug users are rarely covered by the UK press and usually without accompanying photographs. Here we see the construction of female 'deviance' and victimhood, in relation to both voluntary and involuntary, legal and illegal drug use, although it would seem that only certain female victims 'count'.

Why is this important for an understanding of gender and drug use? The socio-cultural hierarchy of drugs and their users is profoundly gendered. This should alert us for example to the ways in which gender is implicated in the artificial division of illicit drugs into 'recreational' and 'problematic'; or of alcohol consumption into 'social' and 'antisocial'.

Heroin is constructed as a 'masculine' drug, often associated with poor, usually white, sometimes 'artistic' males 'heroically' struggling against their social disadvantage and resisting mainstream culture (see Fraser & Valentine, 2008, for a critique). In this sense it is unsurprising that female heroin users (some of whom will be dependent users) are produced as 'doubly deviant', with their heroin use 'spoiling' their gendered identity and representing femininity misplaced and defiled. Ettorre writes of female heroin users:

> In the public sphere she is a 'non-woman'. Her visibility is a direct challenge to the established patriarchal order . . . Whether or not a female heroin addict has ever exchanged her body for drugs or money for her habit, she is characterised as an impure woman, an evil slut or a loose female. (Ettorre, 1992, p. 78)

Women's visible alcohol intoxication is labelled as 'antisocial' and non-respectable, particularly when covered by the British tabloid press. Contrast, for example, the press coverage of female fans behaviour after a Take That pop concert in Manchester city centre as 'worse than drunken football hooligans' (Nathan, 2011), with one of the authors' personal experience of the occasion in which women of all ages were dressed up and confidently dominating the late night city centre streets, with no aggression or disorderly behaviour. Unlike the media coverage, for the author as a woman, walking through the city centre that night was a very different experience compared with previous occasions, with a sense of carnivalesque female solidarity reminiscent of Reclaim the Night marches attended by one of the authors in the 1970s and 1980s.

Given 'female visibility as challenge', it is perhaps unsurprising that dependent female drug users, especially those dependent on illegal substances already demonized by wider society, face immense social stigma. These women do not 'fit' into accepted modes of 'citizenship' within capitalist society as good workers, wives, mothers, and consumers, obliged to enhance their quality of life through her own decisions (McRobbie, 2009). They are, therefore, subject to regimes of post-Fordist governance that involve self-regulation via responsibility discourses through to instances of outright and brutal repression (Fraser, 2003). Feminist scholars have highlighted the ways in which the policing of illegal markets shapes the experiences of women operating within them, as drug users, drug-using mothers, street-level suppliers, drug carriers or 'mules', and sex workers (Erickson, Butters, McGillicuddy & Hallgren, 2000; Fleetwood, 2011; Jacobs & Miller, 1998; Maher, 1997). In this sense any talk of female drug users as empowered, desiring subjects must acknowledge that socio-economic class, age, race and ethnicity, sexuality, disability, and income profoundly shape women's experiences of illicit drug markets and drug use.

Female Drug Use in the First 'Decade of Dance', 1988–1998

Despite the work of feminists and pioneering drugs researchers who focused their efforts on contesting the stigmatization of female drug users, it was not until the advent of rave culture and ecstasy use in the late 1980s and early 1990s that women's 'nonproblematic' drug use was explored in any great detail. Parker, Aldridge & Measham's (1998) longitudinal study of drug and alcohol use by British teenagers applied the concept of 'normalization' to help explain how recreational drug use 'has become too widespread to be explained convincingly in terms of psychosocial disorders or alienated youth cultures' (Heidensohn, 2006: 19). Unlike the new deviancy theories of the 1960s and 1970s discussed above, the normalization thesis suggested that youthful illicit drug use is widespread, that young people are 'drug wise', and that boundaries between drug users and abstainers are blurred, with young nondrug users largely accepting of their peers' drug use and many moving in and out of phases of experimentation as they grow up, leave home, go to college and get jobs. Crucially girls' and boys' experimentation and use of illicit drugs in their teens showed no significant differences.

During this first 'Decade of Dance' 1988–1998, the distinctions of gender and socio-economic class in terms of drug use had blurred amongst both adolescents (Parker, Aldridge & Measham, 1998) and clubbers (Measham, Williams & Aldridge, 2001), with female clubbers experimenting with drugs in numbers closer to their male counterparts than previously evidenced. Some writers argued that women were achieving a rather 'dubious equality' (Henderson, 1999) as prolific 'recreational' drug users. In this sense far from being passive victims of male power, or sad individuals using drugs as an 'escape' from the limited horizons of their lives, young women in the dance scene were found to be self-confident active social beings who chose to use drugs and explore 'new ways of being' as part of a clubbing lifestyle (Hinchcliff, 2001) and who sought pleasure though drug intoxication without infringing upon their future career and family ambitions (Henderson, 1999; Pini, 2001).

Most importantly as this first Decade of Dance drew to a close, it was recognized that 'doing drugs' remained a core component of the accomplishment of gender within rave/EDM (electronic dance music) club spaces (Measham, 2002). Instead of ignoring gender or framing gender as irrelevant in the face of converging prevalence patterns in UK rave/club spaces, Measham (2002, p. 354) argued that rave was a 'differently gendered drug culture'. Pre-rave there were spaces (such as traditional pubs) where women were 'allowed', albeit largely on male patrons' terms (Measham & Brain, 2005); usually male/female inter-action in such spaces centred around flirting, the possibility of meet-ing a romantic/sexual partner and, problematically, sexual harassment or aggression. As early rave spaces were instead focused on prolonged dancing enhanced by stimulant drugs, specifically ecstasy, the drug cul-tures within such spaces were differently gendered. Men and women did not 'escape' their gender in such spaces, but instead accomplished 'masculinity' or 'femininity' in different ways (see also Hunt, Moloney & Evans, 2010). Hence for Measham (2002) not only does gender influ-ence drug use and drug use influence gender, but 'doing drugs' can itself be seen as a way of 'doing gender'. This means that, for women, 'doing drugs' whether legal or illegal, involves an enactment of gender through the performance of specific femininities – from 'good mother' to 'club babe' – with the consumption of legal or illegal drugs (and their effects) shaping the attainment of these gendered identities. One of the processes by which women 'do gender' through 'doing drugs' is the 'controlled loss of control' (Measham, 2002) in relation to the desired and actual level of intoxication, which remains profoundly shaped by gender norms and expectations. For example, in the authors' research with ketamine users (Moore & Measham, 2008), it was found that some female interviewees hid their ketamine use from male partners for fear of being judged by them. Such concerns about gendered 'respectability' appeared not to be misplaced, as some male ketamine users illustrated the gendered dou-ble standards applying to young people's recreational drug use (as with alcohol and sex) through their expressed distaste at female users becom-ing visibly intoxicated on ketamine, yet whilst recounting stories about similar levels of intoxication by themselves and male friends. Here we can see how drug use is a way of enacting gender and drawing the bound-aries of 'acceptable' 'masculinity' and 'femininity'. If we consider this process in relation to female drug use, we might question whether female drug use, at least in the context of British EDM club culture, is really as 'empowering' or 'emancipatory' as has been claimed (at least during the early rave era and during the celebratory era of the 'ladette').

Such research highlights that work on drug-using cultures needs to balance the celebration of disruptive possibilities with scepticism, via careful attention to issues of gender, power and the body (Ettorre, 2007). Rave/postrave club research provides an example of the contextualized loosening of the norms of masculinity, femininity and heteronormativity in some drug cultures. However, both men and women remain 'accountable' to gender norms even as the embodied emotionality of the ecstasy experience disrupts and engulfs them (Hunt et al., 2010). The continued enforcement of gendered norms within these drug cultures attest to the durability of gendered power structures and relations. Further, gender intersects with other forms of social inequality (age, socio-economic class, ethnicity, sexuality, disability), shaping experiences of club drug use and leisure-pleasure in the NTE. Hutton (2006) notes, for example, the relationship between 'tolerance' of the performance of a 'range of sexualities' in some (but not all) club spaces where ecstasy use dominates, alongside female clubbers' perceptions of (physical) safety, regardless of whether they self-identify as gay, straight or bisexual. On a similar point, Gregory (2009) highlights how age and gender are defining discourses in female ravers' accounts of who does and does not 'belong' in Toronto's contemporary rave scene; young female drug users at raves were marginalized, made 'deviant' and indeed gendered by older female ravers who, despite having themselves attended raves in their early teenage years, constructed their younger counterparts as 'so young and so fragile . . . They should have been home playing with their Barbies, not snorting cocaine and taking Ecstasy' (Gregory, 2009, p. 72).

'Drugs': Material Agents in Drug Cultures

The stigmatization of illicit drugs has an impact on drug users. Moore (2004) comments on how the concept of 'drugs' is often used, both in the media and in state antidrug policies and practices, as a 'catch-all' term to denote what are perceived to be *inherently* problematic substances and their deviant users. She notes that there are many different types of drugs, used in different ways by differently gendered social actors and that greater differentiation should occur to highlight that not all illegal drugs, nor indeed all drug users, are the same. Gender emerges as crucial to this process of differentiation, in that drugs may be differently gendered, with UK researchers (Henderson, 1999) and US researchers (Hunt et al., 2010) highlighting the 'feminization' of ecstasy for example.

Even what are ostensibly the 'same' substances (e.g. alcoholic beverages, caffeine drinks) are made to mean very different things as they are experienced by different embodied subjects. In contemporary Britain, a glass of *Chateau Lafite* by theatre-goers lays claim to an easy 'respectability' that a glass of *Lambrini* by teenage girls in a public park cannot, given the structural and symbolic shaping of consumption practices. Similarly, illegal drugs are gendered, classed, aged and racialized within and beyond the contexts of their consumption. The paraphernalia of heroin injection such as needle, tourniquet, foil or spoon is masculinized as 'having your own works'. Thus the 'material' intersects with the sometimes romanticized macho-heroism of urban heroin-using cultures (Bourgois & Schonberg, 2009). Ettorre (2007) argues that the assumption that drug use entails a degree of 'loss of control' marks embodied gendered subjects; for example even within contemporary NTE leisure/pleasure playspaces only a 'controlled loss of control' is permissible (Measham, 2002). In Hunt et al.'s US study (2010), male ravers spoke of working to protect their female friends 'from themselves' and from the 'Other' (predatory male ravers). In this way women's bodies *may* become the primary focus of (paternalistic) control within drug cultures.

Gendering Drugs Research

Clearly considerations of gender need to be at the heart of research on drug cultures in all their myriad forms. Relationships between power, pleasure, embodiment, emotions and drug use must be more thoroughly investigated if we are to 're-vision' women and drug use (Ettorre, 2004, 2007) beyond a narrow focus on sex (differences), risk and harm through the dominant lenses of medical and epidemiological research, the 'epistemologies of ignorance' that neglect gender (Campbell & Ettorre, 2011) or perhaps the 'epidemiologies of indifference' that merely offer a cursory acknowledgement of gender issues but do little to advance or address them.

There are precedents that highlight that such a re-visioning project is possible and indeed desirable. The leisure/pleasure-orientated approach of UK cultural studies, cultural criminology and Club Studies research into rave and EDM club cultures have provided alternative perspectives over the past 20 years to the problem-orientated approach which dominates elsewhere (Hunt & Evans, 2008). One criticism of this body of work is the lack of critique of the (often undisclosed) use of (partial) insider knowledge to build a picture of the gendered club drug user in the context of the leisure/pleasure playspaces of the NTE which can obscure the possibilities open or closed to male and female researchers (Measham & Moore, 2006). It is interesting for example that accounts of the cultural producers of rave, clubs and parties around the world have been written by male researchers, such as D'Andrea's (2007) engaging work on counter cultural trance parties in Ibiza and Goa, as have ethnographic accounts of club security staff (Hobbs, Hadfield, Lister & Winlow, 2003, although see Hobbs, O'Brien & Westermarland, 2007), including the physical and legal risks involved (Calvey, 2000; Monaghan, 2002, 2003) of violence in the NTE more generally (Winlow & Hall, 2006), and of drug economies within clubs (Sanders, 2005).

The gendering of drugs research may be subtle. From her ethnographic study of the ways in which gender, ethnic and economic inequalities are reproduced in a Brooklyn street drug market, Maher (1997, p. 193) notes how the 'choices' her impoverished female participants made occurred under conditions not of their own choosing. In the face of male dominance in the local illicit drug economy (not least through threatened and actual violence), homeless female drug users' 'choices' were predominately restricted to sex work: 'women are virtually absent from the drug business, under-represented in non-drug hustles and grossly over-represented in sexwork' (Maher, 1997, p. 83). Similarly the 'choices' Maher made throughout the research process were constituted in the context of concern about her vulnerability as a *female* researcher, particularly (male) collegial resistance to a (white) woman undertaking street ethnography in an impoverished (largely nonwhite) community where the perceived threat of rape, robbery or worse loomed large (Maher, 1997, p. 220). Our own experiences as alcohol and drug researchers echo that of Maher's with regards to university ethics committees. The 'riskiness' of nightclub research and our 'vulnerability' as female researchers has repeatedly been flagged as a problem on our seeking ethics approval, despite our decades of untroubled experience in such venues as researchers and as keen clubbers (Measham & Moore, 2006; see Winlow & Hall, 2012 for an extended discussion of institutionalized research ethics). In light of Maher's comments, it is perhaps more understandable that research on daily dependent (typically male) injecting drug use – particularly medical, epidemiological perspectives on blood-borne viruses and their transmission – is perceived as 'proper' drugs research and is largely but not exclusively populated by male academics. It is in this way that we argue that not only is drug use gendered, but also that drugs research is gendered.

Karenza Moore and Fiona Measham

(Still) Doing Gender, (Still) Doing Drugs: Where Do We Go from Here?

Throughout our work over the decades we have sought to place gender at the centre of our research and challenge claims by colleagues and peers that gender is no longer important to drug use. Our own and others' empirical data disrupt the simplistic convergence thesis in drug and alcohol use between women and men. We note that important differences remain in terms of prevalence and patterns of drug use, in part shaped by the differentiated gender norms across diverse NTE leisure spaces and across the life course (Measham, Williams & Aldridge, 2011). Drug use remains 'gendered' – as a way of enacting *both* 'masculinities' and 'femininities'. Indeed it is also increasingly crucial that 'gender and drugs research' embraces consideration of male drug use and conceives of both men and women as subject to social processes and cultural influences. In this regard, the reproduction and disruption of normative femininities, masculinities and heteronormativity in relation to different forms of drug use across diverse spaces is ripe for exploration.

Furthermore, structures and relations of gender as aspects of drug use are best considered alongside other social inequities and intersections. The intersections between gender, socio-economic class, age, race and ethnicity, sexuality and disability are crucial to understanding drug discourses and embodied experiences of drug users (e.g. Fazio, Joe-Laidler, Moloney & Hunt, 2010). Within rave, club and club drug research, for example, there has been a tendency to concentrate research efforts on 'underground' and spectacular EDM scenes (supposedly) populated by enlightened middle-class women defined against a denigrated and feminized 'mainstream' populated by 'oppressed' working-class women (Hutton, 2006). There is a danger that without sufficient attention to the nuances of how the NTE and drug use is gendered, classed, racialized and so on, we will reproduce the very social inequities we aim to contest (in relation to exclusion from clubland and ethnicity, see Measham & Hadfield, 2009). In the workplaces and playspaces of our supposed postfeminist era, where women dress for success and consume to 'please themselves', there remain normative pressures surrounding demeanour and appearance. The older, larger or supposedly less attractive female clubber may be marginalized and ridiculed within supposedly 'inclusive' postrave club spaces, experiences that the authors have witnessed on many occasions. Also, in relation to exclusion from clubland and women's body size, there has been a least one instance reported by the press of a nightclub that barred entry to a group of 20 women for being too fat (Mail Online, 2008).

As we have noted above, the model of the passive female drug victim has been challenged by experiential accounts of the embodied pleasures of female drug use by participants in music and club scenes across the NTE. New perceptions of female users' bodies (Ettorre, 2007, p. 125) and to a lesser extent male users' bodies (Hunt et al., 2010) have emerged from drug research since the early 1990s. Reflexive and critical accounts of the emotional involvement of both the researcher and research participants in drug cultures (here contemporary NTE scenes) may yet lead to fruitful research endeavours (Measham & Moore, 2006: 17), not least in light of the growing attention by feminists to issues of emotionality, embodied emotions and specifically 'the affective dimensions of gendered drug use' (Ettorre, 2007, p. 125). There is a further need for drugs research to consider emotions and affect as producing of and produced by drug-using bodies.

Despite the advances outlined in this chapter regarding gender and drugs research over the last four decades, we suggest that drugs research still needs to engage more thoroughly with feminist theorizing. Gender remains little more than an 'add-on' to mainstream considerations of drug use, as with criminology and sociology more generally. Taking our focus on gender and drug use in the NTE as an example, we note that there is little contestation of notions of women's 'choice' and 'freedom' in some club drug cultures, although there has been a critique of the simplistic and unhelpful tendency to polarize women's supposed emancipatory agency of recreational drug-taking and the structural oppression of problem drug use (see Measham, 2002, for a critique). We have also noted (as McRobbie, 2009 does in popular culture more generally) the reconfiguration of female clubbers as being 'reassuringly feminine', part of a broader (re)sexualizing of (some) club cultures.

Conclusion

In our consideration of emerging perspectives in the field of gender and drug use, we note that a key feature is differentiated use within different socio-demographic groupings and musical or stylistic scenes. Much of our own research since the early 1990s has highlighted continuing gender differences in alcohol and illicit drug use, which varies across different leisure spaces, in bars, night clubs, dance clubs, gay-friendly clubs, festivals and so on. There is a tendency for research on female drug users to rest predominately on qualitative methods (notably interviews and participant observation) with little quantitative work that explores gender and drug use through a contemporary feminist lens. For example Hutton (2004, p. 228), through interviews conducted with female clubbers, noted how they preferred to consume illicit drugs (predominately ecstasy) when frequenting the less sexualized 'safe environment' of 'underground' dance clubs. However, from Hutton's analysis, it is unclear how female clubbers' perceptions of the acceptability of pleasurable intoxication, risk/safety and gender respectability map on to drug use prevalence and patterns across NTE spaces. Further, much quantitative work on gender and drug use is undertaken from an epidemiological perspective, which interprets gender and sexuality merely as a variable in the risks and harms assumed to be inherent in illicit drug use of any kind. However, Measham et al. (2011) use longitudinal qualitative and quantitative data sets to explore how gender shapes the drug pathways through different life stages of their cohort of young people followed from early teens to late twenties.

Secondly we have identified experiential diversity in stratified NTE spaces. By this we mean that different forms of intoxication may be more or less 'acceptable' (to others and to oneself) depending on NTE leisure space and gender, but also according to the age, sexuality and ethnicity of participants (Hunt et al., 2010; Hutton, 2006; Measham & Hadfield, 2009). Older female drug users' experiences may differ from those of their younger counterparts (e.g. Gregory, 2009); yet there is little work on experiential diversity amongst female drug users in the postrave era of the stratified and corporatized NTE (Chatterton & Hollands, 2003; Measham & Brain, 2005). For example, women's resignation to the inevitability of men's aggressive sexual advances in some alcohol-oriented leisure spaces (Brooks, 2011, pp. 640–641) may have been disrupted in some but not all rave and postrave dance club spaces (Hutton, 2004, 2006). Such experiential diversity and complexity in terms of leisure scenes and spaces could be further explored in the marriage between Club Studies, NTE research and critical epidemiological studies (Hunt et al., 2010; Measham & Moore, 2009).

Our final point relates to debates about contested postfeminist representations and practices in which confident, sexually active, drug-consuming women dominate. How do critiques of postfeminism relate to those female drug users located in the UK NTE in the postrave era? Women at play are presented as having agency: they 'please themselves' in the way they dress for a night out, and if they 'happen' to attract men's approval and desire in the process 'so be it'. Yet the classed and gendered abject figures of white working-class women (Skeggs, 1997, 2004, 2005; Tyler, 2008), specifically when at play in public spaces, point to the 'symbolic violence' of national public morality as played out in the cultural sphere. Critiques of postfeminism highlight the contradictions inherent within contemporary representations and practices of women at work and at play. For whilst some women may have 'won' their new-found 'freedom' to pursue (or rather purchase) pleasure in the United Kingdom's postrave NTE, this pursuit of pleasure is circumscribed by the cultural obligation on women to retain control and remain 'respectable' or (at best) risk being labelled a 'pill-popping chavette' (Urban Dictionary, retrieved March 13, 2013 from http://www.urbandictionary.com/define.php?term=chavette) or (at worst) risk 'inciting' male alcohol-fuelled sexual aggression.

For those teaching in the contemporary academy (or working elsewhere in contact with young women), hearing our female students say 'I'm not a feminist but . . .' will be achingly familiar, based on the perception that feminism is an archaic irrelevance at best, a disruptive force that homogenizes women at worst, and ultimately seen as irrelevant in an era of 'gender mainstreaming' and postfeminist versions of equality (Walby, 2005). As McRobbie (2009, p. 12) points out in relation to British popular culture, 'the "taken-into-accountness" (of feminism) permits all the more thorough dismantling of feminist politics and the discrediting of the occasionally voiced need for its renewal.' In this context, we argue that drugs researchers need to engage more thoroughly with contemporary feminist theorizing than is currently the case. Whilst writers such as Ettorre, Fraser and Miller continue to infuse their work with a concern for the advancement of drugs research through feminist theory, they remain the exception rather than the rule.

References

Bourgois, P. & Schonberg, J. (2009). *Righteous Dopefield*. Berkeley, CA: University of California Press.

Brooks, O. (2011). 'It's more like, guys, stop doing it!' Young women's adoption and rejection of safety advice when socialising in bars, pubs and clubs. *British Journal of Criminology*, 51(4), 635–651.

Burgess, A., Donovan, P. & Moore, S. (2009). Embodying uncertainty? Understanding heightened risk perception of drink spiking. *British Journal of Criminology*, 49, 848–862.

Calvey, D. (2000). Getting on the door and staying there: A covert participant observational study of bouncers. In G. Lee-Treweek & S. Linkogle (Eds.) *Danger in the field: Risk and ethics in social research* (pp. 43–61). London: Routledge.

Campbell, N. & Ettorre, E. (2011). *Gendering addiction: The politics of drug treatment in a neurochemical world*. Basingstoke: Palgrave Macmillan.

Chatterton, P. & Hollands, R. (2003). *Urban Nightscapes: Youth cultures, pleasure spaces and corporate power*. London: Routledge.

Curran, V. & Golombok, S. (1985). *Bottling it up*. London: Faber.

D'Andrea, A. (2007). *Global nomads: Techno and New Age as transnational countercultures in Ibiza and Goa*. Abingdon: Routledge.

Erickson, P., Butters, J., McGillicuddy, P. & Hallgren, A. (2000). Crack and prostitution: Gender, myths and experiences. *Journal of Drug Issues*, *3*(4), 767–788.

Ettorre, E. (1992). *Women and substance use*. London: Macmillan.

Ettorre, E. (2002). Editorial: Is gender still a non-field? *Social and Preventative Medicine*, *47*(1), 1–5.

Ettorre, E. (2004). Revisioning women and drug use: gender sensitivity, embodiment and reducing harm. *International Journal of Drug Policy*, *15*, 327–335.

Ettorre, E. (2007). *Revisioning women and drug use: Gender, power and the body*. Basingstoke: Palgrave Macmillan.

Fazio, A., Joe-Laidler, K., Moloney, M. & Hunt, G. (2010). Gender, sexuality, and ethnicity as factors of club drug use among Asian Americans. *Journal of Drug Issues*, *40*(2), 405–432.

Fleetwood, J. (2011). Five kilos: penalties and practice in the international cocaine trade. *British Journal of Criminology*, *51*, 375–393.

Fraser, N. (2003). From discipline to flexibilization? Rereading Foucault in the shadow of globalisation. *Constellations*, *10*(2), 160–171.

Fraser, S. & Valentine, K. (2008). *Substance and substitution: Methadone subjects in liberal societies*. New York: Palgrave Macmillan.

Gregory, J. (2009). Too young to drink, too old to dance: The influences of age and gender on (non) rave participation. *Dancecult: Journal of Electronic Dance Music Culture*, *1*(1), 65–80.

Gregory, J. (2010). (M)Others in altered states: Prenatal drug use, risk, choice and responsible self-governance. *Social and Legal Studies*, *19*(1), 49–66.

Hannah-Moffat, K. (2007). Gendering dynamic risk: Assessing and managing the material identities of women prisoners (Chapter 11). In K. Hannah-Moffat & P. O'Malley (Eds.) *Gendered risks*. London: Routledge.

Hebdige, D. (1979). *Subculture: The meaning of style*. London: Routledge.

Heidensohn, F. (2006). Gender and justice: New concepts and approaches. Portland, OR: Willan Publishing.

Henderson, S. (1999). Drugs and culture: the question of gender. In N. South (Ed.) *Drugs: Cultures, controls and everyday life* (pp. 16–48). London: Sage.

Hinchcliff, S. (2001). The meaning of ecstasy use and clubbing to women in the late 1990s. *International Journal of Drug Policy*, *12*(5–6), 455–468.

Hobbs, D., Hadfield, P., Lister, S. & Winlow, S. (2003). *Bouncers: Violence and governance in the night-time economy*. Oxford: Oxford University Press.

Hobbs, D., O'Brien, K. & Westermarland, L. (2007). Connecting the gendered door: Women, violence and doorwork. *British Journal of Sociology*, *58*(1), 21–38.

Hunt, G. & Evans, K. (2008). The great unmentionable: Exploring the pleasures and benefits of ecstasy from the perspectives of drug users. *Drugs: Education, Prevention and Policy*, *15*(4), 329–349.

Hunt, G., Moloney, M. & Evans, K. (2010). *Youth, drugs and nightlife*. London: Routledge.

Hutton, F. (2004). Up for it, mad for it? Women, drug use and participation in club scenes. *Health, Risk and Society*, *6*(3), 223–237.

Hutton, F. (2006). *Risky pleasures? Club cultures and feminine identities*. Aldershot: Ashgate.

Jacobs, B. A. & Miller, J. (1998). Crack dealing, gender and arrest avoidance, *Social Problems*, *45*(4), 550–569.

Kalant, O. J. (1980). *Research advances in alcohol and drug problems*. Volume 5, Alcohol and drug problems in women. New York: Plenum Press.

Maher, L. (1997). *Sexed work: Gender, race and resistance in a Brooklyn drug market*. Oxford: Oxford University Press.

Mail Online (2008). Storm over nightclub that barred women 'for being too fat'. Retrieved March 13, 2013 from http://www.dailymail.co.uk/news/article-1039500/Storm-nightclub-barred-women-fat.html.

McRobbie, A. (2009). *The aftermath of feminism: Gender, culture and social change*. London: Sage.

Measham, F. (2002). Doing gender – doing drugs: Conceptualising the gendering of drugs cultures. *Contemporary Drug Problems*, *29*(2), 335–373.

Measham, F., Aldridge J. & Parker, H. (2001). *Dancing on drugs: Risk, health and hedonism in the British club scene*. London: Free Association Books.

Measham, F. & Brain, K. (2005). 'Binge' drinking, British alcohol policy and the new culture of intoxication. *Crime, Media, Culture: An International Journal* *1*(3), 263–284.

Measham, F. & Hadfield, P. (2009). Everything Starts with an 'E': exclusion, ethnicity and elite formation in contemporary English clubland. *Adicciones*, *21*(4), 363–386.

Measham, F. & Moore, K. (2006). Reluctant reflexivity, implicit insider knowledge, and the development of club studies. In B. Sanders (Ed.) *Drugs, Clubs and Young People: Sociological and Public Health Perspectives*. Aldershot: Ashgate.

Measham, F., Williams, L. & Aldridge, J. (2011). Marriage, mortgage, motherhood: What longitudinal surveys can tell us about gender, 'drug careers' and the normalization of adult drug use. *International Journal of Drug Policy*, 22(6), 420–427.

Millman, M. (1982). Images of deviant men and women. In M. Evans (Ed.) *The Woman question: Readings on the subordination of women* (pp. 334–343). London: Fontana.

Monaghan, L. (2002). Regulating 'unruly' bodies: work tasks, conflict and violence in Britain's night-time economy. *British Journal of Sociology*, 53(3), 403–431.

Monaghan, L. (2003). Danger on the Doors: Bodily risk in a demonized occupation. *Health, Risk and Society*, 5(1), 11–31.

Moore, D. (2004). Drugalities: the generative capabilities of criminalized 'drugs'. *International Journal of Drug Policy*, 15, 419–426.

Moore, K. & Measham, F. (2008). 'It's the most fun you can have for twenty quid': Meanings, motivations, and consequences of British ketamine use. *Addiction Research and Theory* (special issue: social and cultural aspects of ketamine use), 16(3), 231–244.

Moore, S. (2009). Cautionary tales: Drug-facilitated sexual assault in the British media. *Crime, Media, Culture: An International Journal*, 5(3), 305–320.

Mulia, N. (2002). Ironies in the pursuit of wellbeing: the perspectives of low-income, substance using women on service institutions. *Contemporary Drug Problems*, 29(4), 711–748.

Nathan, S. (2011). The Take That effect: How middle-aged fans go mad when the ageing boy band comes to town. *Mail Online*. Retrieved March 13, 2013 from http://www.dailymail.co.uk/femail/article-2004447/The-Take-That-effect-How-middle-aged-fans-react-ageing-boy-band-comes-town.html.

Parker, H. (1974). *View from the boys: A sociology of down-town adolescents*. Newton Abbot: David & Charles.

Parker, H., Aldridge J. & Measham, F. (1998). *Illegal leisure: The normalization of adolescent recreational drug use*. London: Routledge.

Pini, M. (2001). *Club cultures and female subjectivity: The move from home to house*. New York: Palgrave.

Reeves, J. & Campbell, R. (1994). *Cracked coverage: Television news, the anti-cocaine crusade and the Reagan legacy*. Durham, NC: Duke University Press.

Reinarman, C. & Levine, H. (2004). Crack in the rearview mirror: deconstructing drug war mythology. *Social Justice*, 3(1–2), 182–199.

Sanders, B. (2005). In the club: ecstasy use and supply in a London nightclub. *Sociology*, 39(2), 241–258.

Skeggs, B. (1997). *Formations of class and gender: Becoming respectable*. London: Routledge.

Skeggs, B. (2004). *Class, self, culture*. London: Routledge.

Skeggs, B. (2005). The making of class and gender through visualising moral subject formation. *Sociology*, 39(5), 965–982.

Tyler, I. (2008). 'Chav mum, chav scum': Class disgust in contemporary Britain. *Feminist Media Studies*, 8(1), 17–34.

Walby, S. (2005). Gender mainstreaming: Productive tensions in theory and practice. *Social Politics, 12*(3), 321–343.

Winlow, S. & Hall, S. (2006). *Violent night: Urban leisure and contemporary culture.* London: Berg.

Winlow, S. & Hall, S. (2012). What is an 'ethics committee'? Academic governance in an epoch of belief and credulity. *British Journal of Criminology, 52*(2), 400–416.

Young, J. (1971). *The drugtakers: The social meaning of drug use.* London: McGibbon & Kee.

6

Embracing Children and Families in Substance-Misuse Treatment

Lorna Templeton

Introduction

The plight of family members affected by substance misuse has long been discussed in both academic research literature and other popular media (Orford, 2012). As far back as 1969 those affected by parental drinking were referred to as the 'forgotten children' (Cork, 1969) and until relatively recently the children and families of substance misusers have been largely marginalized from policy and practice (Copello & Templeton, 2012; Velleman, 2010). However, developments since the late 1990s in the United Kingdom, in terms of recognizing the needs of family members and addressing those needs through practice and policy, have been a step in the right direction and therefore very much welcomed. Several key drivers for these steps forward include the Hidden Harm agenda, which focused attention on the children of drug misusing parents (Advisory Council on the Misuse of Drugs, 2003); the recovery agenda (e.g. National Treatment Agency for Substance Misuse, 2010; Wardle, 2009), which highlights the importance of social capital for families and communities as part of recovery; and various government initiatives aimed at society's most complex and vulnerable families (most recently called 'troubled families'). This chapter will discuss four areas, presenting an overview of the progress made in supporting children and families affected by a relative's alcohol or drug misuse, as well as the gaps and challenges which remain. The focus will be England, but literature

Emerging Perspectives on Substance Misuse, First Edition. Edited by Willm Mistral.
© 2013 John Wiley & Sons, Ltd. Published 2013 by John Wiley & Sons, Ltd.

and lessons from the rest of the United Kingdom and further afield will inform the chapter where relevant.

The four areas to be discussed are:

- Increased recognition of the numbers of children and families who have one or more relative with an alcohol or drug problem, and of the burden this places on families and society.
- Improved understanding of the wide range of ways in which children and families are affected by substance misuse.
- Progress in considering how to include these children and families within relevant policy agendas.
- Development of a more holistic practice response to the needs of these children and families.

The Size of the Problem and its Burden

. . . it is estimated that several million family members in the UK are affected by the substance misuse of a relative. Putting a notional financial value on the support provided by families, the impact of substance misuse on families and the resource savings of their support and care is extremely difficult . . . Overall, significant gaps in knowledge and information. . . .need to be urgently filled if support and services to families is to evolve. (Copello, Templeton & Powell, 2010a, p. 71)

It is widely recognized that the number of children and family members affected by a relative's alcohol or drug problem is unclear, as well as of the size of the burden in social and monetary terms. Attempts to provide such estimates in UK alcohol and drug policy have been largely absent. The last few years, however, have seen an increase in studies, largely from highly developed countries, attempting to address this. For example, in New Zealand a telephone survey of over 3,068 residents found that 29% said there was least one person in their life (friend, family or other) who they considered to be a heavy drinker (Casswell, You & Huckle, 2011). In Norway, a study of social harms related to others' drinking, found a fifth of the 2,170 respondents reported being kept awake at night by drunk people, with 12% saying they had been frightened as a result of someone else's drinking, 15% harassed in public, and 3% physically hurt. Such burdens were more commonly carried by women, and the authors also reported a correlation between higher levels of drunkenness and victimization or the experience of social harms (Rossow & Hauge, 2004). A third study, in Australia, reported that nearly a quarter of those with caring responsibilities for one or more children, recognized that those children had been adversely affected in the previous year by someone else's alcohol consumption (including neglect, abuse, being left in unsafe or unsupervised situations, or exposed to violence) with children living with a single carer seemingly at greater risk of harm (Laslett, Ferris, Dietze & Room, 2012).

Several UK studies have made important contributions to understanding the scale of the problem. One study employed data from several household surveys (Health Survey for England, General Household Survey, National Psychiatric Morbidity Survey, British Crime Survey and Scottish Crime Survey) to estimate the numbers of children living with substance misusing parents (Manning, West, Faulkner & Titherington, 2009). The headlines from this study are that over three million children live with at least one parent who is, at minimum, a binge-drinker; nearly 750,000 children live with a dependent drinker; and approximately one million children live with a parent who has used illegal drugs in the previous year. Manning further estimated that there are 93,500 children under one year of age living with a parent who is a problem drinker and 50,650 children under one year of age living with a parent who has used drugs in the past year (Manning, 2011). While these estimates give no indication of the levels of harm experienced by these children, when the data are seen alongside other research evidence summarized below, of how children can be affected, it is likely that the problem is a very sizeable one. In addition to this work, there is further evidence from England of high numbers of children who live with parental substance misuse (and often domestic violence) who are known to social care services (Cleaver, Nicholson, Tarr & Cleaver, 2007; Forrester & Harwin, 2011).

Another study modelled, for the first time in the United Kingdom, estimates of the numbers of adult family members affected by a relative's illegal drug misuse, and of the costs associated with both the harms they experience and the care they provide (Copello et al., 2010a). Acknowledging the challenges associated with making such calculations, and highlighting that the cautious approach taken is likely to mean that the figures presented are underestimates, the authors propose that at least 1.5 million family members in the general population may be affected by a relative's drug misuse. Furthermore, the study estimated the cost of the harms experienced by these family members at £1.8 billion, and the savings associated with the care and support they provide to their relatives to be in the region of £750 million. Currently, no UK study has undertaken a similar exercise for family members affected by alcohol misuse.

While these studies represent significant steps forward in filling a major gap in our understanding of families affected by substance misuse, they are also important for an additional reason. Manning's study, with its focus on children, considers not just those affected by dependent alcohol or drug users but also children affected at a range of levels of consumption, including binge-drinking. Similarly, the Copello study considers not just adult family members who have a relative with a drug problem who is in treatment, but also adult family members in the general population. Hence, both studies make an important contribution to understanding the potential scale of the problem, rather than taking a narrow focus on, for example, treatment populations, those affected by dependent drinkers, or children known to social care services. Manning et al. emphasize the importance of this broader focus, with their conclusion that 'widespread patterns of binge-drinking and recreational drug use may expose children to sub-optimal care and substance-using role models' (Manning, West, Faulkner & Titherington, 2009: 377). This has implications for the practice response needed for these children and their families, as will be discussed below. Ultimately, however, while such studies are important, the overall dearth of work in this area is one of the main barriers to further progress in greater prioritization of family members within policy. This progress is needed in order to increase service provision in line with demand.

How substance misuse can affect the family

> ... living with a relative with a drinking or drug problem ... brings together in some combination elements of stress, threat, and even abuse, often simultaneously affecting different family functions and different members of the family. Worry about the loved relative is a core characteristic. It is bad for the health of family members and for the health of the family as a whole. (Orford et al., 2005, p. 117)

Perhaps where there has been the greatest volume of work in recent years, and where the greatest progress has been made, is in an increased understanding of how families can be affected by substance misuse, and how this can permeate, in both short term and the long term, deep into all aspects of individual and family lives. There is now a wealth of evidence showing how adult family members and children can be affected, and these two groups will be considered separately.

Adult Family Members

Historically, adult family members, with the focus usually on female spouses or partners, were viewed in pathological terms, seen as partially to blame for their relative's drug or alcohol problem, as possessing certain character deficits, and maintaining a stake in their relative's continued addiction (Orford, 2012). A dominant feature of many such relationships was presumed to be 'co-dependency', where both 'addict' and family member were seen to be responsible for the problems and benefiting from their continuation. An important change in recent years has been a shift away from viewing family members as dysfunctional or deficient, and towards framing their experience within stress-coping models of health. These models propose that family members affected by problems such as substance misuse are ordinary people exposed to highly stressful circumstances and adversities that are often longstanding and which can place great strain on individuals and families (Moore, Biegel, and McMahon, 2011; Orford et al., 2010a; Orford, Velleman, Natera, Templeton & Copello, 2013). The experience can be likened to living with other chronic adversities and traumas such as severe illness, disability or disaster. One American survey with 110 'concerned and significant others' assessed the impact of their relative's substance use across seven domains using the Significant Other Survey (Benishek, Kirby & Leggett-Dugosh, 2011). The majority of those surveyed had experienced problems in at least one domain over the past 30 days (with the exception of legal issues which were reported by less than a fifth of respondents). All respondents reported experiencing emotional and relationship problems, with between 65–91% reporting problems in the areas of finance, family, health and violence. Problems were more common for female family members, spouses or partners, and for those living with their relative. A telephone survey in New Zealand, where over a quarter of the 3,068 respondents reported having at least one person in their life who they considered to be a heavy drinker, noted an association between this and ill health and poor wellbeing (Casswell et al., 2011). A study of a nonprofit healthcare provider in the USA compared over 25,000 family members of someone with an alcohol or drug problem to matched groups of family members of someone with no alcohol or drug problem (over 20,000), someone with diabetes (over 17,000) and someone with asthma (just under 20,000). The authors found that the families of people with alcohol or drug problems were more likely to be diagnosed with a number of serious health problems (substance use, depression or trauma), and experienced higher healthcare costs than the other groups (Ray, Mertens & Weisner, 2009).

A study in Singapore also illustrated the application of stress-coping models to Asian communities, with family members of substance misusers reporting greater levels of stress, depression and psychiatric morbidity than matched controls (Lee et al., 2011). These findings of how another's substance misuse can affect family members, are similarly reflected in the experience of families seen in the UK, Mexico City, Aboriginal communities in the Northern Territory of Australia, and Italy (Arcidiacono et al., 2010; Orford et al., 2005) although there are inevitable nuances influenced by, for example, culture, family and religion. An international study of alcohol-related negative consequences for drinkers (which included items related to relationships, family, friends and social life) highlighted the need to consider both gender and culture when understanding alcohol consumption and its consequences for drinkers and others (Graham et al., 2011). The implications of this shift in understanding in terms of the help made available to family members will be discussed later in the chapter.

Children

There is now a wealth of recent evidence demonstrating the wide range of ways in which children can be affected by a parent's alcohol or drug misuse. This includes work from Australia (Burke, Schmied & Montrose, 2006), New Zealand (Girling, Huakau, Casswell & Conway, 2006), Scotland (Wales, Gillan, Hill & Robertson, 2009), Ireland (Horgan, 2011), and England (Adamson & Templeton, 2012). This library of work very clearly highlights how children, at all ages and stages of development, can be affected in both the short term and the long term by parental substance misuse. All domains of individual and family life are at risk, including mental health, development, behaviour, education, relationships and parenting (Cleaver, Nicholson, Tarr & Cleaver, 2011). For example, the Family Life Project interviewed 50 young people aged 10–18 years, from five areas of England, all of whom had been affected by parental substance misuse in the previous year (Houmoller, Bernays,

Wilson & Rhodes, 2011). Some of the key points to come out of the study in understanding the young peoples' experiences are:

- Parents make a lot of effort to conceal their misuse, employing strategies of ambiguity and damage limitation, believing this is better for their children.
- Nevertheless, young people often sense the misuse before it is fully understood, and this is often accompanied by shame, embarrassment and recognition that family life is not normal.
- Young people go to great lengths to conceal family life from the outside world to protect themselves and their family. This can sometimes inadvertently sustain the harms of the parental substance misuse.
- Despite not often receiving unconditional love from their parents, young people maintain a very strong sense of 'family' and there can be conflict between caring for family and caring for self.
- Relationships between siblings are important, offering opportunities for sharing, protection and coping. Older siblings, especially girls, often take on caring roles, at the expense of their own needs.
- Young people think very carefully about who to trust and talk to, and often do not talk to other family or friends.
- Young people talked about disrupted relationships with professionals who do not really understand their experiences (Houmoller et al., 2011)

Until relatively recently there was a belief that the most likely future for children living with parental substance misuse was a bleak one, with children at risk of a wide range of negative outcomes including developing their own substance misuse or mental health problems. However, a welcome alternative viewpoint has emerged that not necessarily all these children will be adversely affected. Many children seem to be 'resilient' (Backett-Milburn, Wilson, Bancroft & Cunningham-Burley, 2008; Moe, Johnson & Wade, 2007; Velleman & Orford, 1999) and there is now an increased understanding of protective factors and processes, operating at individual, family and environmental levels, which can buffer children from their family circumstances and minimize the likelihood of negative outcomes (Velleman & Templeton, 2007). This new understanding has important implications for meeting the needs of children, and their families, who are affected by substance misuse, although it has been highlighted in at least one study that '. . . the protective factors classically thought to promote resilience were seldom in place for them unconditionally and without associated costs' (Backett-Milburn et al., 2008,

p. 476) and that resilience cannot be presumed because a child is supported by protective factors or appears to be coping and doing well.

Inclusion in Policy

> There is still . . . a major need to increase the visibility both of the needs of *all* family members, including spouses and parents of substance misusers, to be able to access appropriate help in their own right . . . and of their important role as part of the treatment that their substance-misusing relatives might receive. (Velleman, 2010, p. 8)

Until relatively recently alcohol and drugs policy tended to focus rather narrowly on the individual with the substance-use problem. A key catalyst for change came in 2003 with the publication of the Advisory Council on the Misuse of Drugs report *Hidden Harm* (Advisory Council on the Misuse of Drugs, 2003), which focused on the children of drug misusing parents. Since then, across the UK, alcohol and drugs policy has become more holistic, and the children and families of substance misusers have been identified as a priority areas within national policy in Scotland, Wales and Northern Ireland, although the focus and detail varies. Other than the *Hidden Harm* agenda this issue has not been given such a high priority in England and adult family members have tended to be overlooked. An important statement, therefore, in the recent English drugs strategy (Home Office, 2010, p. 21) was the need to support family members 'in their own right'. There is no such statement in the alcohol strategy. Additional positive developments have been seen with policy guidance in this area in England, which has included, for example, the National Treatment Agency for Substance Misuse's (2010) guide for commissioners and providers on developing services for families as carers as well as involving them in treatment, and the National Institute for Health and Clinical Excellence's quality standard on alcohol dependence and harmful use, which included a statement that 'families and carers of people who misuse alcohol have their own needs identified, including those associated with risk of harm, and are offered information and support' (National Institute for Health and Clinical Excellence, 2011, p. 14). Another policy development has come from the alignment of family members within the wider carers' agenda, although the challenge with this is that many family members do not identify themselves as carers. Overall, however, despite these positive developments, beyond broad policy statements there is often a lack of detail of how a practice response to family members should be developed. There is also a tendency to take a narrow focus on substance misusing parents and their children, at the expense of consideration of the many other groups of family members who can be affected by the alcohol or drug misuse of any relative (Velleman, 2010).

Another area of policy with the potential to emphasize the needs of families affected by substance misuse is that which targets society's most vulnerable families. Previously called *Every Child Matters*, *Think Family*, and *Respect*, the current programme is called *Troubled Families* and aims to offer specific support to 120,000 of England's most vulnerable families. However, this initiative does not include parental substance or alcohol misuse as one of its seven defining criteria, but rather says that this is a discretionary measure that may be applied at the local level when identifying target families. Furthermore, criticism can be levelled at the focus only on the most vulnerable families, and on children identified as 'at risk' and hence known to social care services. There is a need for policy to broaden its focus to consider the far larger numbers who are less likely to be known to services but where children may be in need (Adamson & Templeton, 2012). Furthermore, families affected by substance misuse are relevant to a range of different policy agendas, and there is an additional need for joint work to ensure a consistent response, including drugs and alcohol, children, families, and carers as well as other key areas such as domestic violence and mental health.

In summary, while some good progress has been made in terms of developing a more holistic and family- oriented response to substance misuse, significant gaps and limitations remain and much more work is needed.

Developing an Holistic Response to the Needs of Children and Families

Whilst there has been welcome development in terms of acknowledgement of the importance of adult family members affected by a relative's drug problem, there is still a significant challenge in terms of identifying this specific group and developing a robust and integrated service commensurate with need and with the potential to reduce significant harm . . . there is interest in and appetite for improving provision. (Copello & Templeton, 2012, p. 22)

Following on from the increased recognition and understanding of the impact of someone else's alcohol or drug misuse on children and families, another area which has seen quite significant change is the practice response to this population. There has been a notable shift from a treatment system that has been largely individualistic in focus towards one which is more holistic and better able to meet the needs of children and families (Copello, Velleman & Templeton, 2005; Templeton, Velleman & Russell, 2010). This is despite a lack of clear data on prevalence, which, as discussed above, limits developments in this area (Copello & Templeton, 2012). However, while there has been some major progress, discussed below, it is still the case that services for children and families are lacking and that, overall, the response remains inconsistent across the United Kingdom – something of a 'postcode lottery'.

A web survey of 253 service providers was conducted across the United Kingdom in 2011 to find out more about the support available to the adult family members of drug misusers (Copello & Templeton, 2012). Over half of the respondents were from drug services which also offered help to family members, a further quarter of the respondents were from services which worked solely with family members of substance misusers, and the remainder were from a range of other services such as carer services or social care. Where the work was part of the remit of a larger service for substance misusers the support available to family members tended to be a low percentage of the overall workload. Support to family members tended to be offered in the nonstatutory sector by services which were smaller in size (with less than ten members of staff). Overall, based on available prevalence estimates, the level of provision does not seem to be close to that which is required.

Examples of Interventions

A review of provision for family members broadly identified three categories of intervention: those that target family members as mediators who can increase the engagement of users in treatment; those that work with users and family members together (usually through couples therapy); and those that aim to respond to the needs of family members in their own right (Copello et al., 2005). The positive contribution that family members can make to the engagement and retention of an alcohol or drug user in treatment, and the benefits associated with a range of couples and network therapies, has been well recognized (Copello et al., 2005). However, the findings from the survey reported above suggest that the use of some evidence-based approaches, such as behavioural couples therapy, which has been recommended by NICE, remains low (Copello

& Templeton, 2012), and this issue will be discussed further below. Two areas have seen particular developments in recent years and are worth further consideration. One is the growth in interventions and services to support family members in their own right, rather than viewing them as vehicles through which to engage substance users in treatment or as necessary partners in couples or family therapy approaches. The other is the increase in ways of working to support children (on their own or with their families). A number of studies have demonstrated how such interventions and services can benefit individuals (adults and children) and family units, although it should be highlighted that the evidence is mainly qualitative and based on an assessment of short-term benefits (Adamson & Templeton, 2012; Copello, Templeton, Orford & Velleman, 2010b). Nevertheless, the evidence is encouraging. Six examples of services or interventions that have demonstrated promise in the United Kingdom are briefly summarized below.

- The Five-Step Method: for family members in their own right (Copello, Templeton, Orford & Velleman, 2010c; Velleman et al., 2011). Developed in England and based on stress-coping models of understanding the experiences of family members (Orford et al., 2010a), the Five-Step Method is an evidence-based and internationally recognized intervention to support adult family members who are living with a relative's substance misuse. It is a brief, structured, psychosocial intervention that aims to support family members to explore their situation, gain information, consider the coping dilemmas they face, think about how their support networks could be enhanced and explore options for further support. Research has demonstrated that the Five-Step Method can significantly reduce symptoms of ill health, support family members to feel more informed, and provide an opportunity for them to consider and change their coping responses (Copello et al., 2010b), all changes that can be sustained at 12 months (Velleman et al. 2011). This programme of work has also piloted web-based materials and an adapted form of the intervention to support children and young people who are living with parental substance misuse and/or parental mental health problems.
- CRAFT (Community Reinforcement and Family Training): working with family members to support treatment engagement. Developed in the United States, CRAFT is an extension of CRA (the Community Reinforcement Approach) and aims to work with family members to encourage a treatment-resistant substance misuser into treatment or to maintain sobriety. CRAFT also offers additional support to

family members with regards to their own happiness and well-being. A number of research studies have demonstrated, first, that CRAFT can improve rates of engagement for treatment-resistant individuals and, second, that family members' own physical symptoms, depression, anxiety and anger can be reduced (Barefoot Research & Evaluation, 2012; Meyers, Roozen & Ellen Smith, 2011; Roozen, de Waart & van der Kroft, 2010).

- Social Behaviour and Network Therapy (SBNT): for substance users and their social networks (Copello, Orford, Hodgson & Tober, 2009). Developed in England, SBNT aims to work with a substance misuser and any number of people identified as having a positive role to play in the client's social network, with the aim of developing positive social support for change, both during treatment and beyond (including any relapses which occur). Social Behaviour and Network Therapy was compared with an individual treatment (Motivational Enhancement Therapy) as part of the UK Alcohol Treatment Trial (UKATT research team, 2001, 2005) with results demonstrating similar outcomes for the two treatments in terms of drinks per day, days abstinent and mental health quality of life. The two treatments were also equitable in terms of cost savings and cost effectiveness. Other studies have also piloted SBNT with drug users and their networks.

- Option 2: for families where substance misuse is having serious consequences and where a child is at risk of being removed (Forrester, Copello, Waissbein & Pokhrei, 2008). Option 2 is informed by work in the United States, and is now widely used across Wales and England. The service model is an intensive one, working with a family at crisis point by offering them as much support as they need over a four week period. An evaluation of the service reported that it was greatly appreciated by families and could result in significant benefits, changes that produced cost savings in, for example, time to entry in the care system, length of time in care and likelihood of being at home at follow-up. However, the authors cautioned that for families with more complex and long-standing problems changes were less likely to be sustained.

- M-PACT (Moving Parents and Children Together): a family programme developed by one of England's largest treatment providers, Action on Addiction, M-PACT brings together several families (including children), where parental substance misuse is present, for a structured 8-week group programme. Evaluation to date has focused on qualitative data, with the programme demonstrating promising outcomes for individuals and families. This includes the opportunity to talk about addiction; awareness raising about the impact of addiction on children, parenting and families; developing closer relationships between family members and within family units; and improving communication and reducing conflict (Templeton, 2012).

- Family Drug and Alcohol Court (FDAC): a specialist court that aims to support a family through intervention with a drug using parent (Harwin et al., 2011). Informed by a model developing in the USA, FDAC is a specialist family court (supported by two district judges and a multidisciplinary team), which operates within the care system where parental substance misuse is the key factor. Evaluation of FDAC shows promising findings for this innovative intervention, with a family more likely to be reunited with their children by the end of the court process (39% compared with 21% for the comparison group), with the intervention facilitating swifter processes for alternative placements when a child could not remain in the family, and with parents more likely to control their substance misuse or engage with treatment.

Regardless of the approach, it seems that there is encouraging evidence of the benefits of a range of interventions for children, families, and misusers, although it is acknowledged that further research and evaluation in this area is needed, particularly to consider long-term benefits, to engage larger groups of families, and to conduct more experimental or quasi-experimental work. What also remains unknown is the active ingredients for change – is it the intervention itself, the worker-client relationship, other characteristics of the help received, or combinations of these, which may vary according to a number of factors, such as individual characteristics of the client, or the length and severity of the problem? There has been little work exploring these issues in relation to interventions for family members, and this is an area that needs attention. In addition to this, there are a number of challenges limiting progress in this area.

Challenges

In addition to the web survey discussed above (Copello & Templeton, 2012) the same study completed 100 interviews with commissioners and service providers in 20 areas across five English regions, and with co-ordinators and service providers in eight alcohol and drug partnerships in Scotland. The data highlighted the areas presenting the main challenges to developing services for families (adult family members in particular) and where attention is needed. Gaps were identified in terms of the response of nonspecialist settings, assessment of need, provision of services to adult family members in their own right, engaging family members in services for drug users, and a low implementation of family-based, evidence-informed therapeutic interventions (such as those noted above). Moreover, the qualitative data from commissioners highlighted six themes that capture the successes and challenges in this area, namely identifying adult family members as a target group with their own needs, the need for local estimates of prevalence, enhancing engagement of family members in commissioning processes, promoting and improving access to services (with stigma a particular challenge), prioritizing family members on commissioning agendas, and developing systems (such as recording, targets and outcome monitoring) to inform and support provision.

Another area that presents challenges is that of translating research, usually conducted within standard parameters with the client sample often selected according to particular criteria, to 'real-life' practice situations where the client base is likely to be more heterogeneous and where a greater degree of flexibility is often needed in terms of intervention or service delivery. As was noted above there is a low use of evidence-based interventions in practice (Copello & Templeton, 2012), and some research in England has explored the barriers that operate at the levels of the client, the family, the worker, and the organization, and which are limiting routine use of such approaches and the overall development of more family-oriented services (Lee, Christie, Copello & Kellett, 2012; Orford, Templeton, Copello, Velleman & Ibanga, 2010c). Lee et al. suggested that barriers to family work could be overcome by enhanced self-efficacy and role legitimacy; therapeutic commitment and positive support from teams, managers, and organizations; service procedures that are family focused; and therapeutic alliance. The authors also suggested that practitioners can see the introduction of formal intervention approaches as a barrier, concluding that it is necessary to support the use of low intensity and less complex interventions, alongside more widely recognized approaches, in order to advance development of family-focused services.

Further, Orford et al. (2010c) indicated that the capacity of services to work with family members affected by substance misuse of close relatives varies greatly. Where organizations already have a mission to involve family members, capacity is good. Where services have previously focused on substance-misusing individuals, change is difficult but achievable. However, for most nonspecialist organizations, such as primary care centres, and most nonstatutory organizations, capacity is very limited. Sustainability of change also remains an issue. Other challenges to the fuller integration of family focused work include a lack of appropriate outcome measures to support the work (coupled with clinical and organizational resistance to the routine collection of such data), a lack of staff training (this issue has been particularly highlighted among social workers), and insufficient partnership working between, for example, child/adult and drug/alcohol services.

The final challenge is that of demonstrating the cost-effectiveness of interventions and services for children and families, another area where there are notable gaps in the United Kingdom, and where little progress has been made. One systematic review of the cost and clinical effectiveness of psychological interventions involving family and friends in alcohol treatment reported that, overall, studies demonstrated improved outcomes in a number of areas (including abstinence, relationship functioning, and treatment entry) for therapy involving family or friends when compared with individual or group approaches (Meads, Ting, Dretzke & Bayliss, 2007). Another systematic review, which included eight studies, also found that some family-based treatments demonstrated cost-effectiveness (Morgan & Crane, 2010). A study in the United States (Weisner, Parthasarathy, Moore & Mertens, 2010) demonstrated that, whereas family members of those with alcohol or drug problems experienced increased healthcare costs prior to treatment, over time abstinence was related to a reduction in these costs. Overall, while there is some evidence of the cost-effectiveness of family-oriented interventions, there is a need for further work in this area, particularly in the United Kingdom. Such work would have important implications for services often dominated by targets and financial limitations. However, there is some evidence to indicate that cost-effectiveness should not necessarily be the leading factor in decision making about the introduction of support for family members. For example, qualitative data from a primary care trial of the Five-Step Method (see above), comparing two levels of the intervention differing in terms of intensity, suggested that some family members and primary healthcare professionals preferred the additional face-to-face support offered by the more intensive form, and may have gained from this in ways not measurable by the quantitative results, which demonstrated similar outcomes for family members across the two levels (Copello et al., 2010b). Hence, while the less intensive intervention might be more competitive in cost terms, it is also important to consider other clinically relevant issues in making decisions about services and interventions for families.

Conclusion and Moving Forward

There is much to be encouraged about in terms of how children and families affected by a relative's substance misuse are regarded. This chapter has summarized some of the main achievements seen in four areas; recognizing the size of the problem and its burden; understanding how substance misuse can affect the family; including children and families in policy; and developing an holistic response to meeting the needs of children and families. There is every sign that progress will continue but there are nevertheless significant gaps remaining in the attention given to children and families in policy, practice, and research. In particular, there is a need for future work to build on the positive advancements to date, and to focus on the detail that lies beyond the broader developments which have been seen thus far. Only with such continued progress can the needs of children and families be fully and appropriately met.

References

Adamson, J. & Templeton, L. (2012). *Silent voices. Supporting children and young people affected by parental alcohol misuse.* London: Report to the Office of the Children's Commissioner in England.

Advisory Council on the Misuse of Drugs (2003). *Hidden harm: Responding to the needs of children of problem drug users.* London: Advisory Council on the Misuse of Drugs.

Arcidiacono, C., Velleman, R., Procentese, F., Berti, P., Albanesi, C., Sommantico, M. et al. (2010). Italian families living with relatives with alcohol or drugs problems. *Drugs: Education, Prevention and Policy, 17*(6), 659–680.

Backett-Milburn, K., Wilson, S., Bancroft, A. & Cunningham-Burley, S. (2008). Challenging childhoods: Young people's accounts of 'getting by' in families with substance use problems. *Childhood, 15*(4), 461–479.

Barefoot Research and Evaluation (2012). *Community reinforcement approach and family training: Evaluation briefing.* Newcastle: Barefoot Research.

Benishek, L., Kirby, K. & Leggett-Dugosh, K. (2011). Prevalence and frequency of problems of concerned family members with a substance-using loved one. *The American Journal of Drug and Alcohol Abuse, 37*, 82–88.

Burke, S., Schmied, V. & Montrose, M. (2006). *Parental alcohol misuse and the impact on children.* Ashfield, New South Wales: Centre for Parenting and Research.

Casswell, S., You, R. & Huckle, T. (2011). Alcohol's harm to others: reduced wellbeing and health status for those with heavy drinkers in their lives. *Addiction, 106*, 1087–1094.

Cleaver, H., Nicholson, D., Tarr, S. & Cleaver, D. (2007). *Child protection, domestic violence and parental substance misuse: Family experiences and effective practice*. London: Jessica Kingsley.

Cleaver, H., Unell, I. & Aldgate, J. (2011). *Children's Needs – Parenting Capacity. Child abuse: Parental mental illness, learning disability, substance misuse, and domestic violence* (2nd ed.). London: The Stationery Office.

Copello, A., Orford, J., Hodgson, R. & Tober, G. (2009). *Social behaviour and network therapy for alcohol problems*. Hove: Routledge.

Copello, A. & Templeton, L. (2012). *The forgotten carers: Support for adult family members affected by a relative's drug problems*. London: UK Drugs Policy Commission.

Copello, A., Templeton, L., Orford, J. & Velleman, R. (2010b). The 5-Step Method: Evidence of gains for affected family members. *Drugs: Education, Prevention and Policy, 17* (Suppl. 1), 100–112.

Copello, A., Templeton, L., Orford, J. & Velleman, R. (2010c). The 5-Step Method: Principles and practice. *Drugs: Education, Prevention and Policy, 17* (Suppl. 1), 86–99.

Copello, A., Templeton, L. & Powell, J. (2010a). The impact of addiction on the family: Estimates of prevalence and costs. *Drugs: Education, Prevention and Policy, 17* (Suppl. 1), 63–74.

Copello, A., Velleman, R. & Templeton, L. (2005). Family interventions in the treatment of alcohol and drug problems. *Drug and Alcohol Review, 24,* 369–385.

Cork, M. (1969). *The forgotten children*. Toronto: PaperJacks.

Forrester, D., Copello, A., Waissbein, C. & Pokhrel, S. (2008). Evaluation of an intensive family preservation services for families affected by parental substance misuse. *Child Abuse Review, 17,* 410–426.

Forrester, D. & Harwin, J. (2011). *Parents who misuse drugs and alcohol. Effective interventions in social work and child protection*. Chichester: John Wiley & Sons, Ltd.

Girling, M., Huakau, J., Casswell, S. & Conway, K. (2006). *Families and Heavy Drinking: Impacts on Children's Wellbeing. Systematic Review*. Wellington, New Zealand: Families Commission.

Graham, K., Bernards, S., Knibbe, R., Kairouz, S., Kuntsche, S., Wilsnack, S. et al. (2011). Alcohol-related negative consequences among drinkers around the world. *Addiction, 106,* 1391–1405.

Harwin, J., Ryan, M. & Tunnard, J., with Pokhrel, S., Alrouh, B., Matias, C. et al. (2011). *The Family Drug and Alcohol Court (FDAC) evaluation project final report*. London: Brunel University.

Home Office (2010). *Drug strategy 2010: Reducing demand, restricting supply,building recovery: supporting people to live a drug free life*. London: Home Office.

Horgan, J. (2011). *Parental substance misuse: Addressing its impact on children. A review of the literature*. Dublin: National Advisory Council on Drugs.

Houmoller, K., Bernays, S., Wilson, S. & Rhodes, T. (2011). *Juggling harms: Coping with parental substance misuse.* London: London School of Hygiene & Tropical Medicine.

Jayne, M., Valentine, G. & Gould, M. (2012). Family life and alcohol consumption: The transmission of 'public' and 'private' drinking cultures. *Drugs: Education, Prevention and Policy 19*, 192–200.

Laslett, A., Ferris, J., Dietze, P. & Room, R. (2012). Social demography of alcohol-related harm to children in Australia. *Addiction, 107*, 1082–1089.

Lee, C. E, Christie, M. M., Copello, A. & Kellett, S. (2012). Barriers and enablers to implementation of family-based work in alcohol services: A qualitative study of alcohol worker perceptions. *Drugs: Education, Prevention and Policy, 19*(3), 244–252.

Lee, K. M. T., Manning, V., Teoh, H. C., Winslow, M., Lee, A., Subramaniam, M. *et al.* (2011). Stress-coping morbidity among family members of addiction patients in Singapore. *Drug and Alcohol Review 30*, 441–447.

Manning, V. (2011). *Estimates of the number of infants (under the age of one) living with substance misusing parents.* London: Institute of Psychiatry.

Manning, V., West, D., Faulkner, N. & Titherington, E. (2009). New estimates of the number of children living with substance misusing parents: results from UK national household surveys. *BMC Public Health, 9*, 377.

Meads, C., Ting, S., Dretzke, J. & Bayliss, S. (2007). *A systematic review of the clinical and cost-effectiveness of psychological therapy involving family and friends in alcohol misuse or dependence.* Birmingham: University of Birmingham and West Midlands Health Technology Assessment Collaboration.

Meyers, R., Roozen, H. & Ellen Smith, J. (2011). The community reinforcement approach: An update of the evidence. *Alcohol Research and Health, 33*(4), 380–388.

Moe, J., Johnson, J. & Wade, W. (2007). Resilience in children of substance users: In their own words. *Substance Use and Misuse, 42*, 381–398.

Moore, B., Biegel, D. & McMahon, T. (2011). Maladaptive coping as mediator of family stress. *Journal of Social Work Practice in the Addictions, 11*, 17–39.

Morgan, T. & Crane, D. (2010). Cost-effectiveness of family-based substance abuse treatment. *Journal of Marital and Family Therapy, 36*(4), 486–498.

National Institute for Health and Clinical Excellence (2011). *Implementation Programme NICE support for commissioners and others using the quality standard on alcohol dependence and harmful alcohol use.* London: NICE.

National Treatment Agency for Substance Misuse (2010). *Commissioning for recovery. Drug treatment, reintegration and recovery in the community and prisons: a guide for drug partnerships.* London: NTA.

Orford, J. (2012). *Addiction dilemmas: Family experiences in literature and research and their lessons for practice.* Chichester: Wiley-Blackwell.

Orford, J., Copello, A., Velleman, R. & Templeton, L. (2010a). Family members affected by a close relative's addiction: The stress-strain-coping-support model. *Drugs: Education, Prevention and Policy, 17* (Suppl. 1), 36–43.

Orford, J., Natera, G., Copello, A., Atkinson, C., Tiburcio, M., Velleman, R. et al. (2005). *Coping with alcohol and drug problems: The experiences of family members in three contrasting cultures.* London: Taylor & Francis.

Orford, J., Templeton, L., Copello, A., Velleman, R. & Ibanga, A. (2010c). Working with teams and organisations to help them to involve family members. *Drugs: Education, Prevention and Policy, 17*(Suppl.1), 154–164.

Orford, J., Templeton, L., Velleman, R. & Copello, A. (2010b). Methods of assessment for affected family members. *Drugs: Education, Prevention and Policy, 17*(Suppl. 1), 75–85.

Orford, J., Velleman, R., Natera, G., Templeton, L. & Copello, A. (2013). Addiction in the family is a major but neglected contributor to the global burden of adult ill-health. *Social Science and Medicine. 78,* 70–77.

Ray, T., Mertens, J. & Weisner, C. (2009). Family members of people with alcohol or drug dependence: health problems and medical cost compared to family members of people with diabetes and asthma. *Addiction, 104,* 203–214.

Roozen, H., de Waart, R. & van der Kroft, P. (2010). Community reinforcement and family training: an effective option to engage treatment-resistant substance-abusing individuals in treatment. *Addiction, 105,* 1729–1738.

Rossow, I. & Hauge, R. (2004). Who pays for the drinking? Characteristics of the extent and distribution of social harms from others' drinking. *Addiction 99,* 1094–1102.

Templeton, L. (2012). Supporting families living with parental substance misuse: the M-PACT (Moving Parents and Children Together) programme. *Child and Family Social Work,* doi: 10.1111/j.1365-2206.2012.00882.x.

Templeton, L., Velleman, R. & Russell, C. (2010). Psychological interventions with families of alcohol misusers: a systematic review. *Addiction Research and Theory, 18*(6), 616–648.

UKATT research team (2001). United Kingdom Alcohol Treatment Trial: hypotheses, design and methods. *Alcohol and Alcoholism, 36,* 11–21.

UKATT research team (2005). Effectiveness of treatment for alcohol problems: findings of the randomised UK alcohol treatment trial (UKATT). *BMJ, 331,* 541.

Velleman, R. (2009). *Children, young people and alcohol: How they learn and how to prevent excessive use (Findings).* York: Joseph Rowntree Foundation.

Velleman, R. (2010). The policy context: Reversing a state of neglect. *Drugs: Education, Prevention and Policy, 17* (Suppl. 1), 8–35.

Velleman, R. & Orford, J. (1999). *Risk and resilience: Adults who were the children of problem drinkers.* Amsterdam: Harwood Academic.

Velleman, R., Orford, J., Templeton, L., Copello, A., Patel, A., Moore, L. et al. (2011). 12-month follow-up after brief interventions in primary care for family members affected by the substance misuse problem of a close relative. *Addiction Research and Theory 19*(4), 362–374.

Velleman, R. & Templeton, L. (2007). Understanding and modifying the impact of parents' substance misuse on children. *Advances in Psychiatric Treatment, 13*, 79–89.

Wales, A., Gillan, E., Hill, L. & Robertson, F. (2009). *Untold damage: Children's accounts of living with harmful parental drinking*. Edinburgh: Scottish Health Action on Alcohol Problems.

Wardle, I. (2009). *Recovery and the UK Drug Treatment System: Key dimensions of change*. Manchester: Lifeline Project.

Weisner, C., Parthasarathy, S., Moore, C. & Mertens, J. (2010). Individuals receiving addiction treatment: are medical costs of their family members reduced? *Addiction, 105*, 1226–1234.

7

In Their Own Right: Developing Confidential Services for Children and Young People Affected by Parental Alcohol and Drug Use

Louise Hill

First of all, he said, if you learn a simple trick, Scout, you'll get along better with all kinds of folks. You can never really understand a person until you consider things from his point of view – until you climb into his skin and walk around in it.

To Kill a Mockingbird, Harper Lee

Introduction

Since the early 1990s there has been heightened political awareness of the risks for children and young people living in families where there is problematic drug use and, to a lesser extent, problematic alcohol use. In 2003, the UK Advisory Committee on the Misuse of Drugs (ACMD) produced a seminal report, *Hidden harm: Responding to the needs of children of problem drug users*. It estimated, for the first time, the prevalence, impact, level of service provision, and children's experiences of parental problem drug use across the United Kingdom. The report estimated that between 250,000 and 350,000 children of problem drug users were experiencing harm due to parental drug misuse.

> Whilst there has been huge concern about drug misuse in the UK for many years, the children of problem drug users have largely remained hidden from view. The harm done to them is usually unseen: a virus in the blood, a bruise under the shirt, resentment and grief, a fragmented education. (Advisory Council on the Misuse of Drugs, 2003, 90)

Emerging Perspectives on Substance Misuse, First Edition. Edited by Willm Mistral.
© 2013 John Wiley & Sons, Ltd. Published 2013 by John Wiley & Sons, Ltd.

The introduction to the report states that consideration of alcohol was beyond the scope of the review; however 'many of the recommendations we make for protecting and supporting children of problem drug users will also be applicable to the children of problem drinkers' (Advisory Council on the Misuse of Drugs, 2003, p. 7). Since the publication of this report there has been a development of service provision to meet the needs of this hidden group (Advisory Council on the Misuse of Drugs, 2007).

In policy and service developments across the United Kingdom, however, there has been a tendency to homogenize the experiences of children and young people living with parental substance misuse and to overlook their diversity (Gorin, 2004; Templeton, Zohhadi, Galvani & Velleman, 2006; Tunnard, 2002a,b). Children affected by parental substance use are commonly framed as 'at risk of harm' and in need of protection (Bancroft & Wilson, 2007). However, if simply framed as 'at risk', we may inadvertently pathologize these children and young people. An international scoping review on parental drug and alcohol misuse found that 'despite the dominant focus on negative impact, there are studies that found no evidence of heightened risk for children stemming from parental substance misuse alone' (Templeton et al., 2006, p. 1). An influential Department of Health review concluded:

'It is therefore important not to pathologise all children who live in families where a parent suffers from mental illness, a learning disability, problem drinking or drug use or domestic violence' (Cleaver, Nicholson, Tarr & Cleaver, 2010, p. 200).

The present chapter critically explores the development of services for children and young people affected by parental drug and alcohol use. How children and young people are conceptualized, whether as 'helpless victims' or as 'problem solvers and inter-dependent contributors', ultimately affects how services are designed and developed (Alderson & Morrow, 2004, p. 22). The chapter is divided into three sections. The first section, Being Counted, considers the prevalence of children and young people currently living with parental drug and alcohol use, as well as the sources relied upon to identify this often hidden group. The second section, Being Heard, explores common themes emerging from listening to these children and young people, and the effects parental substance misuse has on family and school life, creating multiple problems. The third section, Being Included, considers the development of direct services for children and young people affected by parental drug and alcohol use, and the principles that should underpin their engagement.

119

In identifying new directions for service development, I argue for children's and young people's access to confidential services, in their own right, regardless of parental stage of recovery and involvement in treatment services. All children and young people should have the opportunity to access nonstigmatizing, open and responsive support when living in difficult family circumstances. Although drawing on the experiences of the United Kingdom, many of the issues raised in this chapter will be highly relevant in an international context.

Being Counted

There are significant challenges in estimating how many children and young people are affected by parental drug and alcohol use in the United Kingdom. The secrecy and stigma surrounding problematic substance misuse means estimating a 'hidden population' is difficult; self-disclosure may be more difficult for substance-misusing parents, and more specifically, mothers, due to concerns about children being removed from the family home (Goode, 2000). Despite relying solely on adult treatment figures and adult self-reporting, figures repeated uncritically in a range of UK policy documents have been 250,000 to 350,000 children of problem drug users (Advisory Council on the Misuse of Drugs, 2003) and 780,000 to 1.3 million children of adults with an alcohol problem (Prime Minister's Strategy Unit, 2004). To address these limitations, Manning, Best, Faulkner, and Titherington (2009) have provided new estimates, based on more extensive data sources, for children living with substance misusing parents in the United Kingdom. Five national surveys were considered to meet the data criteria (domestic arrangements, adult substance use, and number of children in household under 16): the General Household Survey, 2004 (UK wide); the Household Survey for England, 2004; the National Psychiatric Morbidity Survey, 2000; the British Crime Survey, 2004/2005; and the Scottish Crime Survey, 2000. By combining data from these various sources, Manning and colleagues estimated that a total of 2.6 million children in the United Kingdom are living with a hazardous drinker (from data sources in 2000) and around 334,000 children are living with a dependent drug user. Furthermore, the study identified the potential heightened risks for 1% of children (119,595) living with an adult problem drinker who also used drugs and had a mental health problem (Manning et al., 2009). The analysis of multiple data sources identified the circumstances of children living with parental drug and alcohol use, ranging from occasional use to daily dependent use. Although the researchers were cautious in attributing consequences for family life, they concluded that the numbers of children affected are much greater than earlier estimates and there is a need for mainstream services to respond to the needs of these children and families.

Children and young people affected by parental alcohol and drug use are represented in a significant proportion of child and family social work caseloads (Cleaver, Nicholson, Tarr & Cleaver, 2007; Forrester & Harwin, 2006, 2011, Fraser, McIntyre & Manby, 2008; Hayden, 2004; Kroll & Taylor, 2003). One audit of Child Protection Registers in London found parental substance misuse was a concern for just over half the children, with alcohol the greater concern at 24% compared to 16% for heroin use (Forrester, 2000). A social work case file study of four London boroughs identified just over a third of families (34%) with parental substance misuse as a concern; 62% of their children were subject to care proceedings and 40% were placed on Child Protection Registers (Forrester & Harwin, 2006). These studies have provided a valuable impetus for greater recognition of the potential impact of problematic parental drug and alcohol use on child welfare. However, there is a need to exercise some caution in equating data on children identified as being at significant risk of abuse or neglect with the wider population of children affected by parental drug and alcohol use.

There have been very few surveys with children and young people exploring parental substance use. One exception is a longitudinal study of adolescent drug use, the Belfast Youth Development Study, that also considered parental problematic drug or alcohol use (Percy, Thornton & McCrystal, 2008). Also, in an NSPCC study of maltreatment in the family with 2,869 young adults aged 18–24 years old, 86 (3% of the sample) indicated they 'often had to look after themselves because parents had problems of their own e.g. alcohol or drugs' (Cawson, 2002, p. 39). Although only indicative, the numbers of children and young people using confidential telephone helplines has demonstrated the impact on their lives of living with parental alcohol and drug use. Analysis of over 9,000 phone calls made by children in Scotland between 2000 and 2003 regarding concerns about parental (or significant carer) health and wellbeing found parental alcohol misuse was the most frequent concern, representing 31% of calls; drug misuse was the next concern at 11%; followed by domestic abuse at 7% (ChildLine Scotland & CRFR, 2005).

In summary, there have been few opportunities for children and young people to participate directly in any prevalence studies; data are usually gathered by proxy through parental self-reporting, parental engagement in treatment programmes, or professional identification of a child who is in need of services. A key recommendation from the work of Hidden Harm (Advisory Council on the Misuse of Drugs, 2003, 2007) was to improve the identification of children and young people affected by parental drug and alcohol use. This has increased efforts in local authorities to establish prevalence figures. As Manning and colleagues (2009) have identified there is clear merit in using the improving data on children affected by parental drug and alcohol use to develop better services. However, even when these data are robustly gathered and analysed we need to exercise caution in our interpretation of what children's and young people's lived experiences are and how they change over time. Furthermore, the collation of local data on how many children are affected by parental substance use rarely considers the provision of services and effectiveness of any interventions.

Being Heard

As mentioned above, there have been few opportunities to hear directly from children and young people about their experiences of parental drug and alcohol use. This results in a reliance on a relatively small number of qualitative research studies and service evaluations, as well as adult retrospective studies and professional insights. Despite the secrecy and stigma surrounding drug and alcohol use in families, it is important to recognize that children often know a lot more about parental problem alcohol and drug use than parents and professionals may assume (Gorin, 2004). Research studies have indicated that children have an awareness of parental drug and alcohol use around the age of five years (Bancroft, Wilson, Cunningham-Burley, Backett-Milburn & Masters, 2004; Hogan & Higgins, 2001; Laybourn, Brown, and Hill, 1996). Some parents may try to conceal their use of substances and any associated paraphernalia (for example, children not allowed in the same room when a parent is taking drugs), although younger children may be more likely to witness this due to parental perceptions that they are 'too young to understand' (Hogan & Higgins, 2001). However, attempts to conceal problematic drug and alcohol use from children are often unsuccessful. Therefore, for those working with families, there needs to be an awareness and sensitivity that even young children are likely to be far more aware of drug and alcohol use in families than presumed by adults.

The secrecy and stigma surrounding problematic use of substances has an impact on 'talking outside of the family' (Barnard & Barlow, 2003). Often parents and children are worried that other people knowing may lead to social work involvement and the removal of children from the family home. Living with parental drug and alcohol use has been described as 'living with an elephant in the room' where everybody pretends the 'elephant' is not there, and therefore is not to be talked about (Kroll, 2004). Yet as Kroll explains, parental secretive behaviour and denial of problematic alcohol or drug use may lead children to question their own perceptions and be unsure whether what they are seeing or experiencing is real or not. Fear of bullying by a peer group if parental alcohol and drug use became known has also been raised frequently as a concern for children and young people, and was a further reason for not disclosing any details of family life (Hill, 2011). Houmøller, Bernays, Wilson & Rhodes (2011, p. 65) conclude 'minimizing the harms of parental substance misuse requires sensitive understanding of the obstacles which parents and young people face in disclosure and the need to tackle hidden and social harms at the same time.'

Family Life

The impact of parental alcohol and drug use on children can be diverse and 'each family has to be assessed in its own right and assumptions cannot be made' (Kroll & Taylor, 2003, p. 173). In some families, alcohol and/or drugs can become the main focus and life revolves around the acquiring, consumption and recovery from the substance. Parents may be physically and emotionally unavailable to meet children's needs; children may not be woken up in time for school; mealtimes may be missed, and sleeping patterns disturbed. Also, problematic alcohol use can involve many different patterns involving drinking in the home, in public houses, with friends and associates and in public spaces, which can impact on the routines of family life in different ways. Periods of absence from the family home may be a source of worry or equally a source of relief for children depending on the associated behaviour of the drinking parent (Laybourn et al., 1996). A Scottish study of 38 young people's experiences found a difference between alcohol and drug use where, 'alcohol would often take the parent out of the home, for example to the pub or on benders for several days or weeks, and separate them from their child', compared to drugs where parents would be physically present, although 'not there' when ingesting drugs (Bancroft et al., 2004, p. 13). Depending on the circumstances, parental drug and alcohol use can also increase risks to children if they become exposed to other unsuitable adults, inappropriate activities and unsafe situations.

Children and young people may feel bewildered, confused, upset and frightened by parental problematic alcohol and drug use and consequent behaviours and, as they grow older they may be increasingly angry and frustrated with a parent (Bancroft et al., 2004). The 'Family Life' longitudinal research study (Houmøller et al., 2011) explored 50 young people's (aged 10–18 years old) lived experiences of parental substance misuse over time across England, and highlighted the dynamics of family life and differing impacts of parental substance misuse on siblings. Some children may take on much greater responsibility within the household (such as washing clothes, cooking and caring for siblings) than their peer group. Compared to illegal drug use when associated with criminal behaviour, the relatively cheaper cost of alcohol is less likely to have a detrimental effect on the family finances, depending on household income (Russell, 2007). If there is sufficient income to ensure the material needs of children are provided, this can help to reduce the impact on a family. Despite multiple challenges, many children and young people express their love for and loyalty to their parent and attempt to negotiate an acceptable family life (Hill, 2011).

School Life

Velleman and Orford (1999) found adult children of problem drinkers were more likely than a comparison group to report a range of childhood problems, including being 'withdrawn, demoralized and having problems at school', and this was significantly greater for daughters than for sons. In Laybourn et al. (1996), a common finding amongst older children and young adults was the negative impact on their education. Direct consequences included not being taken when younger, or not encouraged to attend school; and indirect consequences included frequent moves resulting in changing school, lack of parental interest in achievements, and poor concentration when at school. Although a small sample, the majority of girls in this study reported a positive experience of school, with several excelling; this was in stark contrast to the 11 boys in the study where none had liked school and several were nonattenders (Laybourn et al., 1996, p. 81). This study relied on children's own reporting of school experiences at the present time, rather than reflective accounts as gathered in Velleman and Orford's (1999) study, which may begin to explain some differences.

Across research studies, the following themes emerged as having an impact on children's education: school attendance, academic achievement, ability to concentrate in class, having sufficient time and quiet to complete homework, maintenance of friendships, and relationships with peers and teachers. In a ChildLine study, a small number of children reported not attending school, in some cases due to looking after siblings, and for those attending school, some children had trouble concentrating due to a lack of sleep (Gillan, Wales, Hill & Robertson, 2009). One 15-year-old girl felt teachers should have read the signs of 'homework being handed in late, being very tired – once I fell asleep at school – and being absent' (Brisby, Baker & Hedderwick, 1997, p. 14). In a review of children affected by domestic violence, parental substance misuse and parental health problems, a common theme was children worrying about their parents and siblings while at school (Gorin, 2004). Children may be so concerned that they may need to stay at home to ensure that a parent is okay; for example, Rachel (aged 17, mother alcohol misuser) was worried that her mother might injure herself so rarely attended school. Periods of nonattendance at school also impacted on friendships and sources of informal support (Bancroft et al., 2004). Few children invited friends home due to the unpredictability of parental behaviour, and children were often worried about being bullied if parental alcohol and drug use became known (Gillan et al., 2009; Gorin, 2004; Hill, 2011; Laybourn et al., 1996).

Multiple Problems

Parenting capacity can be affected by the use of alcohol and drugs, but it is important to recognize that many other factors such as poverty, unemployment, mental health, parents' own childhood experiences of abuse and neglect will affect parenting, and these are often overlooked (Social Care Institute of Excellence, 2006). Depending on the developmental age of a child a range of parenting skills is required to meet their needs. For example, very young children rely almost exclusively on caregivers to provide food, warmth, shelter and nurture, compared to an adolescent who may have greater autonomy and ability to meet their own basic needs (see Cleaver, Unell & Aldgate, 1999 and 2010 for a detailed overview of the impact on the child at different developmental stages). For families that face multiple adversities over a continuous period of time, the impact on children is likely to be highly detrimental to their development (Cleaver, Unell & Aldgate, 2010). A study of children's calls to ChildLine, and focus groups with volunteer ChildLine counsellors, found that while parental drinking was rarely the presenting problem, the most common being family relationships and physical abuse, 'in many cases, children viewed parents' drinking as an integral part of their problems' (Gillan et al., 2009, p. 26).

Getting By

Across research studies, many children and young people developed strategies to manage everyday life when living with parental drug and/or alcohol use. Family and friends are the main source of support to children and young people, even when difficulties within families exist (Pinkerton & Dolan, 2007). Many protective factors for children have been identified: for example, having at least one trusted adult in their lives (Cleaver et al., 2010). Wider family can provide a central role in supporting children practically and emotionally; however, family relationships may also be sources of tension and dispute, and cannot always be relied upon by children (Bancroft et al., 2004; Hill, 2011; Houmøller et al., 2011). Studies have highlighted that children may seek to normalize their lives through minimizing any outward signs of difference (e.g. Hill, 2011). As highlighted by some children telephoning the confidential ChildLine, there was recognition of the importance of school in their lives and 'getting on well in the future as a way of countering some of the negative aspects of their lives' (Gillan et al., 2009, p. 40).

The use of the free confidential telephone service, ChildLine, by children and young people affected by parental drug and alcohol use over many years strongly indicates that some children and young people may need a confidential space to talk about their worries and concerns (Brisby et al., 1997; ChildLine, 2010; ChildLine Scotland & Centre for Research on Families and Relationships, 2005; Gillan et al., 2009). A literature review (Gorin, 2004) exploring what children report when affected by parental substance misuse, parental health problems and domestic abuse found that, although accounts of professional help vary, many report negative experiences. They want someone who will listen to them, who they can trust, and who provides reassurance and confidentiality. Children are often afraid that they will not be believed and worry that professional involvement will make things worse. They want help to think through problems, and their most persistent need is for more age-appropriate information and for professionals to talk to them in a language they can understand. Children want to be respected and taken seriously, they say that being involved in finding solutions to problems helps them to cope and, where action is taken, they want to be involved, without having full responsibility for decisions. Since the publication of Hidden Harm, programmes have been developed targeted specifically at children and their families that reiterate the importance of these qualities. Yet, given the numbers of children and young people affected by parental drug and alcohol use, access to specialized services for these children remains limited (Advisory Council on the Misuse of Drugs, 2007).

Being Included

The importance of understanding children's lives from their unique perspectives is vital to support and develop their coping strategies in many cases. It must be acknowledged that whilst some children and young people may not be able to live with a parent who is a problematic drug and/or alcohol user, there will also be many who continue to live in families facing daily challenges and who are likely to be in need of support. It is therefore this group of children, who are not 'at risk of significant harm' but should be considered as children 'in need' who we now consider for support services.

Across the United Kingdom, current government policies for children and young people affected by parental drug and/or alcohol use appear to show little regard for children's and young people's own strategies for managing day-to-day life and seeking help of their own accord. There has been a focus on children of problem alcohol and drug users as 'hidden' and, therefore, an onus on professionals to 'identify' such children (Advisory Council on the Misuse of Drugs, 2003, 2007). We still know very little about what services children and young people require, and access, in their own right. A review of effective support services for children in special circumstances identified the 'limited information about the kinds of services children themselves would find most helpful in situations where their parents have significant difficulties' (Stratham, 2004, p. 593). In general, we do know that when children are experiencing difficulties and seeking any type of formal support, confidentiality and trust are of paramount importance (Franks & Medforth, 2005; Freake, Barley & Kent, 2007). In extending this ethos, the provision of support should not rely solely on professionals' identification of children; rather, it should be innovative and creative in service design to be directly and easily accessible by children and young people themselves.

Provision of Services Directly for Children and Young People

Dalrymple argues that children have a right to confidential services without needing an adult referral, whether this is by a parent or professional. Many other studies and reports have concluded that children and young people have the right to access support services. Velleman & Reuber (2007) highlight in their cross-European study of domestic abuse in families with alcohol problems, that children require a service regardless of whether or not parents are engaging in a service for their alcohol use or violence. Also, parents may often have relapse periods and during these times children may no longer have access to the formal support they require (Bancroft et al., 2004; Hill, 2011; Houmøller et al., 2011). A recommendation stemming from the Family Life research study states 'support should be easily accessible and continuous' (Houmøller et al., 2011). This study also highlighted the dynamics within service provision for these families and the challenges in developing and maintaining trusting relationships when faced with staff turnover and changes in family lives. Furthermore, despite the development of the role of service users in influencing the design and delivery of drug and alcohol services, there remains little consultation of children as users of these services.

In an international review of prevention programmes for children of problem drinkers, Cuijpers (2005) argues there have been too few serious attempts to develop effective interventions programmes for children directly, despite many studies identifying children of problem drinkers as a 'high-risk group'. Furthermore, ethical issues surround the recruitment of children to programmes, such as whether children could self-identify as having a parent who was a problem drinker, and the perceived need for parental consent, which is likely to be difficult to obtain. The additional barrier created if parental consent is a prerequisite increases the potential risk that children most in need of support may be the least likely to be able to access support services.

The importance of young people being able to directly access confidential services was starkly presented in my own doctoral research (Hill, 2011). In recruiting children and young people (aged 9 to 20 years) affected by parental alcohol problems to participate in the study, several discussions revealed the frustrations of practitioners in the voluntary sector who were unable to provide a service for some children and young people due to parental unwillingness to engage. One specific challenge was the perceived need for parental or guardian consent for children and young people to access specialized services, despite the fact that young people can already access healthcare services without the consent of parents or carers if they are deemed as having sufficient capacity by a medical professional (Carlisle, Shickle, Cork, and McDonagh, 2006). This presented ethical dilemmas for practitioners, and voluntary services used many innovative strategies to engage with parents in order to be able to work with the family, including the children. Some services provided a service for children through youth groups which, when framed as a more generic youth service, facilitated parental consent. However, this circumventing of consent processes overlooks the rights of children and young people to access services and reiterates the power dynamics inherent in who can access support. So, with the exceptions of confidential helplines and websites, there have been limited attempts to provide confidential services for children and young people in a social care setting. The concern remains that some children who actively seek support may unfairly be denied this due to the lack of consent of a parent and the oversight of a child's ability to give informed consent in their own right. There needs to be far greater recognition of children and young people's own role in both supporting their parents, and their potential for seeking support for themselves.

However, there is also a degree of uncertainty amongst young people about their right to access confidential services. Carlisle et al. (2006) found some adolescents were not visiting doctors due to concerns about confidentiality. Analysis of children's calls to ChildLine (Vincent & Daniel, 2004) showed that those experiencing abuse and neglect were frequently concerned that, firstly they would not be believed, secondly it might make things worse, and thirdly they would have no control over what happens next. The researchers consider whether there could be 'space for negotiation' where children can seek help without resulting in immediate child protection investigations, although they reflect that this would not be possible in the current system, with the notable exception of ChildLine (Vincent & Daniel, 2004, p. 169). Concerns about confidentiality are similarly highlighted for children living with parental drug and alcohol use who fear that seeking support may result in removal from their parents (Houmøller et al., 2011).

Conclusion

The experiences of children and young people living with parental drug and alcohol use are often framed through a child-protection lens that requires professional identification and intervention. This may be appropriate for some children and young people but does not reflect the experiences of all. In constructing all children as inherently vulnerable and 'at risk' we limit their engagement with support services that could be co-designed to meet their needs. In this chapter, I have argued for a greater understanding of the diversity of children and young people's experiences and for recognition of their varied support need. Many of the concerns of children, young people and their families will prevent them from accessing professional support when it is needed. As part of a range of services, I argue that children and young people have the right to access confidential services to safely explore their own lived experiences of parental alcohol and drug use. Furthermore, I suggest that the common presumption of required parental consent to access services needs to be challenged. We need to seriously listen to children's and young people's repeated concerns about confidentiality, and design services that truly meet their needs.

References

Advisory Council on the Misuse of Drugs (ACMD) (2003). *Hidden harm: responding to the needs of children of problem drug users*. London: Home Office.

Advisory Council on the Misuse of Drugs (ACMD) (2007). *Hidden Harm three years on: realities, challenges and opportunities*. London: Home Office.

Alderson, P. & Morrow, V. (2004). *Ethics, social research and consulting with children and young people*. Ilford: Barnardo's, Ilford.

Bancroft, A. & Wilson, S. (2007). The 'Risk Gradient' in policy on children of drug and alcohol users: framing young people as risky. *Health, Risk and Society*, 9(3), 311–322.

Bancroft, A., Wilson, S., Cunningham-Burley, S., Backett-Milburn, K. & Masters, H. (2004). *Parental drug and alcohol misuse: resilience and transition among young people*. York: Joseph Rowntree Foundation.

Barnard, M. & Barlow, J. (2003). Discovering parental drug dependence: silence and disclosure. *Children and Society*, 17, 45–56.

Brisby, T., Baker, S. & Hedderwick, T. (1997). *Under the influence: coping with parents who drink too much: a report on the needs of children of problem drinking parents*. London: Alcohol Concern.

Carlisle, J., Shickle, D., Cork, M. & McDonagh, A. (2006). Concerns over confidentiality may deter adolescents from consulting their doctors. A qualitative exploration. *Journal of Medical Ethics*, 32(3), 133–137.

Cawson, P. (2002). *Child maltreatment in the family: the experience of a national sample of young people.* London: NSPCC.

ChildLine (2010). *ChildLine casenotes: Children talking to ChildLine about parental alcohol and drug misuse.* London: ChildLine.

ChildLine Scotland & CRFR (2005). *Children's concerns about health and wellbeing of parents and significant others.* Edinburgh: Centre for Research on Families and Relationships.

Cleaver, H., Nicholson, D., Tarr, S. & Cleaver, D. (2007). *Child protection, domestic violence and parental substance misuse: Family experiences and effective practices.* London: Jessica Kingsley Publishers.

Cleaver, H., Unell, I. & Aldgate, J. (1999). *Children's needs – parenting capacity: The impact on parental mental illness, problem alcohol and drug use and domestic violence on children's development.* London: TSO.

Cleaver, H., Unell, I. & Aldgate, J. (2010). *Children's needs – parenting capacity: Child abuse – parental mental illness, learning disability, substance misuse and domestic violence* (2nd ed.). TSO, London.

Cuijpers, P. (2005). Prevention programmes for children of problem drinkers: a review. *Drugs: Education, Policy and Prevention, 12*(6), 465–475.

Dalrymple, J. (2001). Safeguarding young people through confidential advocacy services. *Child and Family Social Work, 6*(2), 149–160.

Forrester, D. (2000). Parental substance misuse and child protection in a British sample: A survey of children on the child protection register in an inner London district office. *Child Abuse Review, 9*(4), 235–246.

Forrester, D. & Harwin, J. (2006). Parental substance misuse and child care social work: Findings from the first stage of a study of 100 families. *Child and Family Social Work, 11*(4), 325–335.

Forrester, D. & Harwin, J. (2011). *Parental substance misuse and children's services, in parents who misuse drugs and alcohol: Effective interventions in social work and child protection.* Chichester: John Wiley & Sons, Ltd.

Franks, M. & Medforth, R. (2005). Young helpline callers and difference: exploring gender, ethnicity and sexuality in helpline access and provision. *Child and Family Social Work, 10*, 77–85.

Fraser, C., McIntyre, A. & Manby, M. (2008). Exploring the impact of parental drug/alcohol problems on children and parents in a midlands county in 2005/06. *British Journal of Social Work, 39*, 846–866.

Freake, H., Barley, V. & Kent, G. (2007). Adolescents' views of helping professionals: A review of the literature. *Journal of Adolescence, 30*, 639–653.

Gillan, E., Wales, A., Hill, L. & Robertson, F. (2009). *Untold damage: Children living with parents who drink harmfully.* Glasgow: ChildLine Scotland & Scottish Health Action on Alcohol Problems (SHAAP).

Goode, S. (2000). Researching a hard-to-access and vulnerable population: some considerations on researching drug and alcohol-using mothers. *Sociological Research Online, 5*(1), 1–17.

Gorin, S. (2004). *Understanding what children say: Children's experiences of domestic violence, parental substance misuse and parental health problems.* London: National Children's Bureau.

Hayden, C. (2004). Parental substance misuse and child care social work: research in a city social work department in England. *Child Abuse Review,* *13*(1), 18–30.

Hill, L. (2011). Revealing Lives: A Qualitative Study with Children and Young People Affected by Parental Alcohol Problems. PhD thesis, University of Edinburgh.

Hogan, D. & Higgins, L. (2001). *When parents use drugs: Key findings from a study of children in the care of drug using parents.* Dublin: Children's Research Centre.

Houmøller, K., Bernays, S., Wilson, S. & Rhodes, T (2011). *Juggling harms: Coping with parental substance misuse.* London: London School of Hygiene and Tropical Medicine.

Kroll, B. (2004). Living with an elephant: growing up with parental substance misuse. *Child and Family Social Work, 9,* 129–140.

Kroll, B. & Taylor, A. (2003). *Parental substance misuse and child welfare.* London: Jessica Kingsley.

Laybourn, A., Brown, J. & Hill, M. (1996). *Hurting on the inside: Children's experiences of parental alcohol misuse.* Aldershot: Avebury.

Manning, V., Best, D. W., Faulkner, N. & Titherington, E. (2009). New estimates of the number of children living with substance misusing parents: results from UK national household surveys. *BMC Public Health, 9,* 377–388.

Percy, A., Thornton, M. & McCrystal, P. (2008). The extent and nature of family alcohol and drug use: Findings from the Belfast Youth Study. *Child Abuse Review, 17,* 371–386.

Pinkerton, J. & Dolan, P. (2007). Family support, social support, resilience and adolescent coping. *Child and Family Social Work, 12,* 219–228.

Prime Minister's Strategy Unit (2004). *Alcohol harm reduction strategy for England.* London: Prime Minister's Strategy Unit, Cabinet Office.

Russell, P. (2007). *A matter of substance? Alcohol or drugs: does it make a difference to the child?* Stirling: Aberlour Childcare Trust.

Social Care Institute of Excellence (SCIE) (2006). *SCIE Research briefing 06: Parenting capacity and substance misuse.* London: SCIE.

Stratham, J. (2004). Effective services to support children in special circumstances. *Child: Care, Health and Development, 30*(6), 589–598.

Templeton, L., Zohhadi, S., Galvani, S. & Velleman, R. (2006). *Looking beyond risk: Parental substance misuse: a scoping study.* Edinburgh: Scottish Executive.

Tunnard, J. (2002a). *Parental problem drinking and its impact on children.* London: Research in Practice.

Tunnard, J. (2002b). *Parental drug misuse: A review of impact and intervention studies.* London: Research in Practice.

Velleman, R. & Orford, J. (1999). *Risk and resilience: adults who were children of problem drinkers*. Amsterdam: Harwood Academic Publishers.

Velleman, R. & Reuber, D. (2007). *Domestic violence and abuse experienced by children and young people living in families with alcohol problems: Results from a cross-European study*. Bath: DAPHNE & ENCARE.

Vincent, S. & Daniel, B. (2004). An analysis of children and young people's calls to ChildLine about abuse and neglect: a study for the Scottish child protection review. *Child Abuse Review, 13*, 158–171.

8

Screening for Alcohol Use Disorders
Lesley Smith

Introduction

The global health and social impact of excessive alcohol consumption is well documented. It results in 2.5 million deaths each year, 320,000 being in young people aged 15 to 29 years, accounting for 9% of deaths in that age group (World Health Organisation, 2011). Globally, alcohol ranks eighth amongst risk factors for death, and is the third largest risk factor for disease burden (World Health Organisation, 2009). Alcohol has been shown to be causally related to over 60 different medical conditions such as neuropsychiatric disorders, gastrointestinal diseases and cancer (Rehm et al., 2009). Women who are heavy drinkers around conception and during pregnancy have an increased risk of giving birth to a baby that is small for gestational age, and/or foetal alcohol syndrome characterized by poor growth while the baby is in the womb and after birth, decreased muscle tone and poor coordination, delayed development and problems in thinking, speech, movement, or social skills (Gray & Henderson, 2006). Most of the deaths attributable to alcohol are from diseases such as liver cirrhosis, cancer, and accidents (Rehm et al., 2009). In the majority of cases, there is a dose-response relationship with the risk of disease increasing with the volume of alcohol consumed (Room et al., 2005). In addition to the adverse impact on health, excessive alcohol intake is also associated with a range of psychosocial consequences such as absenteeism from school or work, domestic violence, neglect and abuse of the family and relationships.

Emerging Perspectives on Substance Misuse, First Edition. Edited by Willm Mistral.
© 2013 John Wiley & Sons, Ltd. Published 2013 by John Wiley & Sons, Ltd.

Epidemiological studies show that, on a population level, the majority of alcohol-related harm is not due to drinkers with alcohol dependence (prevalence 7%) but is in fact attributable to a much larger group of drinkers whose consumption exceeds recommended drinking levels and who largely go undetected (World Health Organisation, 2010a). The health impact of alcohol consumption depends on the cumulative volume consumed and the pattern of drinking. Alcohol consumption patterns include:

- Hazardous drinking, whereby an individual regularly exceeds recommended drinking levels which increase the likelihood of psychological or physical harm in the future (World Health Organisation, 1994). There is no one standard definition of hazardous drinking, and different countries may use different criteria. In the United Kingdom, men are advised not to drink regularly more than four units of alcohol per day, and women not more than three units (Home Office, 2012).
- Harmful drinking, which is drinking at a level such that an individual is likely to be experiencing problems related to alcohol consumption and is diagnosed according to the International Classification of Diseases, 10th Revision (ICD -10) (World Health Organisation, 2010b).
- Alcohol dependence, which refers to a cluster of behavioural, cognitive and physiological phenomena that develop after repeated drinking, and that typically include a strong desire to drink; difficulties in controlling drinking; persisting in drinking despite harmful consequences; a higher priority given to drinking than to other activities and obligations; increased tolerance, and a physical withdrawal state including tremor, sweating, anxiety, nausea and vomiting, agitation, insomnia (World Health Organisation, 1992).

Rationale for Screening

The negative impact on health due to excessive drinking can be improved by preventive measures such as identification of problem drinking and delivery of an appropriate intervention. Screening is distinct from diagnostic testing, which seeks to establish whether an individual has a definitive diagnosis of a disorder. Screening identifies individuals who are likely to have a particular disorder, and may serve as a trigger for further evaluation to establish a definite diagnosis. Alcohol screening is used to assess an individual's drinking patterns to see if alcohol is currently harming their health, or likely to lead to harm in the future if the drinking patterns persist.

The effectiveness and cost effectiveness of brief interventions as well as more intensive treatments provide a sound basis for undertaking screening in order to improve the identification of individuals who are at risk of alcohol-related harm (Kaner et al., 2009; National Institute for Health and Clinical Excellence, 2010). However, the evidence shows little support for universal screening whereby everyone is screened regardless of their risk profile (Beich, Thorsen & Rollnick, 2003), instead opportunistic screening is recommended. In the United Kingdom the recommendation is to limit screening to general health checks and new patient registrations in primary care settings, and to those with special types of consultation (National Institute for Health and Clinical Excellence, 2010).

Screening Tools

Methods for identification of excessive alcohol consumption include clinical physical examination for signs and symptoms of heavy drinking, and testing for blood alcohol concentration or other biological markers such as a liver enzyme, serum gamma glutamyltransferase (GGT). However, these methods are less valid for the detection of hazardous and harmful, as opposed to dependent, drinking. Research shows that standardized alcohol screening questionnaires are a more accurate way of identifying individuals drinking in excess of recommended limits, and have been shown to be more accurate at detecting hazardous and harmful drinking than laboratory tests of biological samples (Aertgeerts, Buntinx, Ansoms, and Fevery, 2002; Coulton et al., 2006). They also have the advantage of being less expensive.

Alcohol screening questionnaires are a quick and simple way to gather information on an individual's drinking prior to delivering an intervention appropriate for a particular screening result. Interventions range from brief advice lasting a few minutes, from a healthcare practitioner or alcohol worker, which aims to reduce alcohol intake to less hazardous levels, to extended advice lasting up to 30 minutes typically delivered by an alcohol worker, to reduce harmful drinking; or further assessment for possible alcohol dependence and onward referral (Parker, Marshall & Ball, 2008). Alcohol screening tools are composed of questions regarding quantity and frequency of alcohol consumption, or effects of drinking and drinking behaviour, or sometimes both. Each question is scored, and the total score calculated by summing these individual scores. The cut-off score for a particular instrument represents the value which is considered positive for the test. It is important to remember that questions about numbers of drinks consumed may need to be adjusted to take into account common drink sizes and alcohol strength in the country in which it is used. For example, AUDIT was developed assuming a standard drink is equivalent to 10 g of alcohol, whereas in the United Kingdom it is 8 g and in the United States 14 g.

Some examples of commonly used valid screening questionnaires are appended to this chapter, and include several of the following:

- Alcohol Use Disorder Identification Test (AUDIT), a 10-item questionnaire about alcohol consumption during the past year, alcohol-related problems and symptoms of alcohol dependence (Babor, Higgins-Biddle, Saunders & Monteiro, 2001). Possible scores range from 0 to 40, and a score of eight or more indicates potential hazardous drinking, 16–19 indicates potential harmful drinking, and a score of 20 or more indicates potential alcohol dependence. The AUDIT takes two to three minutes to complete by the individual. It has been extensively validated in a variety of clinical settings such as primary care and tertiary care and has been translated and validated in many languages. Shorter derivatives of the full AUDIT include AUDIT-C, the first three consumption questions (Bush, Kivlahan, McDonell, Fihn & Bradley, 1998), and AUDIT Primary Care (AUDIT-PC) (Piccinelli et al., 1997) which includes questions 1, 2, 4, 5 and 10 of the full AUDIT.
- CAGE, a four-item screen that enquires about lifetime alcohol dependence (Mayfield et al., 1974). Individuals are considered positive if they answer yes to two or more questions. It takes less than one minute to complete.
- Single Alcohol Screening Questionnaire (SASQ) asks whether a man has recently consumed more than eight drinks in one day (or whether a woman has consumed more than six drinks). Individuals who report exceeding the stated amount within the last 3 months are considered positive for hazardous or harmful drinking (Canagasaby & Vinson, 2005).

Two tests have focused on accident and emergency settings:

- Paddington Alcohol Test (PAT) is a four-item screen for hazardous and harmful drinking for use in accident and emergency settings (Smith, Touquet, Wright & Das Gupta, 1996). It was specifically developed with the intention of making the most of the 'teachable moment', and is a set of questions administered by the clinician.

- Fast Alcohol Screening Test (FAST) is a four-item screening test derived from AUDIT. It was developed for busy clinical settings, such as accident and emergency, as a two-stage initial screening test that is quick to administer, since more than 50% of patients are identified by using just the first question (Hodgson, Alwyn, John, Thom & Smith, 2002).

Two alcohol screening questionnaires have been developed for use with pregnant women. The threshold for a positive score is two or more for both instruments:

- T-ACE is a four-item derivative of MAST (Selzer, 1971) and CAGE (Sokol et al., 1989). It was developed for detecting potential risk drinking during the peri-conception period, usually extending about 2–3 months before and after conception and the beginning of pregnancy. T-ACE takes about one minute to complete.
- TWEAK was also developed to detect alcohol misuse in pregnancy and is a five-item derivative of CAGE (Russell & Bigler, 1979).

Interpreting Results from Alcohol Screening Tests

An essential step in screening for alcohol misuse is to choose the best test for a particular setting taking into account the age and sex of the individual and the level of alcohol intake or alcohol problems to be identified. Tests are evaluated on their ability to discriminate accurately between those who have a condition and those who do not. A gold standard is a test that, ideally, correctly identifies every person with the condition and, conversely, every person without the condition. There are no perfect gold-standard simple tests for alcohol misuse. The accepted gold-standard methods for diagnosing alcohol-use disorders are lengthy structured diagnostic interviews such as the World Health Organisation (WHO) Composite International Diagnostic Interview (CIDI) (Wittchen, 1994), and the Alcohol Use Disorders and Associated Disabilities Interview Schedule (AUDADIS) (Grant, Dawson, Stinson, Chou, Kay & Pickering, 2003). These were developed based on criteria for alcohol disorders according to the Diagnostic and Statistical Manual-IV (DSM-IV) (American Psychiatric Association, 1994) and the WHO International Classification of Diseases (ICD-10) (World Health Organisation, 1992). These gold standard interviews are often time consuming and expensive, making their use for mass screening unfeasible. They are useful, however, for making definitive diagnoses, or for acting as the reference standard against which another screening test can be validated. They are not adequate for assessing alcohol consumption at the lower, or hazardous, level.

The process of validating a screening test involves comparing it with a reference 'gold standard' by testing a group of people with and without the condition of interest with both tests. Assuming that the reference standard test always makes the correct diagnosis, participants are classified in one of four groups:

- True positives – people who have a positive screening test and who have the condition according to the reference standard
- False positives – people who have a positive screening test but do not have the condition according to the reference standard
- True negatives – people who have a negative screening test and do not have the condition according to the reference standard
- False negatives – people who have a negative screening test and do have the condition according to the reference standard

Sensitivity

Measures of a test's ability to correctly identify people include sensitivity and specificity. Sensitivity refers to the proportion of people with the condition of interest such as hazardous drinking (determined by the reference standard) who are correctly identified by the test. Sensitivity values range from 0 to 1 (0% to 100%) and is the ratio of true positives over all individuals who have the disorder (i.e. true positives plus false negatives).

Higher sensitivity (i.e. a value closer to 1) can be achieved by lowering the threshold score that is used to define a positive screening result. For example as noted above, an AUDIT score of eight is generally recommended as the cut-off score for a positive screen for hazardous drinking. If the threshold is lowered to four, then sensitivity is even higher (Table 8.1). However, the consequences of high sensitivity can be a higher proportion of false positives. Although more individuals who are truly hazardous drinkers (true positives) are identified, high sensitivity also leads to more individuals being mistakenly classified as hazardous drinkers (false positives) as shown in Table 8.1.

Table 8.1 Cutoff Scores and Performance of AUDIT for Identification of Heavy Drinking in Women in the General Population

Cutpoint score	True positive	True negative	False positive	False negative	Sensitivity	Specificity
4	50	518	442	1	0.98	0.54
5	50	672	288	1	0.98	0.70
6	43	749	211	8	0.84	0.78
7	40	826	134	11	0.78	0.86
8	30	864	96	21	0.59	0.90
9	27	883	77	24	0.53	0.92
10	23	902	58	28	0.45	0.94

Note: Heavy drinking was defined as at least 10 standard drinks (120 g of absolute alcohol) on average in a week during the past 28 days (Aalto, Alho, Halme & Seppa, 2009).

Specificity

Specificity is the proportion without the condition that is correctly identified by the screening test. Like sensitivity, specificity values range from 0 to 1 (0% to 100%), and are the ratio of true negatives over all individuals who do not have the disorder (true negatives plus false positives). Higher specificity can be achieved by increasing the threshold score used to define a positive test. If the AUDIT cutoff score is increased from eight to ten a greater proportion of individuals who are not hazardous drinkers will have a negative screening result (true negatives). However more individuals who are hazardous drinkers will also have a negative screening result (false negatives) thereby reducing the test's sensitivity as shown in Table 8.1.

An ideal screening test would have a sensitivity and specificity close to 1 (or 100%) meaning that most people are correctly identified and only a small minority would have a misleading result. In practice this is a rare occurrence and a balance between sensitivity and specificity has to be made. The consequences of false positive results versus false negative results should be considered to help with this decision. Priority is usually given to high sensitivity over high specificity for alcohol screening tests to minimize the chance of classifying individuals as false negatives. While the adverse impact of false positives is that individuals at low risk of alcohol related harm may receive a brief intervention, these have a relatively low cost and present a low risk to individuals who receive them. It is important to note that the measures described above are dependent on which disorder is screened for. For example AUDIT will have a different sensitivity and specificity for screening for hazardous drinking as opposed to the values for screening for alcohol dependence.

Predictive Values

Other measures used to summarize the performance of a test include the positive predictive value (PPV) and negative predictive value (NPV). Positive and negative predictive values are also known as post-screen probabilities and are useful when considering the value of a test to a clinician. They are dependent on the prevalence of the disorder in the population of interest. Taking into account the prevalence of the disorder in a population, the PPV is the probability that an individual is likely to have a particular disorder given a positive screening test result. So the same test with the same sensitivity and specificity values for a particular cut-point score may have quite different PPVs depending on the prevalence of the target disorder. This has a bearing on using these tests in practice.

The negative predictive value (NPV) is the probability that an individual is not likely to have a particular disorder given a negative screening test result. It represents the proportion of individuals who are true negatives amongst all individuals who test negative. As for PPV, the NPV is dependent on the sensitivity and specificity of a test and prevalence of the condition in the wider population.

Comparisons of Screening Questionnaires in Different Settings

Systematic reviews of alcohol-screening questionnaires that report on their accuracy in various clinical settings are summarized below (see appendices for questionnaires). Individual studies have suggested that performance of screening tests may vary according to ethnicity, however findings are inconclusive (Bradley, Boyd-Wickizer, Powell & Burman, 1998; Kriston, Holzel, Weiser, Berner & Harter, 2008; Reinert &Allen, 2007).

Primary Care

The evidence for the best alcohol-screening questionnaire for detecting alcohol misuse in either primary care or general populations was examined in a Cochrane systematic review (Smith, Foxcroft, Holloway, Minozzi, and Casazza, 2010). Questionnaires comprising 13 questions or fewer were evaluated and included AUDIT, AUDIT-C, and CAGE in comparison with a structured in-depth interview as a reference 'gold' standard.

Based on a meta-analysis for an AUDIT score of eight or more the sensitivity was 0.66 (95% confidence interval (CI): 0.56 to 0.74) and specificity 0.93 (95% CI: 0.90 to 0.96) for the detection of hazardous drinking. The positive likelihood ratio was 9.8, meaning that, with a score of eight or more, there was almost a tenfold increased likelihood of an individual meeting criteria for hazardous drinking. For AUDIT-C, with a score of four or more, sensitivity was 0.89 (95% CI: 0.76 to 0.95) and specificity 0.84 (95% CI: 0.70 to 0.92). The positive likelihood ratio was 5.5 meaning that, with a score of four or more, there was between five- and sixfold increased likelihood of an individual meeting criteria for hazardous drinking.

For the detection of harmful drinking or alcohol dependency, results were very similar for AUDIT as for the detection of hazardous drinking. Sensitivity was 0.67 (95% CI: 0.56 to 0.76), and specificity 0.93 (95% CI: 0.89 to 0.95). The positive likelihood ratio was 9.0 meaning that there was a ninefold increased likelihood of meeting criteria for harmful drinking or alcohol dependency with a score of eight or more. Values for AUDIT-C at a score of four or more were lower than for hazardous drinking. Sensitivity was 0.79 (95% CI: 0.66 to 0.88), specificity 0.78 (95% CI: 0.60 to 0.90), and the positive likelihood ratio was 3.6. Direct comparison of AUDIT score eight with AUDIT-C score four, and AUDIT score eight with CAGE score two, showed that AUDIT was better for detecting harmful drinking or dependence than both AUDIT-C and CAGE.

Gender-specific analyses of a small subset of the studies suggested that an AUDIT cutoff score of six for men and five for women may be more accurate than an AUDIT score of eight for the detection of harmful drinking and/or alcohol dependence. CAGE performed poorly for identification of alcohol-use disorders, and for the other screening questionnaires there was a lack of evidence.

Antenatal Care

The performance of brief alcohol-screening questionnaires to identify problem drinking during pregnancy was assessed in a systematic review

(Burns, Gray & Smith, 2010). Reviewers searched various databases, journals, and reference lists of identified studies current to June 2008. To be eligible for the review, studies had to evaluate a brief (13 or fewer items) alcohol screening instrument against a reference standard consisting of a structured interview to derive diagnoses of risky drinking, alcohol abuse or dependence. Five studies with 6,724 participants met the inclusion criteria.

The studies showed that, for detection of risky drinking, three questionnaires performed well: AUDIT-C (sensitivity values were 95% for cutoff score three or more), followed by TWEAK (71% to 91% for cutoff score two or more), and T-ACE (69% to 88% for cutoff score two or more). Specificity ranges were 85% for AUDIT-C, 71% to 89% for T-ACE, and 73% to 83% for TWEAK. AUDIT-C was also evaluated for past year alcohol dependence and alcohol-use disorder. For a cutoff score of three or more, sensitivity was 100% for past year alcohol dependence and 96% for past year alcohol use disorder, specificity being 71% in both cases. The other two studies evaluated (CAGE and SMAST) performed poorly with sensitivities below 50%.

Therefore, based on these data AUDIT-C, T-ACE, and TWEAK are promising for identification of risk drinking, and AUDIT-C may also be useful for identification of alcohol dependency or abuse during pregnancy. However, there were some limitations with these studies. All were conducted in the United States, mainly with urban-living women of low socio-economic status, and therefore it is unclear whether these results would be replicated in different population groups. The performance of the instruments as stand-alone tools is also uncertain as, in some studies, the instruments were embedded in another questionnaire to reduce the focus on alcohol.

Accident and Emergency

Regarding screening for alcohol problems amongst emergency department patients, the Fast Alcohol Screening Tool (FAST) was found to be the most accurate universal screening tool for identifying alcohol misuse, whereas the Paddington Alcohol Test (PAT) was identified as a cost-effective targeted screening tool for detection of alcohol misuse in a select population, i.e. in people with likely alcohol-related injury such as an accident, fall, assault; or illness such as nonspecific gastrointestinal or cardiac disorder (Jones, 2010). These conclusions were based on a systematic review of seven studies with at least 6,447 participants. The review evaluated the following alcohol screening instruments: FAST, PAT, RAPS-4, or TWEAK, against a reference standard that was AUDIT or standardized diagnostic criteria derived from ICD-10 or DSM-IV obtained during a diagnostic interview (CIDI). The review showed that FAST had the highest values for sensitivity (93 to 94%), and specificity (86 to 88%). A limitation of these studies was the risk of bias due to the instruments being shortened versions of the reference standard tests, which would lead to overestimation of the accuracy of FAST and RAPS.

Another review focused on questionnaires to detect alcohol and other drug misuse in young people aged under 21 years attending an emergency department (Newton et al., 2011). Reviewers searched various databases, journals, and reference lists of relevant articles current to October 2010. The systematic review included six studies with at least 1,228 participants, and evaluated DSM-IV 2-Item, AUDIT-C, FAST, RUFT-Cut, CRAFFT, and RAPS4-QF. The reference standard was an alcohol-use disorder (abuse and dependence) obtained during a standardized diagnostic interview according to DSM-IV criteria.

The 2-Item screen based on DSM-IV criteria was more effective than the other screening instruments for identification of alcohol abuse or dependency. Young people who answered yes to at least one of the two questions had a more than eightfold likelihood of an alcohol use disorder than not. Sensitivity and specificity values were 88% and 90%, respectively. Results for AUDIT-C showed a threefold increased likelihood of an alcohol use disorder with cut-point scores of three in one study and six in another. It is unclear if a targeted or universal screening approach is best in this setting. Again the limitation of these findings is that the accuracy of DSM-IV 2-Item scale may be overestimated as these questions were taken from the reference standard test.

Conclusion

Prevention of, and early intervention in, alcohol-related disorders is an important public health goal. There are reliable and valid alcohol-screening questionnaires to detect levels and patterns of drinking that may lead to health problems in the future, or drinking that is already causing an impact on an individual's health. Therefore, screening for problematic alcohol use with a recommended instrument, followed by appropriate intervention, should lead to health benefits.

Appendices

Alcohol Use Disorders Identification Test (AUDIT)

	Scoring system				
Questions	*0*	*1*	*2*	*3*	*4*
How often do you have a drink that contains alcohol?	Never	Monthly or less	2-4 times per month	2-3 times per week	4+ times per week
How many standard alcoholic drinks do you have on a typical day when you are drinking?	1–2	3–4	5–6	7–9	10+
How often do you have 6 or more standard drinks on one occasion?	Never	Less than monthly	Monthly	Weekly	Daily or almost daily
How often during the last year have you found you were not able to stop drinking once you had started?	Never	Less than monthly	Monthly	Weekly	Daily or almost daily
How often during the last year have you failed to do what was normally expected of you because of drinking?	Never	Less than monthly	Monthly	Weekly	Daily or almost daily
How often during the last year have you needed a first drink in the morning to get going after a heavy drinking session?	Never	Less than monthly	Monthly	Weekly	Daily or almost daily

(*continued*)

Alcohol Use Disorders Identification Test (AUDIT) (continued)

	Scoring system				
Questions	*0*	*1*	*2*	*3*	*4*
How often during the last year have you had a feeling of guilt or remorse after drinking?	Never	Less than monthly	Monthly	Weekly	Daily or almost daily
How often during the last year have you been unable to remember what happened the night before because you were drinking?	Never	Less than monthly	Monthly	Weekly	Daily or almost daily
Have you or someone else been injured as a result of your drinking?	No		Yes, but not in the last year		Yes, during the last year
Has a relative or friend, or a doctor or other health care worker been concerned about your drinking or suggested you cut down?	No		Yes, but not in the last year		Yes, during the last year

Scoring: <8 = sensible drinking; 8–15 = hazardous drinking; 16–19 = harmful drinking; 20+ = possible alcohol dependence.

T-ACE

T	Tolerance: How many drinks does it take to make you feel high?
A	Have people annoyed you by criticizing your drinking?
C	Have you ever felt you ought to cut down on your drinking?
E	Eye-opener: Have you ever had a drink first thing in the morning to steady your nerves or get rid of a hangover?

Affirmative answers to questions A, C, or E = 1 point each. Reporting tolerance to more than two drinks (the T question) = 2 points. A score of 2 or more is considered positive.

CAGE

C	Have you ever felt you should cut down on your drinking?
A	Have people annoyed you by criticizing your drinking?
G	Have you ever felt bad or guilty about your drinking?
E	Eye opener: Have you ever had a drink first thing in the morning to steady your nerves or to get rid of a hangover?

Two positive responses are considered a positive test and indicate further assessment is warranted.

Rapid Alcohol Problem Screen RAPS-4 (Cherpitel, 2000)

During the last year have you had a feeling of guilt or remorse after drinking? (REMORSE)

During the last year has a friend or family member ever told you about things you said or did while you were drinking that you could not remember? (AMNESIA)

During the last year have you failed to do what was normally expected from you because of drinking? (PERFORM)

Do you sometimes take a drink in the morning when you first get up? (STARTER OR 'EYE OPENER')

Scoring: A total score of ≥ 1 indicates a potential alcohol problem.

TWEAK (Russell & Bigler, 1979)

T	Tolerance: how many drinks can you hold ('hold' version ≥ 6 indicates tolerance) or how many drinks can take before you begin to feel the effects ('high' version > 2 indicates tolerance)
W	have close friends or relatives Worried or complained about your drinking in the last year?
E	Eye openers: Do you sometimes take a drink in the morning when you first get up?
A	Amnesia: Has a friend or family member ever told you about things you said or did while you were drinking that you could not remember?
K	Kut down: Do you sometimes feel the need to cut down on your drinking?

Score 2 points each for first 2 items and 1 point each for last 3; range 0–7; positive score threshold ≥ 2

AUDIT, CAGE and T-ACE questionnaires accessed from the National Institute on Alcohol Abuse and Alcoholism: http://pubs.niaaa .nih.gov/publications/aa65/aa65.htm

RAPS4 and TWEAK are freely available. For information please see: http://pubs.niaaa.nih.gov/publications/AssessingAlcohol/Instrument PDFs/54_RAPS4.pdf and http://pubs.niaaa.nih.gov/publications/ AssessingAlcohol/Instrument PDFs/74_TWEAK.pdf.

Fast Alcohol Screening Test (FAST) (Hodgson et al., 2002)

	Scoring system				
Questions	*0*	*1*	*2*	*3*	*4*
How often do you have 8(men)/ 6(women) or more standard drinks on one occasion?	Never	Less than monthly	Monthly	Weekly	Daily or almost daily
Only answer the following questions if your answer above is monthly or less					
How often during the last year have you not been able to remember what happened when drinking the night before?	Never	Less than monthly	Monthly	Weekly	Daily or almost daily
How often in the last year have you failed to do what was normally expected of you because of drinking?	Never	Less than monthly	Monthly	Weekly	Daily or almost daily
Has a relative/friend/ doctor/health care worker been concerned about your drinking or advised you to cut down?	No		Yes, but not in the last year		Yes, during the last year

Scoring: A total score of 3+ indicates hazardous or harmful drinking.

Copies of FAST are available to download from the Health Development Agency website: http://www.nice.org.uk/niceMedia/ documents/manual_fastalcohol.pdf (accessed March 10, 2013).

References

Aalto, M., Alho, H., Halme, J. T. & Seppa, K. (2009). AUDIT and its abbreviated versions in detecting heavy and binge drinking in a general population survey. *Drug and Alcohol Dependence, 103,* 25–29.

Aertgeerts, B., Buntinx, F., Ansoms, S. & Fevery, J. (2002). Questionnaires are better than laboratory tests to screen for current alcohol abuse or dependence in a male inpatient population. *Acta Clinica Belgica 57,* 241–249.

American Psychiatric Association (1994). *Diagnostic and statistical manual of mental disorders.* Washington, DC: American Psychiatric Association.

Babor, T. F., Higgins-Biddle, J. C., Saunders, J. B. & Monteiro, M. G. (2001). *AUDIT. The alcohol use disorders identification test. Guidelines for use in primary care* (2nd ed.). Retrieved 10 March 2013 from http://whqlibdoc. who.int/hq/2001/WHO_MSD_MSB_01.6a.pdf.

Beich, A., Thorsen, T. & Rollnick, S. (2003). Screening in brief intervention trials targeting excessive drinkers in general practice: systematic review and meta-analysis. *British Medical Journal, 327,* 536–542.

Bradley, K. A., Boyd-Wickizer, J., Powell, S. H. & Burman, M. L. (1998). Alcohol screening questionnaires in women: a critical review. *JAMA, 280,* 166–171.

Burns, E., Gray, R. & Smith, L. A. (2010). Brief screening questionnaires to identify problem drinking during pregnancy: a systematic review. *Addiction, 105,* 601–614.

Bush, K., Kivlahan, D. R., McDonell, M. B., Fihn, S. D. & Bradley, K. A. (1998). The AUDIT alcohol consumption questions (AUDIT-C): An effective brief screening test for problem drinking. *Archives of Internal Medicine 158,* 1789–1795.

Canagasaby, A. & Vinson, D. C. (2005). Screening for hazardous or harmful drinking using one or two quantity-frequency questions. *Alcohol and Alcoholism, 40,* 208–213.

Cherpitel, C. J. (2000). A brief screening instrument for problem drinking in the emergency room: The RAPS4. Rapid Alcohol Problems Screen. *Journal of Studies on Alcohol, 61,* 447–449.

Coulton, S., Drummond, C., James, D., Godfrey, C., Bland, J. M., Parrott, S. et al. (2006). Opportunistic screening for alcohol use disorders in primary care: Comparative study. *British Medical Journal, 332,* 511–514.

Grant, B. F., Dawson, D. A., Stinson, F. S., Chou, P. S., Kay, W. & Pickering, R. (2003). The Alcohol Use Disorder and Associated Disabilities Interview Schedule-IV (AUDADIS-IV): Reliability of alcohol consumption, tobacco use, family history of depression and psychiatric diagnostic modules in a general population sample. *Drug and Alcohol Dependence, 71,* 7–16.

Gray, R. & Henderson, J. (2006). Review of the Fetal Effects of Prenatal Alcohol Exposure. Retrieved 10 March, 2013 from http://www.npeu.ox.ac.uk/downloads/reports/alcohol-report.pdf.

Home Office (2012). *The Government's Alcohol Strategy.* http://www.homeoffice.gov.uk/publications/alcohol-drugs/alcohol/alcohol-strategy?view=Binary (accessed 03/12/2012)

Hodgson, R., Alwyn, T., John, B., Thom, B. & Smith, A. (2002). The FAST Alcohol Screening Test. *Alcohol and Alcoholism 37*, 61–66.

Jones, L. A. (2010). Systematic review of alcohol screening tools for use in the emergency department. *Emergency Medicine Journal 28*, 182–191.

Kaner, E. F., Dickinson, H. O., Beyer, F., Pienaar, E., Schlesinger, C., Campbell, F., Saunders, J. B., Burnand, B. & Heather, N. (2009). The effectiveness of brief alcohol interventions in primary care settings: A systematic review. *Drug and Alcohol Review 28*, 301–323.

Kriston, L, Holzel, L., Weiser, A. K., Berner, M. M. & Harter, M. (2008). Meta-analysis: are 3 questions enough to detect unhealthy alcohol use? *Annals of Internal Medicine 149*, 879–888.

Mayfield, D., McLeod, G. & Hall, P. (1974). The CAGE questionnaire: validation of a new alcoholism screening instrument. *American Journal of Psychiatry 131*, 1121–1123.

National Institute for Health and Clinical Excellence (2010). *NICE public health guidance 24. Alcohol-use disorders: preventing the development of hazardous and harmful drinking.* http://www.nice.org.uk/nicemedia/live/13001/48984/48984.pdf.

Newton, A. S., Gokiert, R., Mabood, N., Ata, N., Dong, K., Ali, S. *et al.* (2011). Instruments to detect alcohol and other drug misuse in the emergency department: a systematic review. *Pediatrics, 128*(1), e180–e192.

Parker, A. J. Marshall, E. J. & Ball, D. M. (2008). Diagnosis and management of alcohol use disorders. *British Medical Journal, 336*, 496–501.

Piccinelli, M., Tessari, E., Bortolomasi, M., Piasere, O., Semenzin, M., Garzotto, N. et al. (1997). Efficacy of the alcohol use disorders identification test as a screening tool for hazardous alcohol intake and related disorders in primary care: a validity study. *British Medical Journal, 314*, 420–424.

Rehm, J., Mathers, C., Popova, S., Thavorncharoensap, M., Teerawattananon, Y. & Patra, J. (2009). Global burden of disease and injury and economic cost attributable to alcohol use and alcohol-use disorders. *Lancet, 373*, 2223–2233.

Reinert, D. F. & Allen, J. P. (2007). The alcohol use disorders identification test: an update of research findings. *Alcoholism: Clinical and Experimental Research, 31*, 185–199.

Room, R., Babor, T. & Rehm, J. (2005). Alcohol and public health. *Lancet, 365*, 519–530.

Russell, M. & Bigler, L. (1979). Screening for alcohol-related problems in an outpatient obstetric-gynecologic clinic. *American Journal of Obstetrics and Gynecology*, *134*, 4–12.

Saunders, J. B., Aasland, O. G., Babor, T. F., de la Fuente, J. R. & Grant, M. (1993). Development of the Alcohol Use Disorders Identification Test (AUDIT): WHO Collaborative Project on Early Detection of Persons with Harmful Alcohol Consumption – II. *Addiction*, *88*, 791–804.

Selzer, M. T. (1971). The Michigan Alcoholism Screening Test: The quest for a new diagnostic instrument. *American Journal of Psychiatry*, *127*(12), 1653–1658.

Smith, L. A., Foxcroft, D., Holloway, A., Minozzi, S. & Casazza, G. (2010). Brief alcohol questionnaires for identifying hazardous, harmful and dependent alcohol use in primary care (Protocol). Retrieved March 17, 2013 from http://onlinelibrary.wiley.com/doi/10.1002/14651858.CD008631/pdf.

Smith, S. G., Touquet, R., Wright, S. & Das Gupta, N. (1996). Detection of alcohol misusing patients in accident and emergency departments: the Paddington Alcohol Test (PAT). *Journal of Accident and Emergency Medicine*, *13*, 308–312.

Sokol, R. J., Martier, S. S. & Ager, J. W. (1989). The T-ACE questions: practical prenatal detection of risk-drinking. *American Journal of Obstetrics and Gynecology*, *160*, 863–868; discussion 868–870.

Wittchen, H.-U. (1994). Reliability and validity studies of the WHO – Composite International Diagnostic Interview (CIDI): a critical review. *Journal of Psychiatric Research*, *28*, 57–84.

World Health Organisation (1992). *International Classification of Diseases: Clinical Descriptions and Diagnostic Guidelines*. Geneva: World Health Organisation.

World Health Organisation (1994). Lexicon of Alcohol and Drug Terms. Retrieved 10 March, 2013 from www.who.int/substance_abuse/terminology/who_lexicon/en/.

World Health Organisation (2009). Global Health Risks. Retrieved 10 March, 2013 from http://www.who.int/healthinfo/global_burden_disease/global_health_risks/en/.

World Health Organisation (2010a). Global Information System on Alcohol and Health (GISAH). Retrieved 10 March, 2013 from http://apps.who.int/gho/data/view.main?showonly=GISAH.

World Health Organisation (2010b). *International statistical classification of diseases (ICD) and related health problems, 10th Revision*. Retrieved 10 March, 2013 from http://apps.who.int/classifications/icd10/browse/2010/en.

World Health Organisation (2011). *Global status report on alcohol and health*. Retrieved 10 March, 2013 from http://www.who.int/substance_abuse/publications/global_alcohol_report/en/.

9

From Comorbidity to Multiple Health Behaviour Change

Amanda Baker, Sarah Hiles, Louise Thornton, Amanda Searl, Peter Kelly, and Frances Kay-Lambkin

Introduction

The authors of this chapter form part of a clinical research group focused on understanding co-occurring substance use and mental health problems, and developing and delivering effective and innovative interventions for people experiencing these co-occurring problems. Our approach has evolved over time, broadening the focus of treatment to encompass multiple health behaviour change.

Since the early 1990s, with the benefit of large epidemiological data sets, it has become clear that many people in the community experience mental health and substance use problems in their lifetime and, quite often, experience these problems concurrently. In addition to the physical and social problems associated with substance use in the general population, substance use among people with co-occurring mental health problems is associated with exacerbation of psychiatric symptoms, increased rates of suicide attempts, relapse, homelessness, poor social functioning and reduced medication effectiveness (Carey, Carey & Meisler, 1991; Ziedonis & Nickou, 2001). Despite the high prevalence and associated adverse consequences, treatment services have by and large been designed to service people with either mental health or substance-use problems, not both. It has been increasingly recognized that these 'treatment silos', as they have become known, tend not to provide treatment for coexisting problems, with people attending one type of service being referred on to the other type of service for treatment of the

Emerging Perspectives on Substance Misuse, First Edition. Edited by Willm Mistral.
© 2013 John Wiley & Sons, Ltd. Published 2013 by John Wiley & Sons, Ltd.

coexisting problem. This has tended to result in unsatisfactory outcomes due to conflicting treatment approaches, poor treatment attendance, and client confusion regarding integration of two types of treatment.

In this chapter the term 'mental health problem' refers to both diagnosed mental disorders and the experience of distressing psychiatric symptoms that are insufficient to warrant a diagnosis of a mental disorder (Gadit, 2003). Mental disorders can be defined as clinically significant behavioural or psychological syndromes or patterns associated with a significantly increased risk of suffering distress, disability, pain, death, or an important loss of freedom (American Psychiatric Association, 2000). A substance-use problem exists when the person experiences any type medical, physical, psychological, interpersonal, social, occupation or financial problem related to the use of tobacco, alcohol or other drugs (Daley & Marlatt, 2006). Substance-use disorders involve maladaptive patterns of use leading to impairment or distress manifested by symptoms such as tolerance, withdrawal, failure to fulfil major role obligations, use in situations in which it is hazardous, legal problems, and continued use despite adverse effects (American Psychiatric Association, 2000).

This chapter describes an emerging perspective in the treatment of coexisting mental health and substance-use problems (MHSUP) by summarizing key areas of research. Firstly, we review prevalence to demonstrate how common coexisting MHSUP are, and also to highlight that the most commonly used substances, tobacco and alcohol, are legal. Secondly, we focus on the efficacy of treatment, pointing out that although this can be effective and some progress has been made towards incorporating these practices into clinical services, treatment silos remain. Following this overview, we recommend a way forward in considering MHSUP, suggesting that adoption of a healthy-lifestyles approach may help to break down barriers to provision for coexisting problems within existing treatment services. A case study of a healthy lifestyles intervention is also presented.

Prevalence of Coexisting Mental Health and Substance-Use Problems

As stated above, epidemiological surveys indicate that MHSUP frequently co-occur. Compared to the general population, people with substance-use disorders have twice the rate of mental health disorders, including affective (11% versus 25%) and anxiety disorders (17% versus

36%) (Kessler et al., 1994, 1996). Concurrent mental health disorders are particularly common in people with alcohol-use disorders. This was demonstrated by Grant et al. (2004) in the United States and Teesson et al. (2010) in Australia, with the latter reporting that people with alcohol use disorders were over four times more likely to have a comorbid mental disorder than those without an alcohol use disorder.

Conversely, people with mental health disorders are also more likely than the general population to have substance-use problems. For example, among people dwelling in the community, approximately one-fifth of people with current major depression or schizophrenia also meet criteria for a current substance-use disorder (Farrelly et al., 2007; Grant et al., 2004; Kamali, Kelly, Gerbvin, Browne, Larkin & O'Callaghan, 2000; Kessler, Nelson, McGonagle, Edlund, Frank & Leaf, 1996).

Cannabis is one of the more commonly used illicit substances, yet while the prevalence of cannabis use disorder is only around 2% in the general population (Grant et al., 2004), it is as high as around 50% in people with schizophrenia (Holthausen et al., 2002; Koskinen, Lohonen, Koponen, Isohanni & Miettunen, 2010). Like the general population, the most commonly used substances in people with mental health disorders are legal substances – alcohol and tobacco – rather than illicit substances. While the prevalence of alcohol use disorders in the general population is around 7%, in people with current major depression or schizophrenia, prevalence ranges from 12% to 22% (Grant et al., 2004; Kessler et al., 1996; Teesson et al., 2010). Rates of tobacco smoking in people with mental health disorders are also disproportionately high (approximately 38%, compared to around 20% among people without mental disorders), especially among people with psychotic disorders (62%) (de Leon & Diaz, 2005; Lawrence, Mitrou & Zubrick, 2009). Rates of tobacco use are not in decline in populations with mental disorders as they are in the general population (de Leon & Diaz, 2005).

Even higher rates of comorbid disorders are found within treatment settings. For example, of people who sought treatment for alcohol use disorder in one 12 month period, 41% had a mood disorder and 33% had an anxiety disorder. Likewise, of people who sought treatment for other drug-use disorders, 60% had a mood disorder and 43% had an anxiety disorder (Grant et al., 2004). Among people who sought treatment for mental health problems, criteria for a co-occurring substance-use disorder were met by 21% of people with major depression, 16% of people with an anxiety disorder and 20–34% of people with schizophrenia (Bauer, Altshuler, Evans, Beresford, Williford & Hauger, 2005; Grant et al., 2004; Kamali et al., 2000). Thus, coexisting problems are the norm in treatment settings and require screening, assessment, treatment, and ongoing monitoring (Kay-Lambkin, Baker & Lewin, 2004).

Treatment for Coexisting MHSUP

Available evidence suggests that any treatment is at least partly effective for coexisting MHSUP, including usual care (e.g., Petersen et al., 2007), highlighting the importance of doing something rather than nothing when MHSUP are present. However, in four recent reviews of the literature (Baker, Hides & Lubman, 2010; Baker, Hiles, Thornton, Hides & Lubman, 2012a; Baker, Thornton, Hides & Dunlop, 2012b; Baker, Thornton, Hiles, Hides & Lubman, 2012c), we have reported that manual-guided psychological interventions are consistently associated with better outcomes compared to comparison conditions. We summarize key findings from these reviews, and other research, below.

Alcohol

Among people with psychosis, alcohol consumption has been shown to be significantly reduced following active treatment such as motivational interviewing (MI) and MI combined with cognitive behaviour therapy (CBT). Control conditions including assessment, psycho-education and treatment as usual also appear to be associated with reductions in alcohol consumption (Baker et al., 2012a). However, active treatment appears to be associated with additional benefits over control conditions, in terms of psychiatric symptomatology and functioning. In summarizing this literature, although brief interventions appear effective for alcohol misuse among people with psychotic disorders, longer CBT interventions (up to ten sessions) should be offered to people with psychosis who do not respond to brief interventions, or who have coexisting depression (Baker et al., 2009b).

A review of interventions for outpatients with co-occurring depression and alcohol misuse (Baker et al., 2012c) showed that these conditions are responsive to brief integrated MI interventions (addressing depression and alcohol problems) and CBT of up to ten sessions. The latter were effective when delivered via computer or face-to-face. Additional benefits of CBT over the brief MI intervention were seen on both depression and alcohol outcomes, suggesting that stepped care, where clients receive the simplest, least-intensive treatment first, and then proceed to more intensive treatments if nonresponsive to the first step, is worthy of further investigation (Kay-Lambkin et al., 2004).

In the same review by Baker et al. (2012c) among outpatients with co-occurring anxiety disorders and alcohol misuse, brief behavioural interventions focusing on alcohol were effective for both alcohol and anxiety-related outcomes, with a number of studies also recommending a stepped or staged approach to treatment for these patients (e.g. Toneatto, 2005). Among psychiatric hospital inpatients, primarily with depression, individual (Hulse & Tait, 2002) and group (Santa Ana, Wulfert & Nietert, 2007) MI have been shown to be effective in reducing alcohol consumption. Interpersonal therapy and brief supportive psychotherapy have yet to demonstrate effectiveness when offered to people with coexisting MHSUP. Increasingly, our perspective for the treatment of alcohol problems among people with mental health problems is to recommend a stepped care approach. A brief intervention providing feedback about assessment results (number of standard drinks consumed per day in comparison to recommended health guidelines), consideration of the links between drinking and current concern (including any mental health problems/symptoms), advice to reduce consumption, and MI (if time allows) should be provided to all people with coexisting mental health and alcohol use problems. Alcohol consumption should be monitored, along with mental health symptoms, and more intensive, longer interventions, or more focused interventions offered if alcohol consumption remains problematic or residual mental health symptoms exist.

Cannabis

Among people with mental health problems, brief intervention is effective for a smaller proportion of cannabis users compared to problem drinkers (Baker et al., 2009b, 2010). Longer or more intensive interventions are often required, particularly among heavier users of cannabis and those with more chronic mental disorders. Specific recommendations regarding the type and length of specific psychological treatments cannot be made at this time, although MI and CBT approaches seem promising. We have recently shown that, relative to participants with comorbid depression and alcohol-use disorders, for people using cannabis, Internet-delivered psychological treatments involving limited face-to-face contact may be particularly appealing. For example, our computer-delivered psychological treatment, which comprises CBT and MI techniques and explores the links between mood and cannabis use, has been associated with significantly greater reductions in depression relative to a one-session face-to-face treatment, and superior reductions in cannabis use relative to a face-to-face treatment (Kay-Lambkin, Baker, Lewin & Carr, 2009). In addition, the few available studies in this area indicate that effectively treating the mental health disorder with standard pharmacotherapy for that disorder may be associated with a reduction in cannabis use (Baker et al., 2010).

Regardless of the specific content of treatment for people with coexisting mental health and cannabis use problems, extra attention and effort is required to attract, engage and retain cannabis users in any treatment programme. We have recently shown that compared to users of other drugs including alcohol, people using cannabis report significantly lower therapeutic bond. Therapists treating cannabis users also rated the therapeutic bond with these clients lower than for those using other drugs, including alcohol. Bond decreased as severity of cannabis use increased. Therapeutic bond is akin to the emotional attachment between the client and clinician in therapy, and it is possible that the physiological effects of cannabis use, including time distortion, perceptual alterations, loss of sense of personal identity, memory and attention difficulties may impact on the person's ability to form an emotional connection. In therapy this is often a key component to successful treatment and retention, and in brief treatments in particular (Gibbons et al., 2010). This is vitally important given the above evidence suggesting cannabis users respond better with longer term treatment (Baker et al. 2009b; Kay-Lambkin et al., 2009). Thus, extra time for engagement and targeted clinical supervision of therapists managing cannabis use in their clients will be required to maximize the potential treatment outcomes, particularly when coexisting mental health problems are present.

An emerging perspective is that nicotine replacement therapy (NRT) may be effective in cannabis treatment. Evidence demonstrates similarities in withdrawal symptom profiles and severity between cannabis and tobacco (Budney, Vandrey, Hughes, Thostenson & Bursac, 2008). Thus, pharmacotherapy for nicotine withdrawal may be effective in reducing withdrawal symptoms in individuals who simultaneously quit both cannabis and tobacco. It remains important to address tobacco use among people using cannabis, given our data indicating that tobacco use tends to increase with decreasing cannabis use (Kay-Lambkin et al., in press). Only one small pilot study has tested the impact of NRT among those with cannabis dependence (Diggs, Rabinovich & Gilbert, 2011). Preliminary results among 20 people indicate that relative to a placebo patch, NRT is associated with significantly greater reductions in mood-related craving. No published studies have assessed the effects of nicotine administration on concurrent cannabis and tobacco use, however the low abuse potential of NRT, its high accessibility as an over-the-counter and subsidized pharmacotherapy, and minimal adverse side effects makes it an important treatment option to explore.

Tobacco

Discrepancies exist in the treatment and support offered to people with and without mental disorders to quit or reduce their tobacco use. Research suggests that many mental health professionals are concerned that smoking cessation may negatively impact patients' mental health, and that they are reluctant to implement smoking intervention strategies. In many countries, mental health wards are still exempt from smoke-free legislation, perpetuating this misconception (Banham & Gilbody, 2010; Lawn & Pols, 2005). Nevertheless, the few clinical trials that exist show smoking to be amenable to change in people with coexisting mental disorders, and people with mental health problems are willing to accept smoking cessation interventions.

Alone, psychological interventions for smoking cessation have been found only minimally effective, and pharmacotherapy is suggested as an important part of effective cessation interventions among this population (e.g. Hall & Prochaska, 2009). For instance, the addition of bupropion, an antidepressant, to psychological smoking cessation interventions has been found to improve quit rates significantly among people with psychotic disorders and depression (Banham & Gilbody, 2010; Gierisch, Bastian, Calhoun, McDuffie & Williams, 2010; Tsoi, Porwal & Webster, 2010). Evidence also suggests that bupropion does not adversely affect positive, negative or depressive symptoms among people with mental disorders (George, Vessicchio, Termin, Bregartner, Feingold & Rounsaville, 2002).

Literature reviews have found evidence that with all forms of NRT the chances of stopping smoking were increased by 50% to 70% for a person in the general population, and intensity of support does not appear to be an important moderator of NRT effect (Stead, Perera, Bullen, Mant & Lancaster, 2008). These treatments may also be effective among people with a lifetime history of depression (15%–22%) although cessation rates are lower among people with current depressive symptoms (Gierisch et al., 2010). However, only 4% to 22% of people with psychotic disorders achieve cessation when using bupropion or NRT plus behavioural support (Baker et al., 2006; Banham & Gilbody, 2010). To be optimally effective, additional support may be needed for this population. A recent review (Hitsman, Moss, Montoya & George, 2009) was supportive of repeated longer term psychological and pharmacological interventions for smoking among people with mental disorders.

Further research and large-scale studies are needed regarding the efficacy of smoking cessation treatments, especially psychological treatments, among people with mental disorders (Aubin, Rollema, Svensson & Winterer, 2012; Banham & Gilbody, 2010; Tsoi, Porwal & Webster, 2010). Equally, far more needs to be done to raise the awareness and ability of clinicians treating people with mental health problems to diagnose and treat nicotine dependence (Fagerstrom & Aubin, 2009). As noted by Hughes & Weiss (2009), likely reasons for overlooking tobacco smoking among people with MHSUP include: (a) the absence of behavioural intoxication necessitating immediate attention; (b) nonacceptance of coexisting disorders (or their treatment) as relevant to intervening with smoking; (c) the attitude that intermediate non-abstinence goals (including reduction in use) are less accepted in the treatment of nicotine dependence; and (d) the wide availability of NRT.

Multiple Health Behaviour Change

Noncommunicable diseases, including cardiovascular disease (CVD), cancer and other tumours and respiratory system diseases, are the most common causes of death among people with MHSUP, with a reported average lifespan 25 years less than the general population (Lawrence, Holman & Jablensky, 2001). Smoking, physical inactivity, alcohol misuse and poor diet are the main behavioural risk factors for CVD, accounting for 8%, 7%, 3% and 2% respectively of the burden of disease and injury in Australia (Australian Institute of Health and Welfare, 2010). Thus, high rates of these behaviours among people with coexisting MHSUP affords the opportunity to address multiple health risk behaviours, known as 'risk behaviour bundles' (Spring et al., 2012).

A healthy lifestyle focus represents an important innovation in the treatment of coexisting MHSUP. It reduces stigma, is more appealing to clients, and avoids prematurely focusing on substance abuse, which could evoke client resistance. Our own work is among the first to develop and implement this approach, and shows that clients are willing to target multiple problems simultaneously (Fergusson, Boden & Horwood, 2009), which can make improvements in both mental health and substance-use domains (Baker et al., 2009b; Kay-Lambkin et al., 2009). Taking a healthy lifestyles approach to coexisting MHSUP involves intervening across the range of CVD risk factors within an integrated treatment programme. It allows small changes across a number of health behaviours that increase self-efficacy for further behaviour change and may be associated with a greater net reduction in CVD risk. Spring et al. (2012) have reported that an optimal combination of increasing fruit and vegetable intake paired with reducing leisure screen-time simultaneously achieves a reduction in dietary fat. They have also shown that interventions to prevent weight gain are best delivered after intervention for smoking cessation (Spring et al., 2004).

Healthy lifestyle interventions can be delivered individually (Baker et al., 2009a), by group (currently being trialled in alcohol and other drug residential rehabilitation settings), by telephone (currently being trialled with people with schizophrenia) (Baker et al., 2011), or by combining telephone and Internet-based treatment. Recently we have successfully piloted a face-to-face healthy lifestyles intervention (Baker et al., 2009a) among overweight smokers with severe mental disorder. The intervention consisted of nine individual sessions of MI/CBT plus NRT, in addition to treatment as usual. The intervention was associated with significant reductions in CVD risk scores, smoking and weight. A significant improvement was also reported in moderate physical activity, and a small change was reported in an unhealthy eating index. Based on these promising results, we are currently conducting a randomized controlled trial of face-to-face versus telephone-delivered intervention (Baker et al., 2011; Filia et al., 2012).

The Way Forward: Management of Multiple Health Behaviours

Treatment for coexisting MHSUP is effective. However, treatment silos remain and coexisting problems are often left unaddressed. We believe that a way forward is to adopt a healthy-lifestyles approach to mental health and substance-use treatment. By addressing mental health, substance use, diet and physical activity, a health context serves as the background against which clinicians can monitor, assess and intervene across a range of interconnected domains, regardless of the setting in which they are providing treatment. Specific behaviours, the number of behaviours targeted, and the sequence in which they are targeted (simultaneously or sequential), are the subject of ongoing research.

Group-based approaches are likely to be an effective way to disseminate healthy lifestyles interventions into routine care. They have the advantage that participants can learn from the experiences of other group members, there is an opportunity for positive peer support, and the group may help to keep participants more accountable for their behaviours. The psycho-education components of healthy-lifestyle interventions are particularly well suited to group presentations. It is very common for substance abuse treatment services to use group based approaches, so it is likely that staff will be comfortable delivering these types of interventions. Our research team is currently developing and trialling a group-based intervention for people attending residential substance abuse treatment. The Healthy Recovery programme is an eight-session group intervention that aims to help participants reduce their smoking, improve their intake of fruit and vegetables, and increase their level of physical activity. The core components of the intervention are education, motivational interviewing, goal setting, and monitoring. Participants are encouraged to use NRT, and contingency management is also used to promote behaviour change. Further work needs to be conducted examining the effectiveness of these types of group interventions and how they might be best delivered within routine care. However, early indications from our pilot work indicate that participants understand the need to improve their overall health and are willing to participate in group based healthy lifestyle programmes. The following points illustrate how a healthy-lifestyles session might be conducted with a client of a mental health or substance-use service.

Management of Multiple Health Behaviours

1. Provide rationale regarding the high rate of CVD or other relevant non-communicable diseases among people with MHSUP.
2. Screen for mental health problems, smoking, alcohol, cannabis, other drug use, fruit and vegetables eaten per day, fat in diet, and activity level.
3. Identify stage of change; for example, on a scale of 0–10, how important is it for you to eat two pieces of fruit per day?
4. Use decisional balance: good things/less good things about the behaviours.
5. Ask about possible link between the behaviours to presenting mental health symptoms and/or substance-use problems.

6. Seek permission to provide information.
7. Assess confidence to improve the behaviours; for example, on a scale of 0–10, how confident are you that you can eat two pieces of fruit per day?
8. Explore options for changing each behaviour.
9. Negotiate a change plan: goals typically involve a 25%–50% change, for example, reduce from 10 to 5 drinks per day, then to 2 or 3 drinks per day, and so forth.
10. Regularly monitor mental health symptoms and substance use.

The case study that follows illustrates a longer healthy lifestyles intervention delivered over 17 sessions as part of a Healthy Lifestyles Program (HLP) research trial, funded by the National Health and Medical Research Council of Australia, targeting CVD risk among smokers with a psychotic disorder.

Case Study

John (name altered to ensure confidentiality) is a 49-year-old man diagnosed with schizophrenia who presented as friendly and well mannered, with good social skills including maintaining eye contact, introducing himself and appropriately answering and asking questions. John demonstrated reasonable literacy and concentration skills. He received fortnightly injections for management of psychotic symptoms. His personal hygiene was poor (unclean hair and fingers stained with dirt and tobacco), he was overweight, lived alone, and was socially isolated, although he had a supportive elderly father.

Assessment was conducted over two sessions of approximately 1.5–2 hours. Biomedical measures included weight, height, blood pressure, blood sugar and cholesterol. He reported no ongoing medical conditions. Clinical assessment included psychotic symptoms, depression, and substance use. Results indicated a moderate level of psychotic symptom severity (auditory hallucinations and paranoia) and a significant impairment in social and occupational functioning. Current polydrug use included tobacco from age 13, alcohol, cannabis, and a history of amphetamine use. John presented with strong concern for his current quality of life and poor health behaviours. He expressed motivation to quit smoking, become more physically active, and increase social participation. His current polydrug use and avoidant behaviours exacerbated his mental health symptoms and prevented him from engaging in more meaningful activities.

As John was already highly motivated to change his behaviour, a focus was placed on building self-efficacy and coping strategies. Intervention combined MI, CBT and NRT. John responded well to early stages of therapy; he was easily engaged and set appropriate goals. He quit smoking and increased his daily exercise by scheduling walking and gym activities at home. A problem-solving format was used to help him plan for the achievement of goals and prepare for any challenges. Contingency management was also used to reinforce smoking changes. John received small monetary rewards, a certificate for each week he remained abstinent, and was also rewarded with praise and encouragement. Therapy focused on relapse prevention by assisting John to develop awareness of triggers for smoking, key phrases for refusing cigarettes, and rewarding himself for remaining abstinent during challenging experiences. He found a progressive muscle relaxation audiotape helpful.

John's mood, cravings for smoking, and capacity to engage in activities, were significantly affected by his cannabis use. He believed he was unable to cope without cannabis. MI elicited negative effects of cannabis and he prepared some thought-challenging techniques to increase self-belief about his ability to cope without it, as well as specific behavioural strategies to assist with delaying his drug use. During sessions 7–11, John reported that on most days he was able to delay his cannabis use until evening and achieve goals such as walking his dog, playing guitar, doing a daily weights session, mowing the lawn, and going to the shops. Along with relapse prevention, final sessions also explored goals relating to John's current diet, physical activity and ongoing alcohol and cannabis use. He recognized that smoking cannabis and drinking alcohol interfered with eating well and his fitness programme. Although he had lost weight whilst participating in the programme and was starting to choose low-fat alternatives, he ate unhealthy snacks late at night after smoking cannabis. He did not meet his fitness goals on weekends due to commencing cannabis use earlier in the day and drinking considerably more alcohol. John's ambivalence about changing his drug use was explored. He wanted to stop drug use altogether and gradually reduced his cannabis use during the remaining sessions.

John's final sessions involved consolidating his relapse plan and future management, as well as reviewing his achievements in the programme. Behavioural changes and changes reflected in biomedical results were discussed. In addition to quitting smoking, John felt his physical health was better and he was more able to participate in the community. His functionality had clearly improved (greater structure and planning in days, improved sleeping, improved personal care, and regular eating patterns and daily exercise). He also dramatically increased his physical activity, incorporating a walking and weights programme into his daily plan. He reported consistently exercising 5–6 days per week in the final months of the programme. Despite gaining 4 kg in the initial weeks of smoking cessation, John was then able to reduce by 7 kg. He reported much improved self-confidence, which was reflected in his body language, speech, and improved personal care. He developed skills in problem solving, distress tolerance, and thought challenging and used his determination to achieve goals despite many challenges. A reduction in substance use was also evident. He felt he would never smoke again, was able to delay and reduce cannabis use most days, and reduced his alcohol consumption by more than 50% on average per day. John displayed increased readiness for further change in relation to his drug use and social participation, and was linked with additional supports upon completion of the programme. A focus was placed on reinforcing the coping mechanisms and skills he had developed in the programme, such as using distractions and challenging negative thoughts, as well as his personal characteristics of determination and self-belief, which had allowed him to make these significant lifestyle changes. He reported feeling very proud of his achievements and had noticed that his family and others were treating him more positively. In his final session John stated 'It is not just the changes that I have been able to make, but the fact that I have been able to make them.'

From Treatment Silos to Everyday Practice

A healthy lifestyles approach to treatment appears popular with clients and reduces resistance associated with any premature focus on substance use. In the translation of healthy lifestyle interventions into routine care it is important to consider how systems level changes can be used to support these programmes (Kelly, Baker, Deane, Kay-Lambkin, Bonevski & Tregarthen, 2012). This includes considering the impact of staff beliefs towards the use of these approaches (Guydish, Passalacqua, Tajma & Manser, 2007). It also includes considering how to most effectively introduce policy, procedures and program activities to support sustainable behaviour changes. In addition to addressing mental health and alcohol and other drug use, this should involve introducing sustainable smoking cessation practices, considering the inclusion of structured exercise

164

programmes, and ensuring that healthier food choices are made available to participants (Kelly et al., 2012).

In conclusion, a holistic approach such as the one described enables people with coexisting problems to make positive changes in numerous behaviours. This approach could be rolled out across outpatient and residential treatment services in mental health and alcohol and other drug settings with a minimum of retraining.

References

American Psychiatric Association (2000). *Diagnostic and statistical manual of mental disorders* (4th ed.) (text revision). Washington, D.C.: American Psychiatric Association.

Aubin, H., Rollema, H., Svensson, T. H. & Winterer, G. (2012). Smoking, quitting, and psychiatric disease: a review. *Neuroscience and Biobehavioral Reviews, 36*, 271–284.

Australian Institute of Health and Welfare (2010). *Australia's health 2010*. Canberra: Australian Institute of Health and Welfare.

Baker, A., Hides, L. & Lubman, D. (2010). Treatment of cannabis use among people with psychotic and depressive disorders: A systematic review. *Journal of Clinical Psychiatry,71*, 247–254.

Baker, A., Hiles, S., Thornton, L., Hides, L. & Lubman, D. (2012a). A systematic review of psychological interventions for excessive alcohol consumption among people with psychotic disorders. *Acta Psychiatrica Scandinavica, 126*(4), 243–255.

Baker, A., Kay-Lambkin, F., Richmond, R., Filia, S., Castle, D., Williams, J. et al. (2011). Study protocol: A randomised controlled trial investigating the effect of a healthy lifestyle intervention for people with severe mental disorders. *BMC Public Health, 11*(1), 10.

Baker, A., Richmond, R., Castle, D., Kulkarni, J., Kay-Lambkin, F., Sakrouge, R. et al. (2009a). Coronary heart disease risk reduction intervention among overweight smokers with a psychotic disorder: A pilot trial. *Australian and New Zealand Journal of Psychiatry, 43*, 129–135.

Baker, A., Richmond, R. L., Haile, M., Lewin, T. J., Carr, V. J., Taylor, R. L. et al. (2006). A randomized controlled trial of a smoking cessation intervention among people with a psychotic disorder. *The American Journal of Psychiatry, 163*, 1934–1942.

Baker, A. L., Thornton, L. K., Hides, L. & Dunlop, A. (2012b). Treatment of cannabis use among people with psychotic disorders: A critical review of randomised controlled trials. *Current Pharmaceutical Design, 18*, 4923–4937.

Baker, A., Thornton, L., Hiles, S., Hides, L. & Lubman, D. (2012c). Psychological interventions for alcohol misuse among people with co-occurring depression or anxiety disorders: A systematic review. *Journal of Affective Disorders, 139*(3), 217–229.

Baker, A., Turner, A., Kay-Lambkin, F. & Lewin, T. J. (2009b). The long and the short of treatments for alcohol or cannabis misuse among people with severe mental disorders. *Addictive Behaviors, 34*(10), 852–858.

Banham, L. & Gilbody, S. (2010). Smoking cessation in severe mental illness: What works? *Addiction, 105*, 1176–1189.

Bauer, M. S., Altshuler, L., Evans, D. R., Beresford, T., Williford, W. O. & Hauger, R. (2005). Prevalence and distinct correlates of anxiety, substance, and combined comorbidity in a multi-site public sector sample with bipolar disorder. *Journal of Affective Disorders, 85*, 301–315.

Budney, A. J., Vandrey, R. G., Hughes, J. R., Thostenson, J. D. & Bursac, Z. (2008). Comparison of cannabis and tobacco withdrawal: Severity and contribution to relapse. *Journal of Substance Abuse Treatment, 35*(4), 362–368.

Carey, M. P., Carey, K. B. & Meisler, A. W. (1991). Psychiatric symptoms in mentally ill chemical abusers. *Journal of Nervous and Mental Disease, 179*(3), 136–138.

Daley, D. & Marlatt, G. (2006). *Overcoming your alcohol or drug problem: Effective recovery strategies therapist guide.* New York: Oxford University Press.

de Leon, J. & Diaz, F. J. (2005). A meta-analysis of worldwide studies demonstrates an association between schizophrenia and tobacco smoking behaviors. *Schizophrenia Research, 76*(2), 135–157.

Diggs, H. A., Rabinovich, N. R. & Gilbert, D. G. (2011). Effects of nicotine replacement therapy on marijuana withdrawal symptoms in cannabis-dependent individuals, *Society for Research into Nicotine and Tobacco Abstracts of 17th Annual Meeting.* Retrieved March 10, 2013 from http://www.srnt.org/conferences/2011/pdf/2011%20SRNT%20Abstracts%20Web.pdf.

Fagerstrom, K. & Aubin, H. J. (2009). Management of smoking cessation in patients with psychiatric disorders. *Current Medical Research and Opinion, 25*(2), 511–518.

Farrelly, S., Harris, M. G., Henry, L. P., Purcell, R., Prosser, A., Schwartz, O. et al. (2007). Prevalence and correlates of comorbidity 8 years after a first psychotic episode. *Acta Psychiatrica Scandinavica, 116*(1), 62–70.

Fergusson, D. M., Boden, J. M. & Horwood, J. (2009). Tests of causal links between alcohol abuse or dependence and major depression. *Archives of General Psychiatry, 66*(3), 260–266.

Filia, S., Baker, A., Kulkarni, J. & Williams, J. (2012). Sequential behavioral treatment of smoking and weight control in bipolar disorder. *Translational Behavioral Medicine, 2*(3), 290–295.

Gadit, A. (2003). Subthreshold mental disorders. *Journal of Pakistan Medical Association, 53*(2), 42–44.

George, T. P., Vessicchio, J. C., Termin, A., Bregartner, T. A., Feingold, A. & Rounsaville, B. J. (2002). A placebo controlled trial of bupropion for smoking cessation in schizophrenia. *Biological Psychiatry*, 52, 53–61.

Gibbons, C. J., Nich, C., Steinberg, K., Roffman, R. A., Corvino, J., Babor, T. F. et al. (2010). Treatment processes, alliance and outcome in brief versus extended treatments for marijuana dependence. *Addiction*, 105, 1799–1808.

Gierisch, J. M., Bastian, L. A., Calhoun, P. S., McDuffie, J. R. & Williams, J. W. (2010). *Comparative effectiveness of smoking cessation treatments for patients with depression: A systematic review and meta-analysis of the evidence*. Washington, D.C., Department of Veterans Affairs.

Grant, B., Stinson, F., Dawson, D., Chou, S., Dufour, M., Compton, W. et al. (2004). Prevalence and co-occurrence of substance use disorders and independent mood and anxiety disorders: results from the National Epidemiologic Survey on Alcohol and Related Conditions. *Archives of General Psychiatry*, 61(8), 807–816.

Guydish, J., Passalacqua, E., Tajima, B. & Manser, S. (2007). Staff smoking and other barriers to nicotine dependence intervention in addiction treatment settings: a review. *Journal of Psychoactive Drugs*, 39(4), 423–433.

Hall, S. M. & Prochaska, J. J. (2009). Treatment of smokers with co-occurring disorders: Emphasis on integration in mental health and addiction treatment settings. *Annual Review of Clinical Psychology*, 5, 409–431.

Hitsman, B., Moss, T., Montoya, I. & George, T. (2009). Treatment of tobacco dependence in mental health and addictive disorders. *Canadian Journal of Psychiatry*, 54(6), 368–378.

Holthausen, E. A. E., Wiersma, D., Sitskoorn, M. M., Hijman, R., Dingemans, P. M., Schene, A. H. et al. (2002). Schizophrenic patients without neuropsychological deficits: subgroup, disease severity or cognitive compensation? *Psychiatry Research*, 112(1), 1–11.

Hughes, J. & Weiss, R. (2009). Are differences in guidelines for the treatment of nicotine dependence and non-nicotine dependence justified? *Addiction*, 104(12), 1951–1957.

Hulse, G. & Tait, R. (2002). Six-month outcomes associated with a brief alcohol intervention for adult in-patients with psychiatric disorders. *Drug and Alcohol Review*, 21(2), 105–112.

Kamali, M., Kelly, L., Gervin, M., Browne, S., Larkin, C. & O'Callaghan, E. (2000). The prevalence of comorbid substance misuse and its influence on suicidal ideation among in-patients with schizophrenia. *Acta Psychiatrica Scandinavica*, 101(6), 452–456.

Kay-Lambkin, F., Baker, A. & Lewin, T. (2004). The 'co-morbidity roundabout': a framework to guide assessment and intervention strategies and engineer change among people with co-morbid problems. *Drug and Alcohol Review*, 23(4), 407–424.

Kay-Lambkin, F., Baker, A., Lewin, T. J. & Carr, V. J. (2009). Computer-based psychological treatment for comorbid depression and problematic alcohol and/or cannabis use: a randomized controlled trial of clinical efficacy. *Addiction, 104*, 378–388.

Kay-Lambkin, F., Edwards, S., Baker, A., Kavanagh, D., Kelly, B., Bowman, J. & Lewin, T. J. (in press). The impact of tobacco use on treatment for comorbid depression and alcohol misuse. *International Journal of Mental Health and Addiction.*

Kelly, P., Baker, A., Deane, F., Kay-Lambkin, F., Bonevski, B. & Tregarthen, J. (2012). Prevalence of smoking and other health risk factors in people attending redidential substance abuse treatment. *Drug and Alcohol Review, 31*(5), 638–644.

Kessler, R., McGonagle, K., Zhao, S., Nelson, C., Hughes, M., Eshleman, S. et al. (1994). Lifetime and 12-month prevalence of DSM-III-R psychiatric disorders in the United States. Results from the National Comorbidity Survey. *Archives of General Psychiatry, 51*(1), 8–19.

Kessler, R. C., Nelson, C. B., McGonagle, K. A., Edlund, M. J., Frank, R. G. & Leaf, P. J. (1996). The epidemiology of co-occurring addictive and mental disorders: implications for prevention and service utilization. *American Journal of Orthopsychiatry, 66*(1), 17–31.

Koskinen, J., Lohonen, J., Koponen, H., Isohanni, M. & Miettunen, J. (2010). Rate of cannabis use disorders in clinical samples of patients with schizophrenia: a meta-analysis. *Schizophrenia Bulletin, 36*(6), 1115–1130.

Lawn, S. & Pols, R. (2005). Smoking bans in psychiatric inpatient settings? A review of the research. *Australian and New Zealand Journal of Psychiatry, 39*, 866–885.

Lawrence, D., Holman, D. & Jablensky, A. (2001). *Preventable physical illness in people with mental illness.* Perth: University of Western Australia.

Lawrence, D., Mitrou, F. & Zubrick, S. R. (2009). Smoking and mental illness: results from population surveys in Australia and the United States. *BMC Public Health, 9*, 285.

Petersen, L., Jeppesen, P., Thorup, S., Ohlenschlaeger, J., Krarup, G., Ostergard, T. et al. (2007). Substance abuse and first-episode schizophrenia-spectrum disorders. The Danish OPUS trial. *Early Intervention in Psychiatry, 1*, 88–96.

Santa Ana, E., Wulfert, E. & Nietert, P. (2007). Efficacy of group motivational interviewing (GMI) for psychiatric inpatients with chemical dependence. *Journal of Consulting and Clinical Psychology, 75*(5), 816–822.

Spring, B., Pagoto, S., Pingitore, R., Doran, N., Schneider, K. & Hedeker, D. (2004). Randomized controlled trial for behavioral smoking and weight control treatment: effect of concurrent versus sequential intervention. *Journal of Consulting and Clinical Psychology, 72*(5), 785–796.

Spring, B., Schneider, K., McFadden, G., Vaughn, J., Kozak, A., Smith, M. et al. (2012). Multiple behavior changes in diet and activity: a randomized controlled trial using mobile technology. *Archives of Internal Medicine, 172*(10), 789–796.

Stead, L. F., Perera, R., Bullen, C., Mant, D. & Lancaster, T. (2008). Nicotine replacement therapy for smoking cessation. *Cochrane Database of Systematic Reviews 1*, CD000146.

Teesson, M., Hall, W., Slade, T., Mills, K., Grove, R., Mewton, L. et al. (2010). Prevalence and correlates of DSM-IV alcohol abuse and dependence in Australia: findings of the 2007 National Survey of Mental Health and Wellbeing. *Addiction, 105*(12), 2085–2094.

Toneatto, T. (2005). Cognitive versus behavioral treatment of concurrent alcohol dependence and agoraphobia: a pilot study. *Addictive Behaviors, 30*(1), 115–125.

Tsoi, D. T., Porwal, M. & Webster, A. C. (2010). Interventions for smoking cessation and reduction in individuals with schizophrenia. *Cochrane Database of Systematic Reviews 6*, CD007253.

Ziedonis, D. & Nickou, C. (2001). Substance abuse in patients with schizophrenia. In M. Y. Hwang & P. C. Bermanzohn (Eds.) *Schizophrenia and comorbid conditions: Diagnosis and treatment* (pp. 187–222). Washington, D.C.: American Psychiatric Press.

10

Counselling in Intensive Structured Day Treatment: The Co-production of Recovery

Tim Leighton

This chapter will trace the historical development in the United Kingdom of a model of community-based intensive treatment for people with drug and alcohol dependence who want to achieve a drug- and alcohol-free life. It will explore the role of counsellors currently working in two addiction treatment agencies where this model has been developed, most of whom have graduated from, or are studying on, an undergraduate degree programme in addictions counselling. The practice of counselling will be explored, in particular as it transforms in response to a developing recovery community. This phrase refers to increasingly visible groups of people in local communities who consider themselves in recovery from substance use problems and who organize themselves in various activities to support and empower themselves and others. Although mutual aid groups for people with alcohol and drug problems, such as Alcoholics Anonymous and Narcotics Anonymous, have long been established in the United Kingdom, over recent years there has been a marked increase in their number.

As the chapter considers aspects of programme development and implementation, and presents an organizing framework linking and rationalizing its components, I hope to identify the 'spirit' of this model of intensive treatment, by which is meant the set of principles and values that underlie it and are concretized in human interactions between clients and staff. These dynamic principles developed in practice may not be exclusive to this model but, taken together, they may distinguish it and make it recognizable. The chapter will attempt to illustrate how

Emerging Perspectives on Substance Misuse, First Edition. Edited by Willm Mistral.
© 2013 John Wiley & Sons, Ltd. Published 2013 by John Wiley & Sons, Ltd.

knowledge of evidence-supported approaches is used by counsellors, not mainly to implement discrete forms of these interventions familiar from research, but to shape conversations with clients within a complex multi-goal treatment programme.

What is Addictions Counselling?

In the United Kingdom in the second decade of the 21st century, the term 'addictions (or substance misuse) counselling' covers a wide range of activities, including stand-alone open-ended client-centred counselling (Edwards & Loeb, 2011), in which the counsellor offers a nonjudge-mental, empathic relationship to allow clients to express and explore their concerns; interventions such as motivational interviewing in vari-ous adaptations, usually brief (Marsden et al., 2006), which usually focus on ambivalence, reinforcing the client's reasons for and commitment to behaviour change; and cognitive-behavioural (CBT) or cognitive analytic (CAT) counselling (Leighton, 1997), both of which aim to help the client identify and revise patterns of thinking, behaviour and relationship.

It is probably quite rare for clients of substance-misuse services in the United Kingdom to be offered what are known as 'evidence-supported interventions' (apart from client-centred counselling and possibly moti-vational interviewing) outside of a research study. An *ad hoc* review of websites across England and Scotland, including some large national charities and local community drug and alcohol services, shows that many of these do not offer a service called 'counselling' at all. Some do, and occasionally an intervention such as behavioural couples ther-apy is offered (e.g. Open Road, 2011), in which a couple, of whom one has substance-related problems, are helped to contract with one another to reward desired behaviour change and avoid reinforcing prob-lem behaviour. Interventions such as relapse prevention in individual or group settings are frequently available, but often these are provided by staff identified as drug workers rather than counsellors. These interven-tions aim to build coping responses to situations and emotional states that have been identified as posing a high risk for relapse. At the time of writing the Substance Misuse Skills Consortium, an 'independent sector-led initiative' supported by the National Treatment Agency, lists most of the above-named interventions in their 'Skills Hub', plus others such as social behaviour and network therapy (Copello et al., 2002) and family therapy, but these are identified as specialist, requiring trained and super-vised staff, which many agencies do not have the resources to provide.

It is clear that addictions counselling does not have the same standing this side of the Atlantic as it does in the United States, where federally sponsored role delineation studies in the 1980s produced a list of core functions of the addictions counsellor and began the process of developing professional standards (Birch & Davis Associates, 1984). Since then a number of US publications have described the competencies required for addictions counselling, with the technical assistance publication updated by SAMHSA (Substance Abuse and Mental Health Services Administration) in 2005 being one of the most recent. However it is by no means certain that counsellors on the ground in US treatment services do in fact implement these standards, or practise in a coherent or consistent manner, or receive enough training or support to deliver recognizable evidence-based interventions (Carroll & Rounsaville, 2007; Eliason et al., 2005).

The SHARP Programme

Although there are beacons of good practice offering individual counselling which is both appropriate and of high quality (the Edwards & Loeb, 2011, article mentioned above provides an inspiring example), recent research has shown that, in addition to *individual* support, many people who have substance-dependence problems benefit from *social* support. For example, Kelly, Hoeppner, Stout & Pagano (2011) show how changes in a client's social network (both adding friends in recovery and reducing contact with drug-using people), as well an increase in 'social self-efficacy' (confidence to maintain abstinence in challenging social situations) predict good outcomes among members of Alcoholics Anonymous. Traditionally, models of rehabilitation designed to foster this sense of solidarity and mutual support have been offered in residential forms, most famously as the 'classic' Therapeutic Community and as the 'Minnesota Model' (see below), both of which have their origins in the mid-20th century. The latter, often incorrectly associated with a confrontational therapy style, was founded on the principle of treating people with dignity (Anderson, 1981; Spicer, 1993). It integrated the 'folk-wisdom' of Alcoholics Anonymous, in particular the therapeutic value of recovering people helping one other and the reformulation of the problem as a disease or 'malady', but in a rather different form to the medical disease model as it combined physical, mental, and spiritual aspects.

This chapter will concentrate on the historical development and current challenges of counselling within a model of community-based, structured and intensive treatment, which has attracted the nickname 'community rehab' in recognition of its origins in the residential treatment approaches mentioned. This model, currently implemented in two sites in the north-west and the south coast of England, and which is being rolled out with the assistance of the author's organization in a slightly different form and context in other areas of England, is the subject of ongoing development and research, and offers a good opportunity to observe and reflect on transformations in practice in response to local need. The agencies implementing the model do so under the name of SHARP (Self-Help Addiction Recovery Programme). Here, 'self-help' refers to a principle of the programme as founded, which was that recovery was very much more likely to be durable and rewarding if clients were introduced to, and encouraged to attend, what were then referred to as 'self-help groups', but are now known more accurately as 'mutual aid groups' such as Alcoholics Anonymous (AA) and Narcotics Anonymous (NA). The first SHARP agency opened in London in 1992, although it is no longer running, while SHARP Liverpool opened in 2005. These were operated by a charity, the Chemical Dependency Centre (CDC). SHARP Bournemouth and Poole was opened as a community day treatment programme by the charity Clouds, renamed Action on Addiction after merging with CDC and a research charity in 2007.

SHARP London began as a clearly Minnesota Model-type treatment, with an intensive 5 days per week programme to build a cohesive sense of group participation, using group therapy and educational lectures to help clients develop motivation for change, and to implement change as indicated by individualized treatment plans constructed from a comprehensive psycho-social assessment. The 12-week programme had a strong emphasis on affiliation with 12 Step mutual aid, as exemplified by AA, NA, and Cocaine Anonymous (CA), and promoted acceptance of a 'disease' conception of addiction, with a treatment aim of sustained complete abstinence from all drugs including alcohol. Although there is much from these origins that can be recognized in today's SHARP programmes, there has been a steady line of development, an early example of which was experimentation with different ways of handling lapses to alcohol or drug use while on the programme, with the aim of re-engaging clients who continued to want help while struggling with abstinence, and an attempt to establish a procedure that would not make it either too easy to reaccess the programme (risking a threat to the drug-free community and a failure to address the lapse issue) or too hard (risking losing a client in need).

A recent example of change, and one perhaps more challenging to the original philosophy, has been the development of concurrent 12 Step and non-12 Step streams within SHARP. The original programme not only strongly emphasized the 12-Step approach, but many of the activities (lectures, workshops, individual written assignments) specifically involved exploring the meaning and application of the 12 Steps together with obligatory attendance at several meetings each week. Currently, clients admitted to SHARP are able to choose whether they want a treatment experience that includes the intensive 12-Step exploration, or one that includes the group therapy, community, and counselling components but leaves out the formal 12-Step work. They do not have to choose their preferred path until they have started and are oriented to the programme. The non-12 Step clients are free to attend AA, NA or CA meetings if they wish, and some do so, but there is no requirement for this, and they are also informed about and may attend other mutual aid groups such as SMART Recovery groups if available. SMART Recovery (Self-Management and Recovery Training) is perhaps the best known of newer mutual aid groups, which have arisen as alternatives to the 12-Step programmes, and uses cognitive-behavioural tools in mutually supportive group meetings. Since the counsellors in the original Minnesota Model programmes were often people themselves in 12-Step recovery, it is likely that at one time there would have been anxiety and resistance about moving the 12-Step philosophy from the centre of the programme, but it does not seem to trouble the current counselling teams, which still include counsellors who identify themselves as being in recovery from addiction, but whose recovery status is far less obvious and less used as a treatment tool (i.e. being held up as a role model for recovery) than in the early years of this model.

Integration of Counselling Models

When the first SHARP programme opened in 1992, personal experience of recovery would have been thought of as a qualification for a counselling role, and training in counselling was somewhat rudimentary. In contrast, the counselling teams at the SHARP programmes today have received a much broader and more academically informed training (most of them have taken a specialist degree, which includes a theoretical and practical introduction to motivational interviewing, cognitive therapy, relapse prevention and interpersonal group therapy, and many also have generic counselling qualifications). The problem remains as to how to integrate this knowledge of counselling models into a group-based treatment programme that aspires to be more than the sum of its parts. SHARP does not consist of a series on individual counselling relationships. The core of the therapeutic experience is the group, and the counsellor's task is to support and escort individuals through the programme to make optimal use of its resources to address their particular difficulties. The programme aims to connect clients to a continuing system of support, voluntarily entered into and maintained by the clients themselves, and primarily peer based.

Counsellors seeing themselves primarily as individual therapists risk perpetuating what William White has called the 'pathology and intervention' paradigm of addictions treatment, whereby clinicians are trained to 'diagnose pathology' according to a range of theoretical frameworks, and then intervene to correct or mitigate this pathology (White, 2007). So an addicted client might have 'unresolved conflicts', 'irrational or maladaptive thinking', 'the disease of addiction' (which includes denial as a core symptom), 'insufficient motivation or coping skills', and so on. White (2007) and others (e.g. Orford, 2008) criticize this paradigm as being disappointingly ineffective and, especially, for ignoring natural recovery processes, including the development of recovering communities, which have enabled enormous numbers of people to find and experience recovery, often with minimal or no professional input. What the counselling teams at SHARP are trying to do is use their knowledge and skill in the counselling models in which they have been trained to individualize the treatment experience, to help clients build recovery and self-management skills, and also to connect them as active participants to the recovery resources in the community as described by White.

The way in which this is to be done is currently in the process of clarification with the development of a programme manual and counselling handbook, as will shortly be described. But, rather than attempting to impose demarcated 'evidence-supported' interventions within the programme, these documents have the aim of capturing the practice and analysing what the programme is doing concretely, to create change in the clients. The lack of a clear practice specification up to this point has permitted the creativity and intelligence of the teams, who are committed both to the wellbeing of their clients and to improving practice, to shape the programmes, including local variations. As requests for help in establishing the programme model in other areas arrive, it has become necessary to describe the framework clearly and coherently in a manual, and this process will also aid in improving supervision and staff team development in the established programmes.

Counselling staff at the two agencies currently offering this programme have expressed their ideas about what underpins the counselling practice at SHARP, and there is a shared view that the use of individuated models or approaches, such as cognitive therapy or motivational interviewing are secondary to maintaining a particular community spirit. One counsellor said that the staff '. . . express attitudes and behaviours towards clients that are non-threatening, and convey honesty, respect, caring and understanding. In my view SHARP follows this basic philosophy rather than simply implementing certain counselling techniques or methods.'

Here the implication is that the staff team strives to maintain conditions in which the clients' change processes are most likely to be activated. She goes on:

> There is also capacity to develop good interpersonal relationships as clients learn to relate freely and openly with each other (and staff) on the basis of immediate 'here and now' experiencing, and in so doing developing a richer self-awareness. At times it seems the sense of 'realness' in interactions at SHARP is probably the most important element in client interactions, along with empathy or understanding where our clients seem most anxious and vulnerable.

Another counsellor, who was inspired to apply for a job after experiencing the agency on a social work placement, said that in his view 'the principles of openness, transparency, compassion and love seep right through the very essence of SHARP.' Both of these counsellors stressed the 'integrity' of the agency, which they contrasted with other services at which problem users of drugs and alcohol might find themselves. They felt it was crucial to maintain a culture of inclusivity and respect which they believed, if modelled consistently by the staff, would transfer to the client group and create the conditions for individual participants to take up the resources offered by the programme and make life-changing choices. We can see here that the programme team, to the extent that they succeed in achieving their aspirations, are enacting a 'living theory', which implies certain mechanisms of change. In this case the theory is that by providing a trustworthy, respectful space, participants will open up, connect and develop richer self-awareness, which ought to lead to more adaptive choice making, and thus to the achievement of the aim of the programme. A slightly different version of this theory emerged from an interview with another counsellor who said, when asked what was the most important function of his counselling at SHARP, that his main aim was to have the client leave each session 'with head held high'. The idea here is that a condition inhibiting the mechanisms of change in the programme is one of shame, self-denigration or a feeling of failure. This counsellor makes it clear that he is more concerned with facilitating a state of being in the client which will enable them to take up the resources offered, rather than in specifying the model or approach he is using.

Although there are exceptions to this emphasis on process (one of the counsellors at Bournemouth has more advanced training in cognitive behaviour therapy and clients referred to her are thought to be suitable for this specific approach), for the most part it seems that the counsellors agree that activating change mechanisms can be achieved in a range of different ways and that they use their training in the 'evidence-supported' models to form their interactions, and to 'internally supervise' their work. So a counsellor in conversation with a client struggling with ambivalence might ask herself in an internal reflective process how consonant she is being with the spirit of motivational interviewing or, during a group therapy session, to what extent the group is engaged in interpersonal learning in the 'here and now' and what she might do to help the group work productively. Of course the treatment group consists of individuals – both clients and staff – and these make individual contributions to the process and have their individual aspirations. Their change processes are in large part based on their reasoned responses and choices. However in two senses this also involves social reality. The processes described in the previous section cannot simply be reduced to the interpersonal but must also be seen in a collective, institutional frame: the staff and clients make up a community with 'arrangements, conventions and agreements' (Greenwood, 1994). And so we can attempt to express the ethos that expresses, develops and maintains these as 'the spirit of SHARP'. The second sense in which the interactions within the programme represent a social reality is that individuals' choices are constrained (and enabled) by the social and cultural structures in which they are embedded. A young working-class person in Liverpool, for example, has opportunities and limitations shaped by local and more distal structures of power and tradition, involving issues of class, race and gender and the norms of what Robert Merton (1957) termed 'reference groups'. Choices are not entirely free.

The idea of SHARP as a transformative community involves a three-cornered relationship between the client group in need, the programme, and the local 'recovering community'. Each will influence the others.

One of the advantages of basing a programme like SHARP in the community is that the relationship with local recovery groups and organized recovery resources can be maintained and developed. Compared with an enclosed setting such as a residential centre, clients are exposed to more environmental risks for drug or alcohol use, as drugs and alcohol are more accessible and drug offers and temptations may be experienced. However, the advantages of connection with local recovery organizations are considerable, allowing the clients to encounter and participate in a new 'reference group' while still in the programme. Additionally the self-efficacy that can be developed as a result of not succumbing to such offers and temptations, and understanding the role of peer group support in resisting these and making responsible choices, is of huge value in developing 'recovery capital'. One of the requirements to make these relationships work is that the programme must exhibit what I term 'local congruence'. In my view the programme will only successfully challenge hindrances and create change if it is recognizable by clients and families, if it 'makes sense' in local terms, and if it demonstrates understanding and recognition of local conditions. This is important as the change process is not analogous to a dose of a technological treatment delivered to passive clients. It involves active participation to 'co-produce' change, by creating conditions that allow the mechanisms for change to operate. To achieve this there must be, as Pawson & Tilley (1997, p. 75) point out, some knowledge of the social processes that oppose change.

The Framework

The framework being developed to guide and improve practice is based on identifying four processes, overlapping rather than strictly sequential: 'motivation and engagement', 'generating psychosocial change', 'building recovery capital' and 'reintegration and recovery'. For each of these processes there is a set of assessment tools, a set of core activities essential to the programme, a group of optional activities that can be shaped to the local context. Each of these processes is guided by principles constituting the spirit of SHARP. The domains of recovery capital referred to in the framework derive from an instrument called 'Assessment of Recovery Capital' or ARC (Groshkova, Best & White, 2013) and comprise substance use and sobriety, global psychological health, global physical health, citizenship, social support, meaningful activities, housing and safety, risk taking, coping and life functioning, and recovery experience.

The framework for SHARP is designed so that all core and optional activities contribute to building these domains (in our framework 'citizenship' has been renamed 'community involvement' as the former word is open to misunderstanding). So the introduction of a (noncore) treatment element into a local SHARP programme (for example a workshop or shared group experience like a communal meal) is legitimized by its potential to build recovery capital and its local congruence (as well as its compliance with our organization's code of ethics).

Motivation and Engagement

The first process is that of motivation and engagement. There is considerable research (e.g. Simpson & Joe, 1993; Simpson, Joe, Rowan-Szal & Greener, 1995) indicating that motivation and engagement are associated with better outcomes. There is also evidence that enhancing counselling and creating a good therapeutic relationship improves engagement both during the programme and in continuing care activities (e.g. Harris, McKellar, Moos, Schaeffer & Cronkite, 2006). At SHARP the spirit of this process involves introducing people to the idea that they are invited to become part of a community or joint endeavour. The message is that mutuality leads to empowerment. This starts a journey intended to continue after the programme is completed. Motivation and engagement also involve reaching out and listening to the client. A core activity is assessment of the client's drug or alcohol problem, their family and social situation, and perhaps reviewing the care plan they bring with them from their community-care assessment. The counsellor will adopt the principles of motivational interviewing in the first individual meetings, helping clients assess the need for change, eliciting their hopes and concerns, and identifying resources. They will discuss choosing a drug/alcohol change goal, expecting and accepting some ambivalence, but recognizing and affirming change talk. While counsellors answer questions and provide information about the programme, they sensitively emphasize the sharing of responsibility for change and the importance of becoming an active member of the group. The remaining processes of 'generating psychosocial change', 'building recovery capital' and 'reintegration and recovery' are mutually related and overlapping. However, they have been differentiated for clarity, although each involves increases in domains of recovery capital, in particular social, human and cultural capital (Cloud & Granfield, 2008).

179

Generating Psychosocial Change

The process of 'generating psychosocial change' is based on a collaborative exploration of the clients' social history, assessing their relationships and life goals, as well as personal meaning and values. This process aims to increase recovery capital in the domains of social functioning, attitude to substance use, global psychological health, and meaningful activities. The core therapeutic activities are the development of an individual treatment plan, interpersonal group therapy (Flores, 1997; Leighton, 2004; Yalom, 1995), and individual counselling, with the aims of increasing commitment to recovery, empowerment through responsible choice-making, and developing more fulfilling relationships. Examples of optional activities that support the relevant recovery capital domains are workshops on social functioning, for example dealing with people, responsibility, self-care, substance misuse issues, or an introduction to mindfulness-based relapse prevention. The spirit of SHARP for this process may be expressed as enacting the values of acceptance, valuing and aspiration. Self-acceptance and acceptance of others is attained through participation in an ethos of mutual acceptance. This means acceptance of persons and their potential, not acceptance of destructive or self-defeating behaviour. The belief is that only in a respectful, accepting atmosphere can such problematic behaviours be effectively challenged. This process concentrates on the development of hope and an increase in self-efficacy. Improving clients' ability in interpersonal relating is likely to increase their ability to participate in mutual support (Caldwell & Cutter, 1998; Leighton, 2004).

Building Recovery Capital

The process of building recovery capital involves enhancing resources for recovery such as relapse-prevention skills, improved family relationships, and knowledge of mutual aid available in the local community. As already mentioned, a distinguishing aspect of the spirit of SHARP is the encouragement of clients to participate in a network of mutual support. However the team takes a pluralistic and open-minded view of mutual support. While the history of SHARP has created a highly supportive (but not uncritical) attitude towards the 12-Step mutual aid organizations such as Narcotics Anonymous, Alcoholics Anonymous, and Cocaine Anonymous, wherever possible the counsellors will help clients explore other forms of mutual aid, such as SMART Recovery. So the core activities for this process are:

- the building of a recovery plan that looks beyond the treatment episode;
- using node-mapping, i.e. clients making guided diagrammatic and pictorial descriptions of goals, choices and resources as specified by the International Treatment Effectiveness Protocol (ITEP) (National Treatment Agency for Substance Misuse, 2008);
- mutual aid exploration (visiting meetings of NA, AA, SMART Recovery, reading and discussing literature, and gaining knowledge of how mutual aid works);
- introductory relapse prevention workshops; and
- facilitated family meetings designed to improve communication and, if necessary, to begin the process of repairing relationships.

The domains of recovery capital targeted during this process are 'meaningful activities', 'social support', 'community involvement', 'recovery experience', and managing 'risk taking'. As well as the core activities mentioned, optional workshops might be offered on offending behaviour, financial issues, or risky situations and behaviours. Community activities such as a weekly communal lunch, to which clients bring dishes and beverages, or excursions such as theatre trips or walks, are useful additions to the programme, as are art or creative-writing workshops.

Reintegration and Recovery

The fourth process is 'reintegration and recovery'. Here the core activities are relapse prevention skills-building workshops, and family meetings to discuss expectations and the distribution of responsibilities after treatment. The clients continue to build links with the local recovering community, and optional workshops may be offered on socializing and having fun without drugs or alcohol, parenting, or mindfulness-based relapse prevention. These activities aim to build recovery capital in the domains of 'coping/life-functioning', 'community involvement', 'social support', and 'recovery experience'. In addition, needs assessment, advice and practical help are offered concerning finances (debts, benefits, budgeting) and housing, to increase capital in the 'housing & safety' domain. This may be the responsibility of assigned support workers (as in Bournemouth) or be managed by the team including the counsellors (as in Liverpool). As clients move through the programme they are introduced to linked community resources, such as the Brink, an alcohol-free pub in Liverpool, where there may be volunteering or even employment possibilities, as well as a place where social enjoyment may be experienced in a safe environment. In Bournemouth clients may wish to explore 'Working Recovery', a training programme open to people in recovery. There may be some opportunities for volunteering at the SHARP projects themselves, after a suitable period of sustained recovery.

The SHARP teams are committed to fostering the autonomy of clients. The goal of the programme is to remove barriers to making responsible choices and building the kind of life the clients themselves aspire to. However, there are different varieties of autonomy, and it clear that the type particularly fostered by programmes like SHARP is what Jensen & Mooney (1990) call 'social autonomy', associated with 'the ethical principle of solidarity'. Autonomy in this understanding is an end which is realized only under certain social conditions, whereby "we act as responsible persons in relation to our own lives and those of others" (Jensen & Mooney, 1990, pp. 6, 11). The ethical code of SHARP supports absolutely the right of individuals to be free from coercion and free to choose their own beliefs, values and traditions, but it is by creatively and constructively sharing those values in a spirit of trust and support that true autonomy emerges and recovery for communities becomes a reality.

SHARP Counsellors

This description of the programme framework and its ethical context gives an intimation of the skill, sensitivity, and intelligence required by SHARP counsellors. They need to understand and be able to apply principles and techniques from motivational interviewing, cognitive therapy and interpersonal group therapy. They need to have an excellent knowledge of mutual help groups, including their strengths and limitations, in order to help clients make best and safest use of them, while avoiding dogmatic prescription. They need skills in helping adults to learn, in order to run focused, participatory, and inclusive workshops. They will escort individuals though the experience of the programme, while collectively fostering a healthy, safe, structured and task-oriented community of participants. They must be sensitive to vulnerable clients, offering support and also building the clients' capacity to both receive and offer it. They must be able to work with individuals, couples and groups.

Despite the quotes from the counsellors above, who make it clear that the environment, the relationships, the atmosphere of the programme take precedence over specific 'named techniques', it is clear to me from having run supervision groups and training sessions at SHARP Liverpool and having had discussions with counsellors from SHARP Bournemouth & Poole, that in fact concepts and techniques from the 'evidence-based' models are very much alive in their thoughts and conversations.

Future Directions

It is hoped that the framework described in this chapter will serve as a tool to focus SHARP counsellors' thinking and conversation, so that the training received in the models may be even more effectively integrated in the future. It will, I hope, help to bring those approaches to bear in order to foster 'recovery management' rather than being used within a 'pathology and intervention' paradigm.

We have recently used the framework described to create a new clinical manual, which includes guidance for including activities that suit the local situation. We are currently using the framework to guide the setting up of new projects using the SHARP model. There has been considerable recent interest in the model, and in 2012, in different areas of England, a Drug Action Team decided to run a pilot programme with a view to offering this model at local sites, and an alcohol service was also intending to offer the programme. These provide an excellent opportunity to discover how the model will work in different contexts. Both of these areas as yet lack the range of mutual help support available in Liverpool and Bournemouth, though it could be claimed that the presence of SHARP, together with another 12 Step-based residential programme, was a factor in the rapid development of the recovering community in Liverpool. It may well be that the establishment of the new programmes will also result in a stronger recovery support system in the respective communities, which will in turn support future graduates of the programmes more effectively.

Conclusion

The evidence base, as it appears in guidelines compiled by authoritative bodies such as the National Institute for Health and Clinical Excellence (National Institute for Health and Clinical Excellence, 2008) is equivocal about residential treatment programmes and says virtually nothing about intensive day programmes. The randomized controlled studies required for endorsement by such guidelines are rare and of poor quality. Moreover the sparse evidence for efficacy and cost effectiveness that compares residential and day rehabilitation programmes typically treats these as 'black boxes', that is to say that it does not get to grips with the structure and processes of such programmes. The executive summary of the NICE guideline states that

> the same range of psychosocial interventions should be available in inpatient and residential settings as in community settings. These should normally include contingency management, behavioural couples therapy, and cognitive behavioural therapy. Services should encourage and facilitate participation in self-help groups. (National Institute for Health and Clinical Excellence, 2008, p. 21)

However, it is clear that what is meant is a collection of individually evidenced and discrete interventions. What this chapter has tried to do is to show that in SHARP these elements are combined in relationship to form a complex, multi-stranded and multi-goal programme, the aim of which is to build recovery capital and foster social autonomy, embedded within and mutually supportive of the local recovery community.

References

Anderson, D. (1981). *The Minnesota experience.* Center City, MN: Hazelden Education Service.

Birch & Davis Associates, Inc. (1984). *Development of model professional standards for counselor credentialing.* Rockville, MD: National Institute on Alcohol Abuse and Alcoholism, Rockville MD.

Caldwell, P. E. & Cutter, H. S. G. (1998). Alcoholics anonymous affiliation during early recovery. *Journal of Substance Abuse Treatment, 15*(3), 221–228.

Carroll, K. & Rounsaville, B. (2007). A vision of the next generation of behavioral therapies research in the addictions. *Addiction, 102*(6), 850–862.

Cloud, W. & Granfield, R. (2008). Conceptualizing recovery capital: Expansion of a theoretical construct. *Substance Use and Misuse, 43*(12–13), 1971–1986.

Copello, A., Orford, J., Hodgson, R., Tober, G. & Barrett, C. (2002). Social behaviour and network therapy: basic principles and early experiences. *Addictive Behaviors, 27*(3), 345–366.

Edwards, J. & Loeb, S. (2011). What difference does counselling make? The perceptions of drug-using clients on low incomes. *Counselling and Psychotherapy Research, 11*(2), 105–111.

Eliason, M. J., Arndt, S. & Schut, A. (2005). Substance abuse counseling: what is treatment as usual? In E. Edmundson & D. McCarty (Eds.) *Implementing evidence-based practices for treatment of alcohol and drug disorders.* Binghamton, NY: Haworth Press.

Flores, P. J. (1997). *Group psychotherapy with addicted populations: An integration of Twelve-step and psychodynamic theory* (2nd ed.). Philadelphia, PA: Haworth Press.

Greenwood, J. D. (1994). *Realism, identity and emotion: Reclaiming social psychology.* London: Sage Publications Limited.

Groshkova, T., Best, D. & White, W. (2013). The assessment of recovery capital: Properties and psychometrics of a measure of addiction recovery strengths. *Drug and Alcohol Review, 32,* 187–194.

Harris, A. H. S., McKellar, J. D., Moos, R. H., Schaeffer, J. A. & Cronkite, R. C. (2006). Predictors of engagement in continuing care following residential substance use disorder treatment. *Drug and Alcohol Dependence, 84*(1), 93–101.

Jensen, U. J. & Mooney, G. H. (Eds.) (1990). *Changing values in medical and health care decision making.* Chichester: John Wiley & Sons, Ltd.

Kelly, J. F., Hoeppner, B., Stout, R. L. & Pagano, M. (2011). Determining the relative importance of the mechanisms of behavior change within Alcoholics Anonymous: a multiple mediator analysis. *Addiction, 107*(2), 289–299.

Leighton, T. (1997). Borderline personality and substance abuse problems. In A. Ryle (Ed.) *Cognitive analytic therapy and borderline personality disorder: The model and the method.* Chichester: John Wiley.

Leighton, T. (2004). Interpersonal group therapy in intensive treatment. In B. Reading & M. Weegmann (Eds.). *Group psychotherapy and addiction.* London: Whurr.

Marsden, J., Stillwell, G., Barlow, H., Boys, A., Taylor, C., Hunt, N. et al. (2006). An evaluation of a brief motivational intervention among young ecstasy and cocaine users: no effect on substance and alcohol use outcomes. *Addiction, 101*(7), 1014–1026.

Merton, R. K. (1957). Continuities in the theory of reference groups and social structure. In R. K. Merton *Social theory and social structure* (pp. 335–440). Glencoe, IL: Free Press.

National Institute for Health and Clinical Excellence (2008). *Psychosocial interventions for drug misuse – National Clinical Practice Guideline 51.* London: National Collaborating Centre for Mental Health, British Psychological Society & the Royal College of Psychiatrists.

National Treatment Agency for Substance Misuse (2008). *Routes to recovery, Part 2: the ITEP manual.* London: National Treatment Agency for Substance Misuse.

Open Road (2011). Behavioural Couples Therapy. Retrieved March 11, 2013 from http://openroad.org.uk/what_we_do/behavioural_couples_therapy/.

Orford, J. (2008). Asking the right questions in the right way: the need for a shift in research on psychological treatments for addiction. *Addiction, 103*(5), 1–11.

Pawson, R. & Tilley, N. (1997). *Realistic evaluation.* London: Sage Publications.

Simpson, D. D. & Joe, G. W. (1993). Motivation as a predictor of early dropout from drug abuse treatment. *Psychotherapy: Theory, Research, Practice, Training, 30*(2), 357–368.

Simpson, D. D., Joe, G. W., Rowan-Szal, G. & Greener, J. (1995). Client engagement and change during drug abuse treatment. *Journal of Substance Abuse, 7*(1), 117–134.

Spicer, J. (1993). *The Minnesota Model: The evolution of the multidisciplinary approach to addiction recovery.* Center City, MN: Hazelden Educational Materials.

White, W. (2007). Addiction recovery: its definition and conceptual boundaries. *Journal of Substance Abuse Treatment, 33*(3), 229–241.

Yalom, I. D. (1995). *The theory and practice of group psychotherapy.* New York: Basic Books.

11

Movements Towards Recovery
Willm Mistral and Stephen Wilkinson

Society's response to the use (and perceived misuse) of drugs and alcohol has varied dramatically over time both within and between countries, with government policies ranging from *laissez-faire* to legal controls, criminalization of possession of certain substances, and treatment for dependence. The objectives of both government policy and professional practice with regard to psychotropic substance use have met with varying degrees of acceptance, success and failure (amply illustrated throughout other chapters of the present volume). The concept of mutual help to support recovery from problematic use of drugs or alcohol has been around for a considerable time, but recently the concept of recovery has moved up the official agenda and is being presented, in various formats, as the new way forward in government policy.

The United Kingdom was the first country to adopt a managed treatment and substitute prescribing approach to drug use (without, nevertheless, dispensing with legal controls and criminalization), following a report by the Rolleston Committee (1926). From that time, people dependent on heroin and morphine were provided with a medical prescription to obtain a maintenance dose of the drug. This approach continued for about 40 years until the opiate replacement, methadone, was introduced, and this form of substitute prescribing for opiate dependence, using a number of different drugs, continues today in most developed countries.

Across the world the number of people receiving treatment for substance misuse runs into tens of millions. In the United States the

Emerging Perspectives on Substance Misuse, First Edition. Edited by Willm Mistral.
© 2013 John Wiley & Sons, Ltd. Published 2013 by John Wiley & Sons, Ltd.

Substance Abuse and Mental Health Services Administration (SAMHSA) undertakes regular national surveys on substance use and health. For 2009 this survey reported that 23.5 million people needed treatment for an illicit drug or alcohol related problem (9.3% of those aged 12 or older). Of these, 2.6 million (11.2%) received treatment at a specialist facility. There are over 13,000 specialized drug treatment facilities in the United States providing counselling, behavioural therapy, medication, case management, and other services to persons with substance-use disorders. Among these are about 1,400 methadone maintenance programs serving over 254,000 patients, according to a 2006 report (National Institute on Drug Abuse, 2010, 2011).

The European Monitoring Centre for Drugs and Drug Addiction (2012) estimates that at least 1.1 million people received treatment for illicit drug use in the European Union, Croatia, Turkey and Norway during 2010, and more than half of these clients were prescribed opioid substitutes. In England alone there are about 1,200 National Health Service (NHS) and voluntary sector drug and alcohol services treating around 200,000 adults in the community every year. Approximately 150,000 of these service users are being prescribed regular doses of methadone or another substitute drug, with about 40,000 having received this treatment for more than 4 years (National Drug Treatment Monitoring System, 2011).

The logic underpinning the strategy of substitute prescribing, as well as syringe-exchange projects, has been that of 'harm-reduction', and there is evidence that this has reduced the spread of HIV and other severe health problems among injecting drug users (e.g. Hartel & Schoenbaum, 1998; Stimson, 1995); and reduced acquisitive crime to fund drug use (Ward, Mattick & Hall, 2009). However, in recent years voices have been raised insisting that this approach is not only insufficient to tackle drug-related problems, but counterproductive. Many people on prescribed substitute drugs continue to 'top-up' with heroin, or transfer to misuse of other drugs or alcohol (Bell, 2010). Even those service users who adhere to their substitute prescription often report that this treatment can lead to stigma, discrimination, and a life constrained by daily methadone collections (Harris & McElrath, 2012; Neale, Nettleton & Pickering, 2012). Another concern is that providing substitute drugs, such as methadone, simply compounds dependence (Home Office, 2012; Strang, 2011).

A report published in England by the Centre for Policy Studies (Gyngell, 2011) strongly argues that the policy of harm reduction by maintenance prescribing impedes recovery from addiction; that the number of addicts has not reduced; fewer than 4% emerge from treatment free from dependency; and referrals to residential rehabilitation units (see below for evidence of the effectiveness of this treatment) have fallen to an all-time low. However, an opposing view is presented in a report from the National Treatment Agency (National Treatment Agency for Substance Misuse, 2012b), which states that demand for treatment is falling, with the number of young people coming into treatment for heroin use down 62% since 2006. People over 40 years of age now make up almost a third of the treatment population, and it is thought that many of these started using heroin during the epidemics of the 1980s and 1990s, and now their health is failing and they are seeking treatment (National Treatment Agency for Substance Misuse, 2012b).

However one gauges the relative success of substitute prescribing treatment programs, either as a way of reducing harm, crime or demand for illicit substances, in the light of rising costs of state-funded treatment, criminal justice and welfare, and a desire to do more to tackle substance misuse problems, across many developed Western countries there has been a recent change of policy focus from maintaining people in treatment to that of delivering 'recovery' (Neale et al., 2012).

Recovery

Historically, 'recovery' has been associated with the 12-Step programmes of Alcoholics Anonymous and Narcotics Anonymous (see below), which view alcoholism and drug addiction as a disease, with recovery necessitating total abstinence and radical changes of lifestyle. Until recently the term 'recovery' had become used in a pejorative way, in parallel with criticism of the disease model and growth of the controlled drinking and harm reduction movements. Recovery as a valid concept now appears to have been rehabilitated, although not necessarily associated with 12 Step programmes.

The Substance Abuse and Mental Health Services Administration in the United States has a working definition of recovery as a 'process of change through which individuals improve their health and wellness, live a self-directed life, and strive to reach their full potential' (Substance Abuse and Mental Services Administration, 2011). And the UK Drug Policy Commission (UK Drug Policy Commission 2012, p. 14) tells us that 'Recovery from problematic substance use is a process that involves not only achieving control over drug use, but also involves improved health and wellbeing and building a new life, including family and social relationships, education, voluntary activities and employment'. While these aspirational definitions are to be commended, without greater clarity and detail it could prove difficult for public authorities, using a 'top-down' approach, to commission or deliver the personalized care packages required to meet the varied needs of individuals with different presenting and underlying drug-related problems. Also, the absence of a more detailed definition of 'recovery' has allowed it to be seen as in direct opposition to a harm reduction approach (Neale et al., 2012). For example, Gyngell (2011) argues that abstinence-based rehabilitation is by far the best and, in the long run, the cheapest method of helping addicts to recover, and the only way to achieve this is by public authorities de-investing in substitute prescribing and investing more in modern residential rehabilitation.

This chapter now goes on describe residential rehabilitation and evidence supporting its contribution to recovery from drug and alcohol misuse, before considering how merging residential rehabilitation, mutual help, and recovery communities, as well as harm-reduction approaches could assist the 'recovery agenda'.

What is Residential Rehabilitation?

Residential rehabilitation, or 'rehab', has become known in the popular news/entertainment media as a short-term 'drying-out' break for 'celebrities'. In the United Kingdom tabloid newspapers and magazines regularly feature lurid tales of 'stars' who 'check into rehab' having 'hit rock bottom'. And, in the United States, a reality television show (Celebrity Rehab with Dr. Drew) has run over six seasons with a changing cast of celebrities struggling with alcohol and drug addiction. However, the UK National Treatment Agency for Substance Misuse tells us that 'The popular notion of a spell in rehab, beloved of the tabloids, is not representative of mainstream treatment and recovery services provided in England by the NHS and voluntary sector. The reality is more complex' (National Treatment Agency for Substance Misuse 2012a, p. 4).

Residential rehabilitation is a form of treatment usually reserved for people with medium or high levels of alcohol and/or drug dependence, particularly those for whom controlled drinking or drug use has not worked and alternative forms of treatment have not been successful. As the name suggests, people move into a residential facility, for an agreed period of time, often 3 to 6 months or longer. These residential centres offer an environment free of alcohol and drugs where clients, in the care of qualified staff, are able to spend recovery-time in the company of others with similar problems. Compared to community-based treatment, one of the benefits of residential rehabilitation is removing clients from risky communities, and cues that normally result in drinking and drug use, such as a family arguments, or isolation.

Residential rehabilitation clinics have some common defining characteristics, although they also vary in their facilities and approaches. Clients will normally sign a contract that explicitly states that they will be discharged if they breach rules on abstinence. Treatment usually includes psychological and behavioural interventions, counselling, educational courses, and holistic therapies. Days are usually structured, with a combination of one-to-one counselling and group therapy, as well as a choice of activities such as art therapy, sport, life skills, cooking, financial management and family/couples therapy for relatives.

In the United Kingdom, the National Health Service (NHS) and some voluntary services offer access to rehab centres free of cost to the client. Around 100 clinics in England are regularly commissioned by these services to provide residential rehabilitation treatment. Typically NHS-funded residential rehabilitation will be offered as a last resort to individuals for whom other forms of treatment have had little or no success, even though clients themselves may frequently request it and be all too aware of the risks faced by them in the community. One reason for this is that, of all the treatment types and settings available, residential rehab is at the expensive end of the spectrum. Prices vary according to provider, but the average is around £600 a week (although a number of clinics catering for private patients, including 'celebrities', charge substantially more than this). As the average time spent in residential rehab is 13 weeks, commissioners spend around £8,000 each time a person is referred for inpatient treatment. This makes rehab notably more expensive than a comparable period of treatment in a community setting. In England, residential rehabilitation currently accounts for 2% of people in adult drug treatment but 10% of central funding (National Treatment Agency for Substance Misuse, 2012a). So, commissioners have to decide if it is worth the extra cost, although if residential rehabilitation is successful, even as a first positive step towards recovery, it would work out considerably cheaper than a lifetime of methadone prescriptions, often associated with a lifetime of welfare payments (Gyngell, 2011; Hansard, 2010).

Evidence for Residential Rehabilitation

Residential rehabilitation for people with drug and/or alcohol problems has demonstrated positive outcomes in many research studies over the past 30 years (e.g. Bennett & Rigby, 1990; De Leon, Janchill & Wexler, 1982; Gossop, Marsden, Stewart & Rolfe, 1999; Harris, Kivlahan, Barnett & Finney, 2012). Also, clients rate it most highly of all interventions (National Treatment Agency for Substance Misuse, 2006). Completing an agreed time in residential treatment has been consistently associated with positive changes in drug use, psychological health, medical health, criminal activity, and employment. In the United States, the Drug Abuse Treatment Outcome Study (DATOS), showed good outcomes after one year for clients treated in long-term residential or in short-term inpatient treatment modalities. Regular cocaine use (the most common presenting problem in that evaluation) was reduced by about two-thirds among clients in both the long-term and short-term programs, as was regular use of heroin (Hubbard, Craddock, Flynn, Anderson & Etheridge, 1997). In the United Kingdom, the National Treatment Outcome Research Study (NTORS) examined outcomes after end-of-treatment discharge from 16 residential rehabilitation programmes, and found that 51% of clients had been abstinent from heroin and other opiates throughout the three months prior to follow-up. Rates of drug injection were also halved, and rates of needle sharing were reduced to less than a third of intake levels (Gossop, Marsden, Stewart & Rolfe, 1999).

However, for any treatment to be effective a client must be retained for sufficient time for it to have an impact (Meier, Donmall, McElduff, Barrowclough & Heller, 2006). With regard to residential treatment, however, there is conflicting evidence as to the optimum appropriate length of stay. A substantial body of research has found longer stays in community residential care and in therapeutic communities to be linked with better outcomes, as well as lower readmission rates (e.g. Condelli & Hubbard, 1994; Ghose, 2008; Gottheil, McLellan, Druley, 1992; Moos & Moos, 1995). By way of contrast, Witbrodt et al. (2007) found that residential and day hospital treatment for up to 2 months, but not beyond this time, was associated with greater likelihood of abstinence at follow-up. After the first 2 months, these authors suggest, engaging patients in community 12-step programmes (more on this below) is a better use of resources. And, a study of 1,307 patients in 28 randomly selected programmes in the United States reported that 60 to 90 day programmes produced no more improvement than shorter ones, and an average length of stay of more than 90 days could not be justified by the severity of substance use disorder or the magnitude of the clinical improvement observed (Harris et al., 2012).

Problems with Residential Rehabilitation

With some differences of opinion as to the optimal length of time, the above studies demonstrate positive outcomes for many clients who complete their stay in residential rehabilitation. Unfortunately, however, other research shows that a majority of those who enter these facilities fail to complete their agreed time in treatment.

Meier (2005) contacted 87 residential facilities in England and had responses from 65%. Retention data indicated that only 48% of clients completed all treatment as scheduled. On average 32% dropped out, and 19% were asked to leave by the treatment service. Different facilities' retention rates varied dramatically, with between 3% and 92% of clients completing treatment, between zero and 93% dropping out, and between zero and 55% being asked to leave.

Using data from the UK National Drug Treatment Monitoring System (NDTMS) the National Drug Evidence Centre (2005) found that the strongest predictor of retention and completion of treatment was related to the agency rather than the client. At the best performing agency, 9% of new entrants dropped out in the first 2 weeks, and 24% dropped out within the first 6 months. At the worst performing agency, however, over 25% dropped out in the first two weeks and almost 66% dropped out within 6 months. A study for the National Treatment Agency examining characteristics of the treatment regimes (Meier, 2005) identified a number of factors associated with better retention. These included higher rates of single room occupancy, a higher ratio of staff to clients, fewer housekeeping duties, higher service fees, and one to two hours per week of individual counselling. The key conclusion from Meier (2005) was that residential services can be structured to improve retention and that, while client characteristics are important, services must take considerable responsibility for the outcomes they achieve. Improvements in preadmission assessments and preparation so that clients know what to expect in residential rehabilitation should reduce the dropout rate.

Service Users' Views

A relatively small study in England (Wilkinson, Mistral & Golding, 2008) interviewed clients from residential rehabilitation units and found they had only minor complaints, such as activities that they had expected were not available, or compulsory activities, or visiting restrictions. Many had found it difficult when other clients left prematurely or restarted drinking or using drugs. In summary, the most useful aspects of residential treatment were perceived to be as follows:

- a safe place to get well, away from risky, harmful environments or individuals;
- group work, getting feedback, support, and understanding in a non-judgemental way, contributing to a sense of therapeutic community;
- the 12-Step program (more on this below), particularly Steps 1 and 2 about uncontrollability and hope of recovery, which provided a theoretical basis for understanding and combating addiction, along with cognitive strategies for relapse prevention;
- counsellors and key workers who were understanding, nonjudgemental, and provided educational advice and practical assistance.

Despite evidence for the success of completed residential rehabilitation, it does not necessarily provide an exit from the treatment system, and people frequently require ongoing structured support in the community. The quality of the support network on discharge, and an understanding family, were seen as the most important factor in maintaining recovery. It is clear treatment commissioners and providers need to consider arrangements for aftercare, taking a comprehensive holistic approach to client needs, including childcare, housing, training and education, employment, family and relationship concerns.

Emerging Approaches to Rehabilitation

The above feedback suggests that residential treatment should not be viewed as a stand-alone treatment, but as a part of a continuum of care. Responding to this, new providers of rehabilitation services in the United Kingdom are bringing with them innovative ideas and different ways to deliver interventions. Traditionally, residential facilities have been located in large houses in the countryside or by the coast, away from the inner city areas where many users became addicted. This pattern is changing as providers respond to new thinking, and market opportunities, by offering alternative urban arrangements based around housing support. Housing support is help provided to enable a person to manage on a day-to-day basis while living in their own home. It can include assistance with budgeting and bills, planning meals and shopping, emotional support, or help to pursue social or leisure interests, as well as educational and work skills. Among the service providers interviewed for a National Treatment Agency for Substance Misuse (2009) report, a small but growing trend was noticed in residential services whose clients live locally. The reasons for this include meeting specific local needs, facilitating family contact, and having better resettlement and aftercare links. These innovative developments, combining local accommodation and an off-site treatment program, are sometimes called 'quasi-residential' services.

Mutual Help

A very common source of support for people seeking to recover from substance-use problems comes from attendance at local mutual help meetings where people who have shared similar problems with alcohol or drugs offer each other mutual help and support. The practice of mutual help and peer support to combat addiction and sustain recovery has been around for a considerable time. Abstinence-based religious and temperance movements, many of which arose in the 18th and 19th centuries, could be seen as the forerunners of the largest and most well known of ongoing mutual help organizations, Alcoholics Anonymous (AA). This was founded in the United States in 1935, and now counts over 2 million members worldwide (AA Fact File, 2012). Alcoholics Anonymous is based upon mutual help through group meetings and a program of 12 Steps (Alcoholics Anonymous, 2012). Although several of these steps stress turning to God, and the power of prayer, in order to overcome the addicted person's defects and shortcomings, many people attend AA who are not necessarily religious but are willing to work with the 12 Steps principles. These include, in summary, admitting that one cannot control addiction; recognizing that some higher power (however personally defined) can give strength; examining past errors with the help of an experienced AA member; where possible making amends for these errors; learning to live a new life; and helping others who suffer from the same addictions or compulsions.

Alcoholics Anonymous was followed a few years later by Narcotics Anonymous (NA), and then many other offshoot organizations focused on mutual aid to overcome a wide variety of 'addictions'. A number of studies have investigated the relationship between attendance at AA or

NA meetings following professional treatment, and substance-use outcomes (e.g. Gossop et al., 2008; Kelly, Brown, Abrantes, Kahler & Myers, 2008; Kelly, Hoeppner, Stout & Pagano, 2012a; Kelly, Urbanowsky, Hoeppner & Slaymaker, 2012b; Kissin, McLeod & McKay, 2003). These studies indicate that AA and NA have positive effects in facilitating and maintaining recovery from substance misuse, especially if group meetings are attended regularly over an extended period of time. Kelly et al. (2012a) conclude that while AA mobilizes several positive processes, what appears to be of primary importance is facilitating change in the social networks of its members, and enhancing the self-efficacy of members in other, high-risk, social contexts.

Emerging Approaches to Mutual Help

Although mutual help uses regular group meetings, as do many clinical interventions including residential rehabilitation, which is often based on the 12 Steps, many of these approaches view a person with a severe alcohol or drug problem as a victim of their own individual vulnerability. An alternative view is that the problems experienced by the individual are symptoms of dysfunction or breakdown within an *ecological system*. White (2009) tells us there is growing interest in the *ecology of addiction recovery*, a focus on how physical, social, and cultural environments promote or inhibit the growth of substance-misuse problems. While substance misuse is found in all strata of society, the degree to which substance-misuse problems are experienced by people, and their ability to overcome these problems, varies widely according to their social circumstances.

The ecological approach embraces strategies aimed at increasing *recovery capital* (Cloud & Granfield, 2008). Examples of recovery capital include generally good physical and psychological health, close and supportive family and social networks, as well as educational and employment opportunities. Stores of recovery capital can vary dramatically for individuals, families, and communities. Some more fortunate individuals with low to moderate substance misuse problems but moderate to high recovery capital can resolve their problems with support from within their family or community or via a relatively brief professional intervention. There are many people, however, whose substance-related problems are much more severe and who do not have access to sufficient recovery capital to support their recovery. Indeed, for some people, the family and community in which they live may be not only a hindrance to recovery, but an actual encouragement to alcohol or drug misuse (White, 2009).

In these situations, traditional clinical or mutual help approaches aim to increase the individual's resistance, or support them to move away from their harmful environment. However, an emerging view is that what is needed in these circumstances is not simply a recurring series of treatment episodes for the individual, but a focus on building recovery capital in the community environment. Traditional clinical interventions and ongoing monitoring and support for the individual have to be coupled with strategies to deal with the negative cultural, social and economic conditions which underpin substance misuse. Pharmacological, psychological, or mutual-help interventions can help an individual to overcome cravings for drugs or alcohol, but they may also divert attention from the broader social processes within which both addiction and recovery flourish (White, 2009).

Recovery Communities

Reporting from the United States, White, Kelly & Roth (2012) tell us that in recent years there has been a rapid growth of organizations focused on the family, social networks, and on the wider environment in which recovery is supported or undermined. What is interesting about this development is that it appears to be emerging from a grassroots or bottom-up level, with recovery community organizations appearing across America during the 1990s. Contrary to the anonymity that is central to many mutual aid organizations and professional interventions, this new recovery advocacy movement is very public. In September 2011, over 100,000 people took part in more than 200 public Recovery Month celebration events across the United States.

White et al. (2012) report the development of local recovery community centres and the creation, in some states, of regional networks of centres. They provide the type of recovery support not available via traditional treatment or mutual help, as their focus extends beyond the individual. Recovery centres host support meetings and provide recovery coaching, but are also linked to a wide variety of resources including recovery housing, and recovery-conducive education and employment opportunities, and serve as a central hub for recovery-focused social networking and advocacy. The recovery advocacy movement is distinctive in its explicit focus on creating a *public* culture of recovery, and on promoting a policy environment in which addiction recovery can flourish. To that end this new movement advocates the political and cultural mobilization of communities of recovery; recovery-focused public and

197

professional education; pro-recovery laws and social policies; a recovery-focused redesign of addiction treatment; promotion of peer-based recovery support services; support for international, national, state, and local recovery celebration events; and promotion of a recovery research agenda (White et al., 2012). This approach is based upon a public recognition that misuse of drugs and alcohol is a *community* problem, and the way to deal with it is to recognize this and work to improve opportunities for individuals within the community.

Payment by Results

In the United Kingdom, the 2010 drug strategy (Home Office, 2010), contrary to earlier strategies, does not mention harm reduction but stresses recovery and introduces a plan for payments to drug services according to their results in helping people to recover from problems brought about by substance misuse. Payment by results (PBR) aims to incentivize the drug treatment system to move away from long-term substitute prescribing, and to improve delivery of recovery from drugs of dependency. Payment to drug services will be subject to achieving high level outcomes for clients:

- after leaving treatment free from drugs of dependence, individuals must not re-present within 12 months;
- reduced criminal activity, as measured by 12-month nonappearance on the Police National Computer (PNC);
- employment;
- improved health and wellbeing (Department of Health, 2011).

The government has launched pilot projects to clarify the details which would indicate different levels of success, and to ascertain the feasibility of attaining these outcomes. This approach is not without critics however. Gyngell (2011) argues that while PBR makes sense as a concept, the proxy measures of results are very blunt instruments and the payment system far too complex. For example, not re-presenting for treatment within 12 months does not necessarily mean that the person is not continuing to use drugs; nonappearance on the Police National Computer means little when crime detection rates remain one in five; drug services as currently constituted are not capable of acting as employment agencies. In order to show success, treatment agencies would also find it difficult to resist 'cherry picking' those clients who already possess sufficient 'recovery capital', such as a supportive family, secure living accommodation, and employment skills.

Gyngell argues that these proxy measures for recovery simply fail to get at the root cause of drug users' criminal activity, lack of employment and poor health and wellbeing, and that root cause is addiction to drugs. Firstly, it is argued that PBR can be made to work if it is based upon one simple single payment criterion: freedom from all drugs, including methadone and alcohol, with a first payment after 90 days' abstinence and a final payment after 6 months' abstinence. How this is achieved would be up to the treatment provider. Other positive outcomes such as education, training, employment, and crime-free living could be included, but only as a bonus. Secondly, restrictions should be set on methadone prescribing, and doctors should be given a positive incentive to refer to modern rehabilitation. Thirdly, harm-reduction services, such as needle exchanges, should only be used as the first step towards rehabilitation. And fourthly, good modern residential rehabilitation expertise should be included at every step of development. Gyngell (2011) argues that the above reforms would concentrate minds on the best way to achieve abstinence, would help addicts to become drug free, and reduce the tendency in treatment services to manage every aspect of their existence. Substitute prescribing is seen as having entrenched long-term drug and welfare dependency whereas recovery depends on the ability of individuals to take responsibility for themselves.

Nevertheless, as the UK Drugs Policy Commission (UK Drug Policy Commission, 2010) reminds us, recovery from drug or alcohol dependence is often a long process with many lapses requiring various types of support and services at different stages. The UKDPC argues that any payment by results should:

- include a wide range of services, from needle exchanges to residential rehabilitation; education and employment providers; housing and peer support groups;
- reward progress across a wide range of domains, taking account of different starting points, which is needed to avoid service providers 'cherry-picking' clients with low severity problems and ignoring those most difficult to treat;
- include measures of sustained recovery, which requires vital aftercare and support;
- recognize that level of community social capital varies between areas, providing differing support and employment opportunities (UK Drug Policy Commission, 2010).

All these indicate the need for flexibility and personalization in service provision to accommodate individuals who are at different stages of problematic substance use. Needle exchange services, drug consumption rooms, substitute prescribing and residential rehabilitation, can all form part of the recovery process. Other factors, such as the availability of mutual help and peer support, as well as employers being able and willing to give jobs, are crucial for sustaining recovery (UK Drug Policy Commission, 2012).

Work and other activities that foster a sense of inclusion and provide opportunities for positive social contact can help to prevent lapse and relapse among drug users (McIntosh, Bloor & Robertson, 2008). Training and work options could include opportunities in the drug and alcohol field, as many people in recovery find their experience to be of significant use to those still struggling with drugs and/or alcohol. However, it must be recognized that obtaining meaningful work that is conducive to recovery is a significant challenge for many people within the current economic climate, and vocational counselling or training, and assertive linkage to recovery supportive employment, are not standard components of most addiction treatment (White, Kelly & Roth, 2012). In some European countries, social enterprise organizations are experimenting with recovery work cooperatives as a transition from treatment to mainstream employment. These recovery work cooperatives are small businesses within the community that support people entering or returning to mainstream employment and, at the same time, have a focus on support, community service and participation in community life. While these programmes may successfully teach employability skills, drug users still have to compete on the labour market at a time of high unemployment in many countries (European Monitoring Centre for Drugs and Drug Addiction, 2012). White et al. (2012), in the United States describe recent community responses to employment needs of people in recovery. Recovery community organizations are establishing employment clearinghouses and incorporating work-related support into the recovery coaching process, and two specialized employment resources are emerging. The first consists of recovery-friendly employers who have had good experiences hiring people in recovery and who remain receptive to providing employment, particularly to people in a structured recovery support process. The second type of specialized employment resources are businesses established by people in recovery themselves who exclusively employ people in recovery. In these settings, people have the opportunity to acquire work skills, establish a recent employment history, and work with and be supervised by other people in recovery as a step along a pathway to continued employment.

Conclusion

Recovery from dependence and other substance-misuse related problems is not a simple or straightforward process. Criminalizing people who use illicit drugs only makes the problem worse as it lessens their chances of obtaining work and reintegrating into wider society. Maintaining individuals in treatment and on substitute drugs can reduce health and social harms, but stigmatizes people and maintains them in dependence on prescribed drugs and often on welfare support. Mutual help recovery movements such as AA and NA, have no negative resource implications for the state or local authorities, as each AA or NA group is fully self-supporting, declines outside contributions, and is not affiliated to any other organization. These self-supporting fellowships provide help to many individuals, both by introducing them to a pathway towards recovery and supporting them in their often faltering steps along this path. However, although counting membership in the millions, not everyone with a substance misuse problem joins AA or NA. To be successful on a much larger scale the recovery agenda requires many more of those people currently lacking sufficient recovery capital to be reintegrated into wider society in terms of accessing educational opportunities, employment, and positive social relationships. Although the 'new' recovery movements as exemplified by White et al. (2012) would seem to be addressing some of the factors that underpin continued dependence on drugs and alcohol, such as stigma and a lack of educational and work opportunities, more research is needed to define and assess the success of these enterprises. It is difficult to imagine that they could flourish in the most needy communities if left entirely to their own devices without investment from local and national authorities.

The state will always be involved to some degree in dealing with psychotropic substance use and related problems. As well as some form of legislative control, and policing of the supply side of substances, there will probably always be a need for professional drug and alcohol workers, and the evidence supports providing residential rehabilitation for many more people with severe addiction problems. However, the state can also help establish the kind of communities that do not initiate or sustain drug and alcohol misuse. Perhaps its most effective role in supporting recovery from drug and alcohol related problems would be to concentrate more resources on the broad community environment. The state could support recovery-oriented charitable and not-for-profit organizations to provide much-needed assistance to people who have been in prison, community-treatment programmes or residential rehabilitation. The state could invest in decent housing, educational opportunities and recovery-conducive workplaces in areas where drug and alcohol problems are rife. This will not come cheaply but taking into consideration the financial costs of keeping people in prison, and on substitute drugs, and on unemployment and other welfare benefits, as well as the psychological and social costs to individuals, families and communities of substance misuse, makes investment in the infrastructure of recovery communities a far more positive step towards improving the life chances of individuals as well as the wider wellbeing of society.

References

AA Fact File (2012). General Service Office of Alcoholics Anonymous. Retrieved March 11, 2013 from http://www.aa.org/pdf/products/m-24_aafactfile.pdf.

Alcoholics Anonymous (2012). *The Big Book Online, 4th edn*. Alcoholics Anonymous World Services Inc. Retrieved March 11, 2013 from http://www.aa.org/bigbookonline/index.cfm.

Bell, J. (2010). The global diversion of pharmaceutical drugs. Opiate treatment and the diversion of pharmaceutical opiates: a clinician's perspective. *Addiction, 105*(9), 1531–1537.

Bennett, G. & Rigby, K. (1990). Psychological change during residence in a rehabilitation centre for female drug misusers. Part I. Drug misusers. *Drug and Alcohol Dependence, 27*, 149–157.

Cloud, W. & Granfield, R. (2008). Conceptualizing recovery capital: Expansion of a theoretical concept. *Substance Use and Misuse, 43*(12/13), 1971–1986.

Condelli, W. S. & Hubbard, R. L. (1994). Relationship between time spent in treatment and client outcomes from therapeutic communities. *Journal of Substance Abuse Treatment, 11*, 25–33.

De Leon, G., Jainchill, N. & Wexler, H. (1982). Success and improvement rates five years after treatment in a therapeutic community. *International Journal of Addictions, 17*(4), 703–747.

Department of Health (2011). *Drug and alcohol recovery pilots supporting material*. Retrieved March 11, 2013 from http://www.dh.gov.uk/health/2011/07/drug-and-alcohol-recovery/.

European Monitoring Centre for Drugs and Drug Addiction (2012). *Annual Report 2012: The state of the drugs problem in Europe.* Luxembourg: Publications Office of the European Union. Retrieved March 11, 2013 from http://www.emcdda.europa.eu/publications/annual-report/2012.

Ghose, T. (2008). Organizational- and individual-level correlates of post treatment substance use: a multilevel analysis. *Journal of Substance Abuse Treatment, 34,* 249–262.

Gossop, M., Marsden, J., Stewart, D. & Rolfe, A. (1999). Treatment retention and one year outcomes for residential programmes in England. *Drug and Alcohol Dependence, 57*(2), 89–98.

Gossop, M., Stewart, D. & Marsden, J. (2008). Attendance at Narcotics Anonymous and Alcoholics Anonymous meetings, frequency of attendance and substance use outcomes after residential treatment for drug dependence: a 5-year follow-up study. *Addiction, 103*(1), 119–125.

Gottheil, E., McLellan, A. T. & Druley, K. A. (1992). Length of stay, patient severity and treatment outcome: sample data from the field of alcoholism. *Journal of Studies on Alcohol, 53,* 69–75.

Gyngell, K. (2011). *Breaking the habit. Why the state should stop dealing drugs and start doing rehab.* London: Centre for Policy Studies.

Hansard (2010). *Written Answer UK Parliament. Unemployment Benefits: Drugs.* Retrieved March 11, 2013 from http://www.publications.parliament.uk/pa/cm201011/cmhansrd/cm100720/text/100720w0005.htm#10072076000056.

Harris, A. H. S., Kivlahan, D., Barnett, P. G. & Finney, J. W. (2012). Longer length of stay is not associated with better outcomes in VHA's substance abuse residential rehabilitation treatment programs. *Journal of Behavioral Health Services and Research, 39*(1), 68–79.

Harris, J. & McElrath, K. (2012). Methadone as social control: Institutionalized stigma and the prospect of recovery. *Qualitative Health Research, 22*(6), 810–824.

Hartel, D. M. & Schoenbaum, E. E. (1998). Methadone treatment protects against HIV infection: two decades of experience in the Bronx, New York City. *Public Health Report, 113*(Suppl. 1), 107–115.

Home Office (2010). *Drug strategy 2010: reducing demand, restricting supply, building recovery: supporting people to live a drug free life.* London: Home Office.

Home Office (2012). *Putting Full Recovery First.* London: Home Office.

Hubbard, R. L., Craddock, S. G., Flynn, P. M., Anderson, J. & Etheridge, R. M. (1997). Overview of 1-year follow-up outcomes in the Drug Abuse Treatment Outcome Study (DATOS). *Psychology of Addictive Behaviors, 11*(4), 261–278.

Kelly, J. F., Brown, S., Abrantes, A., Kahler, C. W. & Myers, M. (2008). Social recovery model: An 8-year investigation of adolescent 12-step group involvement following inpatient treatment. *Alcoholism, Clinical and Experimental Research, 32*(8), 1468–1478.

Kelly, J. F., Hoeppner, B., Stout, R. L. & Pagano, M. (2012a). Determining the relative importance of the mechanisms of behavior change within Alcoholics Anonymous: a multiple mediator analysis. *Addiction, 107*(2), 289–299.

Kelly, J. F., Urbanoski, K., Hoeppner, B. B. & Slaymaker, V. (2012b). Ready, willing, and (not) able to change: Young adults' response to residential treatment. *Drug and Alcohol Dependence, 121*(3), 224–230.

Kissin, W., McLeod, C. & McKay, J. (2003). The longitudinal relationship between self-help group attendance and course of recovery. *Evaluation and Program Planning, 26*(3), 311–323.

McIntosh, J., Bloor, M. & Robertson, M. (2008). Drug treatment and the achievement of paid employment. *Addiction Research and Theory, 16*, 37–45.

Meier, P. (2005). *A national survey of retention in residential rehabilitation services.* London: National Treatment Agency for Substance Misuse.

Meier, P. S., Donmall, M. C., McElduff, P., Barrowclough, C. & Heller, R. F. (2006). The role of the early therapeutic alliance in predicting drug treatment dropout. *Drug and Alcohol Dependence, 83*, 57–64.

Moos, R. H. & Moos, B. S. (1995). Stay in residential facilities and mental health care as predictors of readmission for patients with substance use disorders. *Psychiatric Services, 46*, 66–72.

National Drug Evidence Centre (2005). *Treatment effectiveness: demonstration analysis of treatment surveillance data about treatment completion and retention.* Manchester: University of Manchester.

National Drug Treatment Monitoring System (2011). *Statistics from the National Drug Treatment Monitoring System (NDTMS) 1 April 2010–31 March 2011 Vol. 1: The Numbers.* London: Department of Health.

National Institute on Drug Abuse (2010). Methadone-Treated and Other Patients Fare Equally Well. Retrieved March 11, 2013 from http://www.drugabuse.gov/news-events/nida-notes/2010/12/study-supports-methadone-maintenance-in-therapeutic-communities.

National Institute on Drug Abuse (2011). Drug Facts: Treatment Statistics. Retrieved March 11, 2013 from www.drugabuse.gov/publications/drugfacts/treatment-statistics.

National Treatment Agency for Substance Misuse (2006). *The NTA's first annual user satisfaction survey 2005.* London: NTA.

National Treatment Agency for Substance Misuse (2009). *Residential drug treatment services: good practice in the field.* London: NTA.

National Treatment Agency for Substance Misuse (2012a). *The role of residential rehab in an integrated treatment system.* London: NTA.

National Treatment Agency for Substance Misuse (2012b). *Drug treatment 2012: progress made, challenges ahead.* London: NTA.

Neale, J., Nettleton, S. & Pickering, J. (2012). Does recovery-oriented treatment prompt heroin users prematurely into detoxification and abstinence programmes? *Drug and Alcohol Dependence.* Retrieved March 11, 2013 from http://dx.doi.org/10.1016/j.drugalcdep.2012.06.030.

Rolleston Committee (1926). *Departmental Committee on Morphine and Heroin Addiction Recommendations 8b.* Retrieved March 11, 2013 from http://www.druglibrary.eu/library/reports/rolleston.html.

Substance Abuse and Mental Services Administration (2011). SAMHSA Announces a Working Definition of 'recovery' from mental disorders and substance use disorders. Retrieved March 12, 2013 from http://www.samhsa. gov/newsroom/advisories/1112223420.aspx.

Stimson, G. V. (1995). AIDS and injecting drug use in the United Kingdom, 1987–1993: The policy response and the prevention of the epidemic, *Social Science and Medicine, 41*(5), 699–716.

Strang, J. (2011). *Recovery-orientated drug treatment. An interim report.* London: National Treatment Agency.

UK Drug Policy Commission (2010). Payment by Results for Drug Services: Some Key Issues. Retrieved March 11, 2013 from http://www.ukdpc.org.uk/ publication/payment-by-results-drug-services-key-issues/.

UK Drugs Policy Commission (2012). A Fresh Approach to Drugs. Retrieved March 11, 2013 from http://www.ukdpc.org.uk/wp-content/uploads/a-fresh-approach-to-drugs-the-final-report-of-the-uk-drug-policy-commission .pdf.

Ward, J., Mattick, R. P. & Hall, W. (2009). The effectiveness of methadone maintenance treatment: an overview. *Drug and Alcohol Review, 13*(3), 327–336.

White, W. L. (2009). The mobilization of community resources to support long-term addiction recovery. *Journal of Substance Abuse Treatment, 36*(2), 146–158.

White, W. L., Kelly, J. F. & Roth, J. D (2012). New addiction-recovery support Institutions: Mobilizing support beyond professional addiction treatment and recovery mutual aid. *Journal of Groups in Addiction and Recovery, 7,* 297–317.

Wilkinson, S., Mistral, W. & Golding, J. (2008). What is most and least useful in residential rehabilitation? A qualitative study of service users and professionals. *Journal of Substance Use, 13*(6), 404–414.

Witbrodt, J., Bond, J., Kaskutas, L. A., Weisner, C., Jaeger, G., Pating, D. et al. (2007). Day hospital and residential addiction treatment: randomized and nonrandomized managed care clients. *Journal of Consulting and Clinical Psychology, 75*(6), 947–959.

12

How Current Drug Laws Impede Research and Clinical Treatments

David Nutt

Introduction

In the United Kingdom nonmedical drug use is controlled either by the Misuse of Drugs Act 1971 (MDAct 1971) or, in the case of alcohol and tobacco products, by separate taxation and age-of-purchase controls. The justification for the current illegality of many drugs is that they are harmful and hence criminal sanctions are necessary to reduce use and consequent harms, even though evidence to support this view is not easy to identify. Indeed harms may paradoxically be increased by these drugs being illegal; examples include illness from dirty needles, infected supplies, and exposure to criminal gangs in the purchase of many drugs. Moreover, the illegality of some drugs may encourage the use of more dangerous legal drugs; it could be argued that the rise of binge drinking in the 1990s might have been driven by concerns over potential criminalization for possession of MDMA and cannabis (for more on this topic see Nutt, 2010). However there is another much less considered harm of the MDAct 1971, which is its effect in impeding research, particularly that directed towards finding new medical treatments. This is the subject of the present chapter.

The MDAct 1971

The MDAct was developed in the late 1960s and brought into law in 1971 with the express purpose of taking political machinations out of

Emerging Perspectives on Substance Misuse, First Edition. Edited by Willm Mistral.
© 2013 John Wiley & Sons, Ltd. Published 2013 by John Wiley & Sons, Ltd.

the decision-making process relating to drug harms and classification. Scientific advice relating to drug classification was given to a newly created Advisory Council on the Misuse of Drugs (ACMD). This scientific council was set up under the MDAct to 'keep the drug situation in the UK under review and to advise Government ministers on the measures to be taken for preventing the misuse of drugs or for dealing with the social problems connected with their misuse' (Misuse of Drugs Act 1971). One of its key remits was to decide on the relative harms of drugs and recommend classification in three bands A, B and C. A central feature of the MDAct 1971 is that the position of drugs could, and should, change according to changes in the evidence. However, as can be seen from Figure 1, this hardly ever happens; only cannabis – and then only for a few years – has had its position in the MDAct 1971 reduced. All others have moved in or up.

Drugs controlled under the MDAct 1971 include a raft of medicines such as morphine, heroin, benzodiazepines, ketamine and amphetamine. These medically-used drugs are put in Schedules 2–4 depending on how dangerous they are perceived to be, with Schedule 2 being the most dangerous (heroin, morphine, methadone, methylamphetamine, etc.) so requiring greater security in safekeeping and handling than those

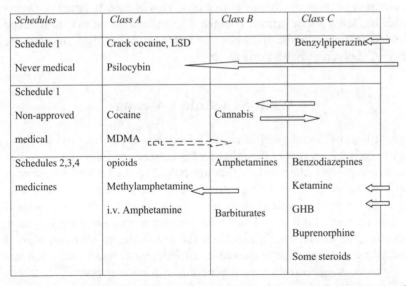

Schedules	Class A	Class B	Class C
Schedule 1 Never medical	Crack cocaine, LSD Psilocybin		Benzylpiperazine
Schedule 1 Non-approved medical	Cocaine MDMA	Cannabis	
Schedules 2,3,4 medicines	opioids Methylamphetamine i.v. Amphetamine	Amphetamines Barbiturates	Benzodiazepines Ketamine GHB Buprenorphine Some steroids

Figure 1 Classes and schedules of MDAct 1971. Arrows show movements of drugs between classes. The dashed arrow shows the ACMD recommendation that MDMA be downgraded to B that was rejected by the government in 2009.

in Schedules 3 and 4. However, other drugs that are not currently medicines, even if they previously were, have been put in Schedule 1. So cannabis, LSD and MDMA which were used therapeutically before being banned under the act are included in Schedule 1, alongside crack cocaine. And new drugs with therapeutic potential such as psilocybin (the active psychedelic in 'magic' mushrooms) are included as well. Recent research has shown that these drugs vary enormously in terms of their harms both to individuals and society (Nutt et al., 2010) but in Schedule 1, unlike in the other Schedules, there is no discrimination according to relative harms. It seems absurd that it is easier for clinicians or researchers to work with heroin than cannabis – particularly when the MDAct 1971 puts cannabis in a less harmful class!

The situation worsens almost monthly as more so-called 'legal high' compounds are controlled. Following on from the banning of mephedrone and naphyrone and their analogues, the ACMD has just recommended banning a vast tranche of ketamine analogues as well as a range of cannabis agonists (an analogue is a substance that is chemically 'substantially similar' to a controlled substance, while a cannabis agonist is a substance that acts like the active ingredient of cannabis, THC). Thus more and more compounds that need to be researched, because they are being used on the street and because they may have medical potential, are now much harder to study. This blanket banning of chemicals has led a senior organic chemist to comment to me that almost any undergraduate organic synthesis chemistry course is now running the risk of inadvertently breaking the law!

What Schedule 1 Means

Regardless of the relative harms, all Schedule 1 drugs have to be held at a level of security higher than that for the other Schedules. This requires secure safes or locked fridges that are bolted to the wall and floor with at least two locks controlling entry. Moreover, possession of Schedule 1 drugs requires a special licence that now costs £3,000 plus annual retaining fees; and licence holders are subject to random visits by police working for the Home Office. Even the most sought-after and abused Schedule 2 drugs such as heroin and methadone, which are considerably more dangerous than most Schedule 1 drugs (see Nutt et al., 2010) do not require this level of safety and surveillance. For these reasons few establishments hold Schedule 1 licences; in fact I know of only one hospital in the United Kingdom that does, which means that almost no research clinicians can, if they desire, work with these compounds. Moreover prescribing them would be enormously difficult even if efficacy was proven. Getting a licence is not only costly but tedious – one group I know has waited over 10 months for one – a long chunk of time within most research grants which are usually 3 years. As getting a licence before obtaining a grant can be an expensive waste of money if the research application is not funded, few if any do so. What is peculiar about this situation is that NHS hospital and university departments that conduct biomedical research that requires controlled drugs in Schedules 2–4, are exempt from the need to purchase a license to hold these (Home Office, 2012) but must purchase one if they wish to work with a Schedule 1 drug – even one as easily available and relatively harm-free as cannabis. Finally, the controls required for Schedule 1 mean that few chemistry companies want to deal with the complicated regulations, so making obtaining these drugs for research – particularly clinical research – extremely costly and difficult. Further, for the same reasons, very few pharmaceutical companies can be bothered to work in this arena. One particularly bemusing aspect of the Scheduling rules relates to the status of Sativex. This is a liquid preparation of natural cannabis that now has a licence for treating pain and spasticity in conditions such as multiple sclerosis. This is currently a Schedule 4 drug whereas the very same molecules in the living plant are Schedule 1! Such anomalies not only slow scientific progress but also make a mockery of the MDAct 1971 so that its credibility is even more compromised.

How the Law has Denied Research Advances

Clearly the law is not based on evidence of relative harms. But does this matter? I contend that not only does it matter but the impact that the law has had on research has been so profound as to amount to a scandal of wasted opportunity with few if any equals in modern times; the George W. Bush limitation of stem cell research in the United States is perhaps the only example of comparable restriction. All the Schedule 1 drugs I have mentioned have huge importance in our understanding of brain function and in developing new treatments for a range of brain and other diseases. Yet since each has been controlled (i.e. banned) under the MDAct 1971, research has stopped or has been severely limited. For example, before LSD was controlled there were over 1,000 published papers reporting its actions in 40,000 patients. Since its banning there has been no new research. MDMA was extensively used to augment psychotherapy but since its banning there have been only two studies in the UK and a handful more worldwide. We have recently conducted the first studies on psilocybin ever in the UK (Carhart-Harris et al., 2012a,b) to complement less than a handful worldwide, despite this drug being used widely and safely used for recreational purposes for decades.

From the neuroscience perspective it is obvious that the changes of brain function produced by drugs such as LSD and psilocybin (psychedelics), cannabis and MDMA need to be understood in terms of changes in brain neurotransmitter function and brain connectivity. I would argue that it is impossible to study consciousness adequately without perturbing it, and the psychedelics produce some of the most profound and interesting effects on this state. The fact that they have not been studied using new imaging techniques, particularly MRI, is a massive wasted opportunity for consciousness research.

MDMA provokes marked alterations of brain function, notably enhanced mood and increased empathy (it was originally known as *empathy* and it appears that a media campaign to get it banned originated when the name was changed to *ecstasy*, as it was marketed at youth). These effects are hugely important subjects for neuroscience research on areas such as consciousness and mood, which are hard to alter in such a profound way as MDMA with other drugs or interventions, so research on their brain locations and mechanisms has been limited. Psilocybin can improve mood, often for many months, and we have shown this to relate to its ability to decrease activity in brain regions where depression is generated (Carhart-Harris et al., 2012a,b). Based on these results the Medical Research Council has agreed to fund a clinical trial in patients with resistant depression. This is now starting but the extra costs incurred because of the Schedule 1 status will be substantial. Moreover, if the trial shows psilocybin is effective under current regulations it is hard to see how any doctor could afford the licence to use it!

Lost Clinical Opportunities

Clinically, the lost opportunities are profound. LSD had been shown to be very helpful in allowing people with terminal illness to come to terms with their dying, and psilocybin displays similar efficacy in patients with cancer (Grob et al., 2011). Moreover, studies with LSD conducted in the 1960s found it to be as effective in treating alcoholism as any treatments we currently have (Krebs & Johansen, 2012). Alcohol dependence is the largest cause of disability in men in Europe, with relatively ineffective treatments, yet the opportunity offered by LSD has not been progressed largely because of its controlled status. Post-traumatic stress disorder (PTSD) is another major cause of disability, particularly in the military. Treatments are poor and MDMA has shown remarkable potential in a small proof-of-principle trial (Mithoefer et al. 2010). Extending this work in the UK environment is of high potential value but current regulations militate against this.

Cluster headache is one of the worst pain syndromes known, with limited treatments and high suicide rates. 'Magic' mushrooms are widely used by sufferers but the controlled status of psilocybin means it has not been formally studied. When we approached a charity for this disorder to request support for such as study they replied they could not consider working with 'illegal' drugs! This sentiment was echoed by a member of parliament, Jim Dobbin, who, in reference to our first psilocybin study, used parliamentary privilege to challenge our being allowed to conduct such research (Hansard, 2011). This remarkable (probably unique) level of parliamentary scrutiny of a scientific study illustrates how the 'illegal' status can provoke intense negative interest.

The banning of mephedrone also covered chemically related (analogue) compounds. This meant that the clinically licensed analogue of mephedrone, bupropion (the active ingredient of the antidepressant Wellbutrin and the antismoking agent Zyban) had to be specifically exempted from the law. Of course the exemption was necessary, but let us reflect that had the law been in place *before* the discovery of bupropion then it almost certainly would never have been studied. This would have meant a unique class of therapeutic agent that has saved many lives would never have been available for treatment. Given that bupropion is the only drug that has been shown to reduce dependence on tobacco through a mechanism other than acting on nicotine receptors it seems likely that analogues might also be effective, but this will now almost certainly never be tested. This blind faith in the efficacy of a policy of banning analogues to reduce illicit drug use flies in the face of common sense, international evidence, and justice (see King et al. 2012).

It is humbling to remember that mephedrone and naphyrone were discovered from a programme to make new drugs to treat addiction – a route made much harder now they are illegal – particularly as it seems likely that the emergence of mephedrone in the UK reduced the number of deaths from cocaine (Nutt, 2011).

Cannabis and ketamine derivatives are two new groups of compounds that have recently been controlled. Cannabis agonists are sold as 'spice' or herbal products for smoking or making psychoactive tea. This is a means to circumvent the illegal status of cannabis itself. Many of these compounds were made as potential therapeutic agents in the latter part of the last century and now are being resynthesized in China for sale over the Internet. Many are very potent agonists and so can cause severe 'stoning'. However the net thrown to ban these potent THC-like substances now appears to include other nonpsychoactive compounds such as tetrahydrocannabivarin (THCV), which may have utility in anxiety disorders and as a treatment for cannabis dependence. This drug is now treated by the Home Office as Schedule 1 even though there is no evidence or expectation of it being harmful or abused.

Ketamine, as well as being a respiratory-sparing anaesthetic, is a useful treatment for pain and has an emerging role for treatment-resistant depression. It is also an important research tool for the study of the brain mechanisms of psychosis. However, in recent years ketamine has become a popular drug of misuse in the young, with severe lethal intoxication and a few deaths reported. The long-term use of ketamine is also associated with an inflammatory cystitis and possibly cognition impairments, so there is a real need to find safer and more effective alternatives.

Such research is in its infancy but promising leads were being worked on. One of these is methoxetamine (mexxy), made by a chemist with chronic postamputation pain, to be a safer version of ketamine particularly in relation to the bladder problems. In the last year mexxy entered the youth market and some cases of severe intoxication were reported with adverse effects somewhat different to those of ketamine. Because of these it was made subject to a temporary banning order and now the recommendation of the ACMD is not only to make this ban permanent but also to ban a whole range of other ketamine analogues just in case!

The lessons of bupropion have not been learned. Exemptions have had to be made for one analogue, tiletamine as it is a useful veterinary anaesthetic, which suggests that some of the other analogues might also be useful treatments, or at least safer than ketamine. If the ACMD recommendation is put into law then we shall probably never know.

How Can We Move Forward?

We need to make laws that facilitate, not impede, research on these most scientifically interesting drugs, to further neuroscience and to optimize their therapeutic uses. The 40-year-old MDAct 1971 and the Schedule system is clearly not now fit for purpose. It seriously impairs research without having any obvious impact on recreational use. There is an urgent need to change the Act to empower research and (hopefully) accelerate the development of new treatments. A straightforward solution would be to remove the specific licence requirements for Schedule 1 drugs, treating them in the same way as those in Schedule 2, for production, research, and clinical establishments. This would greatly ease barriers to research and allow clinical use of these drugs when evidence supports this. There is little, if any, likelihood of this change affecting 'illicit' use. All research and clinical bodies with an interest in this field should be working together to this end. The Independent Scientific Committee on Drugs (ISCD) is leading a campaign to achieve this – join up and follow progress on our website www.drugscience.org.uk.

References

Carhart-Harris, R. L., Erritzoe, D., Williams, T. M., Reed, L. J., Colasanti, A., Tyacke, R. J. et al. (2012a). Neural correlates of the psychedelic state as determined by fMRI studies with psilocybin. *Proceedings of the National Academy of Sciences of the United States of America, 109*(6), 2138–2143. Retrieved March 17, 2013 from http://www.pnas.org/content/109/6/2138.short.

Carhart-Harris, R. L., Leech, R., Williams, T. M., Erritzoe, D., Abbasi, N., Bargiotas, T. et al. (2012b). Implications for psychedelic-assisted psychotherapy: functional magnetic resonance imaging study with psilocybin. *British Journal of Psychiatry, 200*, 238–244. Epub. Retrieved March 12, 2013 from http://www.ncbi.nlm.nih.gov/pubmed/22282432.

Grob, C. S., Danforth, A. L., Chopra, G. S., Hagerty, M., McKay, C. R., Halberstadt, A. et al. (2011). Pilot study of psilocybin treatment for anxiety in patients with advanced-stage cancer. *Archives of General Psychiatry, 68*, 71–78.

Hansard (2011). Written answers for 26 January 2011. Retrieved March 12, 2013 from http://www.publications.parliament.uk/pa/cm201011/cmhansrd/cm110126/text/110126w0004.htm#11012688000126.

Home Office (2012). Controlled Drug Domestic Licences. Companies. Retrieved March 12, 2013 from http://www.homeoffice.gov.uk/drugs/licensing/domestic-licences/companies.

King, L. A., Nutt, D. J., Singleton, N. & Howard, R. (2012). Analogue Control: An Imperfect Law. ISCD & UKDPC, London. Retrieved March 12, 2013 from http://www.ukdpc.org.uk/publication/analogue-controls-an-imperfect-law/.

Krebs, T. & Johansen P.-O. (2012). LSD for alcoholism: A meta-analysis of randomized controlled trials. *Journal of Psychopharmacology, 26*, 994–1002.

Mithoefer, M., Wagner, T., Mithoefer, A. C., et al. (2010). The safety and efficacy of 3,4-methylenedioxymethamphetamine-assisted psychotherapy in subjects with chronic, treatment-resistant posttraumatic stress disorder: the first randomized controlled pilot study. *Journal of Psychopharmacology*, 25(4), 439–452.

Nutt, D. J. (2010). The role and basis of the drug laws. *Prometheus: Critical Studies in Innovation*, 28(3), 293-297. doi.org/10.1080/08109028.2010.518052.

Nutt, D. J. (2011). Perverse effects of the precautionary principle: How banning mephedrone has unexpected implications for pharmaceutical discovery. *Therapeutic Advances in Psychopharmacology*, 1, 35–36.

Nutt, D. J., King, L. A. & Phillips, L. D. (2010). Drug harms in the UK: a multicriteria decision analysis. *Lancet, 376*, 1558–1565.

Index

Emerging Perspectives on Substance Misuse, First Edition. Edited by Willm Mistral.
© 2013 John Wiley & Sons, Ltd. Published 2013 by John Wiley & Sons, Ltd.